EOG Test Scores and Chinese Language Immersion Programs

An Inference from
A Comprehensive Evaluation of a
K-5 Chinese Language Immersion
Program

By
Dr. Shoufen Jacobson

East West Pro Publishing,
P.O. Box 470851
Charlotte, NC 28247
United States of America

EOG Test Scores and Chinese Language Immersion Programs

Copyright © 2017 by Shoufen Jacobson

All right reserved. No part of this publication may be reproduced or utilized in any form or by any means, electronic or mechanical, including photocopying, recording, or by any information storage or retrieval systems, without the written permission of the publisher.

Library of Congress Control Number: 2017918788
Shoufen Jacobson, Charlotte, NC

Jacobson, Shoufen, 2017
EOG Test Scores and Chinese Language Immersion Programs
An Inference from
A Comprehensive Evaluation of a K-5 Chinese Language Immersion Program

ISBN-13: 978-0692990247
ISBN-10: 0692990240

East West Pro Publishing,
P.O. Box 470851 Charlotte, NC 28247 United States of America
Eastwestpropublishing@gmail.com
EastWestProPublishing.com
First published in 2017
First Edition

The book can be found at: www.amazon.com/dp/0692990240

To my husband Todd Jacobson and my daughter Amanda Jacobson

Preface

Will Chinese language immersion programs improve students' EOG test scores? In this study of K-5 students, overwhelming evidence has demonstrated that the students in this K-5 Chinese Language Immersion Program (CIP) scored significantly higher than the similar students, in non-immersion programs, in the key instructional areas of English reading, math, and science. Furthermore, CIP students clearly demonstrated consistently strong higher academic performance measured by the EOG test scores starting from the 3rd and continuing through the 5th grade.

The synergistic component of the CIP is an exciting new concept and this study may be the first one to have comprehensively and statistically evaluated the CIP program in effort to prove or disprove this thesis. Based on the results of this study, the conclusion would be that yes indeed there is a strong correlation. CIP has a strong synergistic impact on other critical instructional areas. Although one study alone certainly does not resolve all questions, it clearly that CIP has much potential from the synergistic learning perspective. This is surely a very exciting development in K-5 education. This book is an exact copy my doctorate dissertation. My next book, which will be coming soon, will be the synthesized version designed to more directly explain how to set up and establish effective CIP programs in a K-5 setting to have maximal impact on both the direct goal of teaching Chinese language, and as well as the secondary and synergistic goal of helping the students who are in the CIP to have positive and synergistic improvement in the other important subject areas. This study demonstrates, although not conclusively, this positive synergistic relationship exists.

Please contact me at shoufenjacobson@gmail.com if you have any questions.

Acknowledgements

My genuine thanks first go to my professors at Gardner-Webb University, in particular, to Dr. Dennis Triplett for his invaluable insights, guidance, and confidence in my ability to complete my study and to Dr. Doug Eury, Dr. John Reynolds, and Dr. Jeffery Rogers for their valuable assistance. In addition, I want to thank my advisory group, Dr. Zhining Chin, Mr. Bernd Nuss, and Ms. Debra Lentz for their expertise in the field of language immersion and their generous support and guidance. I owe much to those who participated in this study: Ms. Ynez Olshausen, Dr. Jeff Linker, Ms. Yanhong Ye, and the entire Chinese team. They have offered their discerning perspectives for the findings of this study. Without their participation, this study would not have been possible. Many thanks go out to Dr. Kelly Gwaltney, who inspired me for selecting this particular dissertation topic. Much gratitude is also obligated to Ms. Sarah Thomas who diligently edited the unusually long document. Her expertise was instrumental to my finished dissertation, which is consistent with the rigorous academic standards associated with this genre. Finally, I want to express my deepest appreciation to my dearest husband, Todd Jacobson, and my darling daughter, Amanda Jacobson. They have unselfishly offered their support and encouragement in my long journey.

Abstract

A Comprehensive Evaluation of a K-5 Chinese Language Immersion Program. Jacobson, Shoufen, 2013: Dissertation, Gardner-Webb University, Chinese Language Acquisition/Language Immersion/Program Value/Program Evaluation/CIPP Evaluation Model

This dissertation was designed to provide a comprehensive data-driven evaluation of a Chinese language Immersion Program (CIP) for the stakeholders. CIP was implemented in 2006 with a goal for students to become proficient in the Chinese language and develop increased cultural awareness while reaching at least the same level of academic achievement as their peers in non-immersion programs. Yet, CIP had never been fully evaluated. It was not known how and to what extent this CIP met the needs of immersion students.

This study employed Stufflebeam's (2003) CIPP program evaluation model to determine the CIP's Context, Input, Process, and Product. A mixed method was employed for this study. Finally, a meta-evaluation survey was used to determine the level of the utility, feasibility, propriety, and accuracy of the evaluation.

The findings of the study showed that (a) 3 out of 3 program planners and 11 out of 14 Chinese teachers (75.91%) agreed that the goals met the addressed needs; (b) 3 out of 3 program planners and 12 out of 14 Chinese teachers (83.50%) agreed that the selected approach and plans were feasible, compatible, successful, and cost effective; (c) 3 out of 3 program planners and 11 out of 14 Chinese teachers (78.61%) agreed that CIP was implemented as designed, that the concerns and ideas for improvement were handled efficiently, and that negative side effects were analyzed and minimized; (d) CIP students scored significantly higher than the similar students in non-immersion programs in English reading, math, and science. Furthermore, CIP students clearly demonstrated consistently strong higher academic performance measured by the EOG tests starting from the 3rd and continuing through the 5th grade; (e) CIP students scored significantly higher in mathematics than in English. In addition, CIP students scored significantly higher in mathematics than that of all comparable schools across all measures. CIP has reduced the achievement gap in mathematics between the majority and minority students, which was substantiated by 3 years' CIP EOG test results; and (f) there was no significantly statistical difference between combined CIP students' YCT listening and reading scores and that of a Chinese immersion program in Minnesota, with students of less diverse population and higher socioeconomic status. This revealed that the modified CIP Chinese language immersion model served the needs of the diverse students effectively. Finally, 3 out of 3 advisory panel members scored the evaluation process at least 80% for the utility, feasibility, propriety, and accuracy of the process.

In conclusion, the criteria for each of the evaluation questions were met or exceeded by the substantiated results; therefore, although the recommendations for CIP's improvement were made, CIP was successful as designed.

Table of Contents

Page

Chapter 1: Introduction 1
Nature of the Problem 1
Impact of the Problem 3
Background of the Problem 4
Significance of the Problem 17

Definition of Terms 19
Chapter 2: Literature Review 27
Theoretical Framework 27

Use of Chinese Language 29
Research on Language Immersion Acquisition 30
Development of Chinese Pinyin Skill 48

Development of the Four Chinese Language Skills 50

Chinese Language Immersion Program Development 57

Program Evaluation Design 67
Purpose Statement 74
Evaluation Questions 74
Chapter 3: Methodology 76
Statement of the Problem 76
Statement of the Purpose of the Study 76
Evaluation Questions 77
Evaluation Methodology 85
Evaluation Sequence Model 85
Procedures 87
Participants 90
Instrumentation 95
Data Collection Procedure 98
Administration Data Collection Instruments 100
Data Analysis and Expected Outcomes 101
Assumptions 108
Limitations 108
Delimitations 109
Chapter 4: Results 111
Semi-Structured Interview Analysis 112
Chinese Instructional Environment Analysis 112
Analysis for Evaluation Question 1 123
Analysis for Evaluation Question 2 126
Analysis for Evaluation Question 3 131
Analysis for Evaluation Question 4 134
Analysis for Evaluation Question 5 166

Analysis for Evaluation Question 6 177
Meta-Evaluation Survey Analysis 194
Chapter 5: Discussions..196
Overview of the Findings..197
Discussion of Results..198
Conclusions...214
Meta-Evaluation Results...218
Recommendations...218
Implications of Study..221
References...226

Appendices
A   The 5th National Chinese Language Conference 2012 238
B   Comprehensive Chinese Language Immersion Program Sequence Model........240
C   Chinese Curriculum Articulation...242
D   Chinese Tri-Input Model..246
E   Meta-Evaluation Survey..248
F   Interview Questions 253
G   Proposal Timetable 255
H   Chinese Immersion Instructional Environment Survey................................257
I   Quantitative Data Collection Analysis Organizational Chart.......................261
J   Informed Consent Forms 263

Tables
1   Staff Age 7
2   Years of Teaching Experience 7
3   Comparable School Student Demographics 17
4   Chinese Language Immersion Program Evaluation Plan 79
5   Chinese Language Immersion Teacher Educational Profile........................91
6   CIP Class Participants...94
7   District Comparable Class Participants 94
8   YCT Chinese Immersion Program Participants...95
9   Short-Term, Medium-Term, and Long-Term Class Participants..................95
10   Chinese Immersion Instructional Environment Survey Results 114
11   Chinese Instructional Environment Frequency Distribution 120
12   Reading, Math, and Science EOG Participants 136
13   Reading, Math, and Science EOG NCEXTEND I Participants.................137
14   NCEXTEND I Reading, Math, and Science Scale Score Conversion 138
15   Combined Grades Mean Scores and Standard Deviations for All Measures 139
16   Grade 3 Mean Scores and Standard Deviations for All Measures.............139
17   Grade 4 Mean Scores and Standard Deviations for All Measures.............139
18   Grade 5 Mean Scores and Standard Deviations for All Measures.............140
19   Summary of t-test for Combined Grades 141
20   Combined Grades t-test Results for CIP and School NSS in Reading 141
21   Combined Grades t-test Results for CIP and School MSS in Reading.....142
22   Combined Grades t-test Results for CIP and School NSL in Reading 142
23   Combined Grades t-test Results for CIP and School NSS in Math 143
24   Combined Grades t-test Results for CIP and School MSS in Math 144

25	Combined Grades t-test Results for CIP and School NSL in Math	144
26	Summary of t-test Results for Different Terms	146
27	t-test Results for CIP and School NSS Short-Term Impact on Reading	147
28	t-test Results for CIP and School MSS Short-Term Impact on Reading	148
29	t-test Results for CIP and School NSL Short-Term Impact on Reading	148
30	t-test Results for CIP and School NSS Short-Term Impact on Math	150
31	t-test Results for CIP and School MSS Short-Term Impact on Math	150
32	t-test Results for CIP and School NSL Short-Term Impact on Math	151
33	t-test Results for CIP and School NSS Medium-Term Impact on Reading	152
34	t-test Results for CIP and School MSS Medium-Term Impact on Reading	152
35	t-test Results for CIP and School NSL Medium-Term Impact on Reading	153
36	t-test Results for CIP and School NSS Medium-Term Impact on Math	154
37	t-test Results for CIP and School MSS Medium-Term Impact on Math	154
38	t-test Results for CIP and School NSL Medium-Term Impact on Math	155
39	t-test Results for CIP and School NSS Long-Term Impact on Reading	156
40	t-test Results for CIP and School MSS Long-Term Impact on Reading	156
41	t-test Results for CIP and School NSL Long-Term Impact on Reading	157
42	t-test Results for CIP and School NSS Long-Term Impact on Math	158
43	t-test Results for CIP and School MSS Long-Term Impact on Math	158
44	t-test Results for CIP and School NSL Long-Term Impact on Math	159
45	t-test Results for CIP and School NSS Long-Term Impact on Science	160
46	t-test Results for CIP and School MSS Long-Term Impact on Science	160
47	t-test Results for CIP and School NSL Long-Term Impact on Science	161
48	Mean Scores for CIP and School NSL Reading and Math	167
49	Summary of t-test Results for Math and Reading Scores	168
50	t-test Results for Grade 3 CIP Reading and Math Scores	168
51	t-test Results for Grade 3 NSL Reading and Math Scores	169
52	t-test Results for Grade 4 CIP Reading and Math Scores	169
53	t-test Results for Grade 4 NSL Reading and Math Scores	170
54	t-test Results for Grade 5 CIP Reading and Math Scores	171
55	t-test Results for Grade 5 NSL Reading and Math Scores	171
56	t-test Results for CIP Grades 3-5 Reading and Math Scores	172
57	t-test Results for NSL Grades 3-5 Reading and Math Scores	173
58	Percentage of Students Achieved at or above Grade Levels	173
59	Mean Scores and Standard Deviations for CIP Chinese Report Cards	181
60	The 2nd Grade YCT Frequency Distribution Table for All Measures	183
61	The 3rd Grade YCT Frequency Distribution Table for All Measures	184
62	The 3rd Grade YCT Frequency Distribution Table for Writing	185
63	YCT Mean Scores and Standard Deviations for All Measures	186
64	Summary of YCT t-test Results	187
65	t-test Results for the 2nd Grade YCT Listening Scores	187
66	t-test Results for the 2nd Grade YCT Reading Scores	188
67	t-test Results for the 2nd Grade YCT Combined Scores	189
68	t-test Results for the 3rd Grade YCT Listening Scores	190
69	t-test Results for the 3rd Grade YCT Reading Scores	190
70	t-test Results for the 3rd Grade YCT Combined Scores	191

71	Meta-Evaluation Survey Results	195

Figures

1	CIP 2nd grade YCT Participant's Chinese Report Card Grade	179
2	CIP 2nd Grade YCT Non-Participant's Report Card Grades	179
3	CIP 3rd Grade YCT Participant's Report Card Grades	180
4	CIP 3rd Grade YCT Non-Participant's Report Card Grades	180

Chapter 1: Introduction

Nature of the Problem

In North America, the language immersion approach has commonly been acknowledged as the most effective way to teach students a second language at no perceptible cost to their English academic skills (Curtain & Dahlberg, 2004; Finnamore, 2006; Fortune, 2012; Genesee, 1987, 1994; Met, 2012). Widespread inquiries on language immersion have been continuing, at least from the creation of the Saint Lambert immersion program in Canada in 1965, and uphold the conclusion above (Cummins, 1998; Finnamore, 2006; Fortune, 2012; Genesee, 1987). Most research on language immersion focuses on French and Spanish, alphabet-based languages (Genesee, 1984, 1985; Swain & Lapkin, 1981), and much less on Chinese, the pictographic language (Chao, 1993; De Courcy, 1997). Chinese immersion education has developed rapidly in the recent decade as the importance of the bilateral relationship between China and the United States has become more critical than ever in modern history (See Appendix A). There were 75,000 students studying Chinese in K-12 schools and 50,000 students studying Chinese in colleges (National Chinese Language Conference, 2012), yet there was only one study on a Chinese immersion program evaluation, which was conducted and reported by the Center for Applied Linguistics (CAL, 2012):

> CAL's Foreign Language Education Division recently conducted an evaluation of an independent Chinese partial immersion school. A team of educators visited the school on multiple occasions to conduct a comprehensive review of the program that included observations of English and Mandarin classrooms; review of English and Mandarin curricula; interviews with staff, parents, and students; and questionnaire protocols completed by staff, students, and parents. (p. 1)

Chinese immersion program designers replicated the program models from the studies and practices of French immersion programs (Fortune & Tedick, 2003), though Chinese is linguistically different from English, just as Kanagy and Hai (2001) stated that immersion students who learned to read first in a language that was markedly different from English, such as Arabic or Chinese, would need to learn and practice literacy skills that were specific to each language. Met (2000) posited, "As existing research base and professional experience often guide decision about programs in French and Spanish. The same decisions are required of planners in Chinese programs, yet decision makers must take into account the differences between those languages and English" (p. 139). Met (2000) also stressed

> Immersion researchers have long held that literacy skills gained by students in their second language transfer to their first language. In immersion programs where the first and second languages use the same alphabet, students seems to have little difficulty reading in their first language once they read successfully in the second language. Thus, students learning to read in French or Spanish do not have to be taught from scratch how to read in English. Obviously, differences between the writing systems of English and students' second language suggest that each must be taught independently. There is no basis for assuming that second language literacy will or will not transfer to the first language. The question of transfer of literacy skills when two languages do not share a writing system is an important research questions for the field. (p. 147)

The need of researching, investigating, developing, and improving Mandarin Chinese immersion pedagogy and curriculum for elementary schools has surfaced. This was not only a result of ineffective, limited, and under-researched programs that have been established for early language learners (Loke, 2002; Met, 2000; Walker, 1996), but also a result of recognizing the Chinese language is fundamentally a different language from English (Kanagy & Hai, 2001; Met, 2000, 2012; S. C. Wang, 2010; T. T. Wang, 2008).

The Chinese immersion program (CIP) was implemented at an urban school in North Carolina in 2006, yet had not been evaluated. It was not known how and to what extent CIP met the needs of immersion students. This study was designed to answer the evaluation questions by obtaining substantial data from the school district and the comparable schools. The criteria for evaluating CIP were based on the North Carolina Standard Course of Studies in math, English language arts, world languages guidelines, and the CIP Chinese curriculum.

The purpose of this study was to evaluate the effectiveness of the K-5 Chinese immersion program (CIP) developed and implemented at a school that served a diverse population in its school district. To accomplish this purpose, the study employed Stufflebeam's (2003) revised Context Input Process and Product (CIPP) design. Stufflebeam's (2003) model divides the program that is being evaluated into four separate components: Context, Input, Process, and Product. This program evaluation utilized all four components of the model.

Impact of the Problem

The lack of research on the impact of the Chinese language immersion program might not only impose a threat to the development of new emerging programs at the national level but also be detrimental to the stability of such programs. There were some studies on the effectiveness of Chinese instruction in immersion settings but very few program evaluation studies were conducted on Chinese immersion in North America. It was time to think about how to sustain the Chinese immersion programs in the United States and how to ensure the accountability of the Chinese immersion programs (National Chinese Language Conference, 2012). The interviews with the world language curriculum specialist at the district, the Chinese immersion school principal, and the language immersion facilitator revealed that there were not any curriculum review processes in place for world language curricula or for language immersion programs, including CIP, at the district or school level. The primary purpose of this program evaluation was to render judgments about the value of whatever was being evaluated (Fitzpatrick, Sanders, & Worthen, 2011). According to Stufflebeam (2004), "Evaluation's most important purpose is not to prove but to improve" (p. 262). In order to assist stakeholders in making value judgments and decisions about CIP and to improve CIP, a comprehensive Chinese language immersion program evaluation was needed for the school using Stufflebeam's CIPP program evaluation model. In addition, program theory was utilized to build the program sequence model (See Appendix B).

Background of the Problem

Setting of the problem. An urban K-8 language immersion magnet school located in southern North Carolina provided the setting for this study. This school offered French, German, Japanese, and Chinese instruction to the students in immersion settings. The school made the expected growth in the NC ABC's program and met 33/33 Adequate Yearly Progress (AYP) goals under No Child Left Behind guidelines (No Child Left Behind, 2001). It was also an NC School of Distinction 2006-2007, 2007-2008, 2008-2009, 2009-2010, and 2010-2011. The standards were based on North Carolina Standard Course of Study (NCSCOS), and the students were assessed in English in the state mandatory summative assessment, for example, End Of Grade (EOG) or End of

Course (EOC). The K-5 CIP was implemented in 2006 when the other three language immersion programs had already been up and running. CIP provided all students with at least 65% of instruction in Chinese, with English instruction provided at each grade level beginning in Kindergarten.

This study was designed not only to collect CIP students' EOG test data and investigate CIP's outcomes but also to examine the Chinese instructional environment and to evaluate its effectiveness. From many perspectives, CIP behaved as an organism in this school environment, an open system that had many unique students' needs, such as student's academic, linguistic, and social development. In addition, this open system also had to fulfill teachers' professional needs. If the program could address each student's needs and satisfy teacher's needs at different levels of Maslow's hierarchy, it would lead a full and healthy life and perform effectively for its mission (Morgan, 2006). More specifically, how the school administrators provided administrative supports to the teachers and how the school environment cultivated healthy working conditions for the teachers would impact CIP's effectiveness. In addition, how the teachers utilized the teaching strategies and created the optimal Chinese immersion learning environment would also impact CIP's effectiveness.

Identifying and implementing strategic changes at the program level was critical for CIP's success. Pettigrew (1972), in his study "Organizational Change and Learning," "underlines the particular complexity of the interacting factors of context, content, and process with which managers have to grapple to execute an effective strategic change. Strategic change is a complex, situation-dependent, continuous process" (p. 173). How to identify and execute the strategic change in a timely manner was a challenge and need, which was addressed by this formative evaluation guided by the CIPP evaluation model.

In summary, examining the instructional environment and its outcomes using the CIPP program evaluation model enabled this study to comprehensively portray CIP as a living system and to diagnose its strengths as well as areas for improvement.

Staff classification. The school had 95 certified staff members, and 42 of them were target language teachers. In addition, 71% of teachers possessed a Bachelor's Degree or equivalent; 29% held a Master's Degree or equivalent; and 8.4% had National Board certification.

The target language teachers were native speakers or had near-native proficiencies in the target languages. Teachers and staff were from Europe, Asia, Africa, North America, South America, and Australia. A majority of the staff was bilingual with 30% of the total professional staff being non-US citizens. Among the 42 K-5 target language classroom teachers, 10 were German immersion teachers; 11 were French immersion teachers; two were late immersion French teachers; six were Japanese immersion teachers; and 12 were Chinese immersion teachers. The school principal, being the language immersion school principal for 12 years, had 36 years in education and 24 years in administration.

Table 1 illustrates staff age distribution patterns within every 10 years. The dominating age group was 40-50 year-old. The group of 21-30 year-old had the least representation in CIP (See Table 1).

Table 1

Staff Age

Age Group	21-30	31-40	41-50	51-60	61-70	Total
Number	12	30	37	20	24	123
Percentage (%)	10	24	30	16	20	100

Table 2 illustrates the years of teaching experience in the different age groups listed. Approximately 40.4% of the teachers had 0-5 years of experience, which was the biggest group in the school. All the visiting international faculty (VIF) teachers and 75% of the Chinese language immersion teachers were in this group (See Table 2).

Table 2

Years of Teaching Experience

Years of Teaching Experience	0-3	4-5	6-7	8-10	11-15	16-20	21+	Total
Number	18	16	14	17	8	6	5	94
Percentage (%)	21.4	19.0	16.7	20.2	9.5	7.1	6.0	100

As there were many professionals switching from other fields to education through alternative lateral entry programs under NCDPI, the relationship between the staff age and years of teaching experience was different from that of traditional schools. Some of the younger teachers had more years of teaching experience than those of the older teachers in this school.

Program description. Learning Chinese and developing Chinese cultural competencies became a need for the immersion students of the United States. The rapid economic growth of China has drawn attention from the western world. Eight years ago, several district educational leaders who were fascinated by the global economy became anxious about investing the students in the Chinese language. *The World is Flat*, published in 2005, was a snap shot of the context of the world at that time (Friedman, 2005). The need of implementing a Chinese language program surfaced. The director of the magnet office and a language immersion school principal took this opportunity and made a strategic change—initiating CIP.

CIP was a full Chinese language immersion program. Modeled after the pioneering early total French immersion programs developed in Canada in the 1960s, CIP was designed to enrich the education of native-English-speaking students by teaching them all of their academic subjects in Chinese (Fortune & Tedick, 2003). CIP provided all students with at least 65% of instruction in Chinese, with English instruction provided at each grade level in one 45-60 minutes session per day, beginning in Kindergarten. In addition, five teachers provided instructions to the students respectively on the subjects of media, physical education, music, art, or dance, on a weekly basis. There were 12 Chinese immersion classes with 12 Chinese immersion teachers and three assistants.

CIP students came from diverse socioeconomic and demographic families. Specifically, 31.9% of the students were white; 27.8% were African American; 12.5% were Hispanic; 19.4% were Asian; and 8.3% were Multiracial. In addition, 34.6% of the K-8 students qualified for reduced or free lunch.

In summary, CIP full Chinese language immersion program was a customized version of an early total French language immersion model that was designed to address the needs of its diverse student population.

Program goals and objectives. The goal of CIP was for students to become proficient in the Chinese language and develop increased cultural awareness while reaching at least the same level of academic achievement as their peers in non-immersion schools. The objectives of CIP were defined by NCSCOS in all the subject areas. In the context of the goals and objectives of Chinese immersion language, the curriculum leaders at the school level were making independent curricular decisions based on the guideline of the American Council on the Teaching of Foreign Languages (ACTFL) standards, NCSCOS for Language Arts, and curriculum guideline of *International Curriculum for Chinese Language Education* and *Chinese Language Proficiency Scales for Speakers of Other Languages*.

More specifically, the program established that students should (a) reach the immersion exit proficiency expectations for logographic languages defined by the NCSCOS for World Language Essential Standards (NCDPI, 2010); (b) be able to master Pinyin skills by the end of the 2nd grade; (c) be able to produce 1,750 Chinese characters by the end of the 5th grade; (d) be able to recognize 3,500 Chinese characters, of which 2000 Chinese characters to be produced, by the end of the 8th grade; (d) be able to function in China for studies or vacations; for example, they should be able to read Chinese Newspaper with the aid of Chinese dictionaries or read technical instructions from menus (See Appendix C).

In addition, the Chinese language assessment and curriculum revision were initiated at the school level. First, the students were assessed with multiple measures due to the complexity of the Chinese language. So far, the language acquisition skills have not been assessed by either the state or district. Second, CIP was making language immersion curriculum changes based on the formative assessment from both the teacher-made language assessment instrument and Hanban-made standardized Youth Chinese Test (YCT) instrument. Furthermore, the revision of the CIP Chinese language curriculum was based on the rapid changes in the relationship between the United States and China in recent years to maximize CIP's performance and to best suit the needs of the diverse students and communities.

Program model and Chinese literacy model selection. This section reviews the CIP's full Chinese language immersion model, the reasons of this selection, as well as the Unity-Type Chinese curricula.

First, CIP adopted the full language immersion model with the following characteristics: (a) providing 700 (4 hours X 180 days) Chinese contact hours yearly; (b) generating cognitive engagement in learning tasks that were interesting to students; (c) creating interactive, authentic tasks, and intercultural activities for the students to maximize their learning performance; and (d) emphasizing many learning strategies such as meta-cognitive (paying attention, organizing, monitoring and evaluating), cognitive (making mental links, activating knowledge, thinking in parts, thinking in whole, personalizing, going beyond the data), affective, and socio-cultural interactive strategies to improve the efficiency of learning Chinese.

1. Second, the full language immersion model was adopted for the following reasons: Partial or delayed French immersion did not yield greater proficiency in English, but resulted in reduced French language proficiency. Genesee (1987) pointed out that

    There is no evidence that increased use of English during primary elementary grades as a result of either partial or delayed use of French as a medium of instruction yields greater proficiency in English than that achieved in early total immersion programs. At the same time, the reduced use of French in these alternatives usually results in reduced French language proficiency. (p. 40)

2. Full language immersion provided the most instruction time for immersion students in the Chinese language, which was critical for learning a character-based language with a complicated writing and reading system. The complexity of the Chinese language system required a much longer time to develop Chinese literacy in comparison with developing French, Spanish or German literacy (Met, 2012).

3. The school where CIP was incubated was a full language immersion school, with French, German, and Japanese full language immersion programs. This language immersion atmosphere provided the optimal macro-environment for implementing the full Chinese language immersion program.

Finally, CIP Chinese literacy model was Unity-Type Chinese curricular using simplified character and Pinyin. Initially, simplified character and zhuyin were selected over the traditional character and Pinyin. One year later, zhuyin was replaced with Pinyin, as it was difficult to acquire the teaching materials and computer input system using the combination of simplified character with zhuyin. In addition, it was an inefficient Chinese language system for the students to acquire, and it was time consuming for teachers to develop the Chinese teaching materials. Because of this quick adjustment, the system has run seamlessly and efficiently.

Program implementation. This section, with a brief introduction of CIP's history, concentrates on the seven prioritized components in developing CIP.

First, in 2005, two Chinese teachers were hired to prepare and teach the CIP's first two Kindergarten classes. In the same year, a team of five people, the school principal, two Chinese language immersion teachers, one middle school Chinese teacher, and one English facilitator, flew to California to observe California Association of Independent School (CAIS) and Cupertino school. Both schools offered 50-50 Chinese language immersion programs. CIP was subsequently initiated in 2006, with a vision that learning Chinese language would help American students to develop global competence for this interconnected world. Its mission was to prepare the students to become productive members of the global economy and world community.

Second, its prioritized components were (a) Chinese immersion teacher selection, (b) Chinese immersion teacher training, (c) Chinese program model and curriculum design, (d) Chinese curriculum implementation, (e) administrative and collegial support (f) Chinese language specific teaching strategy inputs, and (g) the CIP outcomes (See Appendix B).

Recruiting Chinese immersion teachers was the first component of CIP development. Three Chinese immersion teacher candidate pools were available for CIP: local Chinese professional communities—75% of the Chinese language immersion teachers were recruited locally and licensed through the alternative lateral entry licensure program in the North Carolina Department of Public Instruction (NCDPI); U.S. college graduates–25% of the teachers were licensed through the regular licensure process; and VIF–the rest of the Chinese teachers were hired from VIF. In short, the local Chinese professional community and two other alternative pools were essential for developing CIP.

The Chinese teacher training was the second component of CIP. Four types of professional development were provided for the newly-hired Chinese language teachers:

(a) a two-week lateral entry training camp which provided regulations, guidelines, and the best practices in classroom management for the new teachers, prior to their reporting to CIP; (b) one-week immersion 101 training workshop at the University of Minnesota which provided the language immersion theoretical framework and research-based practices for teaching in an immersion setting; (c) National Chinese Language Conference, which provided rigorous breakout sessions for the Chinese teachers; and (d) school communities, which provided informal training and classroom observations by the language immersion teachers in the same school building. More relevant local training opportunities were needed.

Chinese curriculum design was crucial; analyzing and revising the curriculum was equally essential for developing CIP. This was the third component of CIP development. First, as Chinese is markedly different from French and English (Wang, 2008; Kanagy & Hai, 2001; Met, 2000; Met, 2012; Wang, 2010), developing a deep understanding of the Chinese language and its didactics, as well as its pedagogy was fundamental. The Chinese Tri-Input Model (See Appendix D) reflected how the Chinese curriculum and instruction were designed and implemented in CIP. The Tri-Input Model was designed based on the findings of the Chinese language acquisition processes in listening, speaking, reading, writing, Pinyin, the application of the three strands of communication, and the observations and experiences of the Chinese language instructions at the classroom level. The Tri-Input Model served as a guide for the designing and refining CIP Chinese language curriculum and instruction. Second, as the Chinese immersion student population changed from one year to another, it was imperative that CIP continuously revisit, develop, and deploy Chinese language-specific instructional strategies and provide an optimal Chinese instructional learning environment for addressing the specific needs of the students.

The designing and implementation of the Chinese curriculum with fidelity was the fourth component of CIP development. CIP has been provided with resources to develop the curriculum for Kindergarten through the 6th grade. The Chinese teachers at the school, as a team, have formed a curricular matrix with emphasis on the relevance, integration, and articulation perspectives of the Chinese curriculum and its implementation. This curriculum matrix served as a Chinese curriculum guide for implementing the program model and curriculum (See Appendix C).

School leaders and learning communities provided continuous support for CIP. This was the fifth component of CIP development. The support included the school: (a) provided mentors to the new teachers, (b) allocated resources for developing the CIP Chinese curriculum, and (c) built an ambassador system for getting CIP parent's involvement in their children's academic and social development.

The CIP's outcomes were measured by the CIP students' academic performance in Chinese language and cultural competencies. The CIP students were required to take the state mandated assessments, for instance, EOG or EOC in English. In addition, the CIP students took Chinese summative tests designed by the CIP Chinese teachers and the YCT Chinese test designed by Hanban, China. The students were also informally evaluated by their voluntarily participations in various speech and writing competitions. Therefore, the information about CIP students' academic achievements in Chinese language and cultural competencies were collected and analyzed to portray CIP's effectiveness.

As planned, two Chinese immersion classes were added to CIP every year until the students reached the 5th grade. The first two Chinese Immersion Kindergarten classes were implemented in 2006.

Change agents and catalysts—the Chinese language teachers. The Chinese teachers grew up and obtained their higher education in China. The teaching philosophies, educational experiences, and the culture instilled shaped their perspectives of students' behavior, classroom management, and expectations, which were significantly different from that of teachers who grew up in the U.S.

The district training camp provided core classroom management concepts and practices that American schools and classrooms customarily accepted. Additionally, the Chinese immersion 101 training workshop at the University of Minnesota provided the core concepts and theories of language immersion education and how to provide effective language immersion instruction in immersion settings. Furthermore, the annual National Chinese Language Conference was another platform provided for these teachers to share innovative strategies for teaching Chinese effectively in immersion settings. Finally the school leadership and community offered administrative and collegial support for the Chinese language teachers. All these supports aimed to build a conceptual bridge between two sets of cultures, educational philosophies, expectations, and practices. The adaptation, integration, and transformation of two sets of concepts were essential for the Chinese teachers to become effective change agents and catalysts and to transform the resources and materials into intellectual assets–the students' academic outcomes in the Chinese language and cultural competencies.

One of the CIP's limitations was that the students who left the program were not easily replaced due to the constraints of the language skills required. No new students were admitted to the Chinese classes above 1st grade level. Combo class strategy, combining different grade levels, has proved not to be a good option for a Chinese language immersion program. That has resulted in sizeable fourth and fifth grade classes, reaching up to 29 students in one class.

Description of comparable schools. Three comparable English schools in the same district were selected. The first one was a neighborhood school with similar economically disadvantage students (NSS); the second one was a magnet school, considered as a high performing school with similar economically disadvantaged students (MSS); and the third one was a neighborhood school, considered as a high performing school with lower economically disadvantaged students (NSL).

The comparable Chinese immersion program was chosen from a school in Minnesota with lower economically disadvantaged students (CIPL). CIPL has adopted the early total French immersion model, which served native speakers of English in an environment where the Chinese language was used exclusively. Content was delivered in the Chinese language. English Language Arts was introduced in Grade 3 in the Chinese language immersion program (Genesee & Jared, 2008).

In this study, five schools were involved, four of which were in North Carolina and one of which was in Minnesota (See Table 3).

Table 3

Comparable School Student Demographics

	EDS (%)	White (%)	African-American (%)	Hispanic (%)	(Sub-total) (%)	Asian (%)	Other (%)
CIP	N/A	30.5	27.8	13.9	41.7	19.4	8.3
CIPS	34.6	42.7	28.9	17.9	46.8	4.6	6
NSS	35	45.5	40.9	5	45.9	5	3.6
MSS	29.5	60.8	31.7	3.1	34.8	1.8	2.6
NSL	17.6	73.5	15	5.8	20.8	3.4	2.4
CIPL	N/A	62.6	6.7	2.1	8.8	27.6	1.1

Note. EDS = economically disadvantaged students; CIPS = the school of CIP; CIPL = the Chinese immersion program in Minnesota.

Significance of the Problem

Chinese immersion programs are seeing a greater demand in North America, yet little research has been aimed at determining the effectiveness of these programs with specifically defined outcomes. Of primary interest was whether or not young learners could benefit from this type of Chinese language immersion program. An examination of the Chinese immersion program in North Carolina that has been promoting Chinese language immersion with character-based language instruction for 7 years had the potential to not only shed light on the strengths and weaknesses of the Chinese immersion didactics and pedagogy in regards to implementation in American public elementary schools but also provide suggestions for future Chinese language program implementation in other contexts in the United States.

First, decision makers across every sector have renewed their focus on questions such as: How did we know if this program worked? How could we ensure that the time, money, and resources devoted to this program were well spent? How would we determine if this program had accomplished what it was meant to do (Nelson & Eddy, 2008)? Based on CAL (2012), only one Chinese immersion program evaluation has been completed in the United States, while there were 70,000 K-12 students studying Chinese and 50,000 students studying Chinese in colleges (National Chinese Language Conference, 2012). The intent of this evaluation was to determine CIP's effectiveness and provide insights for the decision makers, Chinese immersion teachers, and stakeholders.

Second, decision makers and stakeholders also wanted to know how to improve the quality of the Chinese language immersion program. This study not only provided an opportunity for the stakeholders to improve the CIP's quality, as Stufflebeam (2004) stressed, "Evaluation's most important purpose is not to prove but to improve" (p. 262), but also contributed to Chinese language immersion didactics and pedagogy and Chinese program evaluation practices in North America.

Finally, in spite of the increasing number of Chinese language immersion programs in North America, the body of research related to this field is still very limited. The study of the comprehensive Chinese language immersion program evaluation and its methodology is scarce. This study adds to the body of knowledge of Chinese language immersion programs and their evaluation.

Evaluator's role in relation to the organization. The evaluator is the program coordinator and lead teacher. The evaluator developed the CIP Chinese language immersion curriculum with the support of the Chinese team and school. CIP has a 7-year history with noticeable resources invested in this program from the school district and community. It was time to conduct a comprehensive evaluation of CIP, not only to see what has really worked and what has not, but also to determine CIP's merit and worth. To avoid conflict of interests in this evaluation, the advisory panel was created to strengthen the validity and reliability of this study. Detailed discussions are included in Chapter 3.

Definition of Terms

Several terms relevant to the program evaluation are provided in the following text for clarification and they are divided into four congruent groups as follows: Language Immersion, Program Evaluation, Philosophical Views and Evaluation Methodologies, and Accountability Models.

Language immersion. Chinese language immersion is a rapidly developing field in North America, yet this phenomenon is still not well known to the general public. Many terms introduced in this section will facilitate reader to gain deeper understanding of the Chinese language immersion program and its impact in general.

Medium of instruction. Medium of instruction is a language used in teaching. It may or may not be the official language of the country or territory. For example, in the Chinese language immersion program, the medium of instruction is Chinese.

Target language. Target language is the language used in teaching. It may or may not be the official language of the country or territory. For example, in the Chinese language immersion program, the target language is Chinese.

Full language immersion program. CIP is a full language immersion program. In addition, CIP program model is a modified early total French immersion model with the following approach:

The program serves native speakers of English in an environment where the target language is used exclusively. Content is delivered in the target language. English

Language Arts is introduced around grade 2 or later in French or German full immersion programs and at Kindergarten in Chinese or Japanese language immersion programs. The students become bilingual, bi-literate, bicultural, and are equally proficient in both languages with near-native fluency in the target language. (NCDPI, 2010)

Full Chinese language immersion program. CIP is a full Chinese language immersion program, and it is described as follows. The program serves native speakers of English in an environment where Chinese is used exclusively. Content is delivered in Chinese. English Language Arts is introduced since Kindergarten. At least 65% of the instructional time is in Chinese per day. The students become bilingual, bi-literate, and bicultural and are equally proficient in both languages with near-native fluency in Chinese.

Additive bilingualism. According to Genesee (1987), "The immersion program ensures the attainment of second language proficiency without sacrificing first language development and academic achievement" (p. 41).

Young learner's Chinese test. YCT is a standard assessment instrument provided for the non-Chinese speakers. The YCT provides a four-level test based on the mastery of Chinese vocabularies. The 2012-2013 CIP students' YCT test scores were collected and analyzed in this study.

Visiting international faculty. VIF is an organization that brings the qualified foreign language teachers internationally.

Program evaluation. Its root term is value, which is further defined by merit and worth of a program. Program evaluation is to investigate the merit and worth of a program in a systematic manner. The core concepts and theories of program evaluation are discussed with the following terminology.

Value. Value is an idea possessed by a society, group, or individual and can be measured by its relative merit and worth of an object. According to Stufflebeam (2000c),

> The value provides the foundation for deriving the particular evaluative criteria. The criteria, along with questions of stakeholders, dictate information needs. These, in turn, provide the direction for selecting/constructing the evaluation instruments and interpretation standards. (p. 305)

There are seven levels of value and criteria according to Stufflebeam (2000c), and they are: "basic societal values; criteria inherent in the definition of evaluation; criteria in the definitions of Context, Input, Process, and Product evaluation; institutional values; pertinent technical standards; duties of professionals; and idiosyncratic criteria" (p. 308).

Merit and worth. Merit and worth is a root term in program evaluation. The essence of program evaluation is to set up the criteria with regard to the merit and worth of a program. In this study, the merit of CIP was measured by comparing CIP with the excellent programs of the field: the higher performing magnet school (MSS), the higher performing neighborhood school (NSL), and the higher performing Chinese immersion program (CIPL). In addition, the worth of CIP was determined by how CIP addressed the assessed needs for the community. Stafflebeam (2000c) defined merit and worth as follows:

> Merit denotes an object's intrinsic value or quality. Merit assessments address the issue of whether a program, product, or service is sound in concept, design, delivery, material, and outcomes. Evaluators gauge the evaluand's merit by comparing it with the state of the art and critical competitors against established technical criteria. Worth involves an object's extrinsic value or how useful it is in

meeting the assessed needs of a defined group of beneficiaries. (p. 308)

Evaluation. An evaluation is a systematic investigation of the merit and/or worth of a program, project, service, or other object of interest. Stufflebeam (2000c) stressed that, "[o]perationally, evaluation is the process of delineating, obtaining, reporting, and applying descriptive and judgmental information about some object's merit and worth in order to guide decision making, support accountability, disseminate effective practices and increase understanding of the involved phenomena" (p. 280).

Standards for evaluation. According to Stufflebeam (2000c), "They are principles commonly agreed to by specialists in the conduct and use of evaluations for the measure of an evaluation's value or quality." (p. 280) These standards were written by The Joint Committee in 1975, published in 1981, and updated in 1994 and called The Program Evaluation Standards. Stufflebeam (2000b) notes that "The Joint Committee is accredited by the ANSI as the only body recognized to set standards for educational evaluations in the U.S." (p. 440)

Improvement/accountability-oriented evaluation models. They are designed primarily to assess and/or improve a program's merit and worth. Such studies are expansive and seek comprehensiveness in considering the full range of questions and criteria needed to assess a program's value. It calls for multiple qualitative and quantitative assessment methods to provide cross-checks on findings (Stufflebeam, 2000a).

CIPP evaluation model. It is classified as a management/accountability-oriented evaluation model. Based on Stufflebeam (2003), "It is a comprehensive framework for guiding evaluation of programs. This model was developed in the late 1960s to help improve and achieve accountability for U.S. school programs" (p. 31). Stufflebeam

(2003) further posits that,

> [T]his model's core concepts are Context, Input, Process, and Product evaluation. By employing the four types of evaluation, the evaluator serves several important functions. Context evaluations assess needs, problems, and opportunities within a defined environment. They aid evaluation users to define and assess goals and later reference assessed needs of targeted beneficiaries to judge a school program. Input evaluations assess competing strategies and the work plans and budgets of approaches chosen for implementation; they aid evaluation users to design improvement efforts, develop defensible funding proposals, detail action plans, record alternative plans that were considered, and record the basis for choosing one approach over the others. Process evaluations monitor, document, and assess activities. They help evaluation users carry out improvement efforts and maintain accountability records of their execution of action plans. Product evaluations identify and assess short-tem, long-term, intended, and unintended outcomes. They help evaluation users maintain their focus on meeting the needs of students or other beneficiaries; assess and record their level of success in reaching and meeting the beneficiaries' target needs; identify intended and unintended side effects; and make informed decisions to continue, stop, or improve the effort. (p. 31-32)

Stufflebeam's definition of CIPP evaluation provided a conceptual road map for this CIP evaluation.

Program theory. It emphasizes how the programs work. The use of program theory for evaluation has three main purposes: (a) certain types of summative evaluation, which focus on answering questions, such as, "Does the program cause the intended outcomes?" (b) formative evaluations which are intended to suggest how the program can be improved; and (c) ongoing program monitoring, which provides continuous indicators of program performance (Rogers, 2000). Based on the program theory, if the program is very complicated and if the program needs to be replicated, designing a program logic model is worth the effort.

Philosophical views and evaluation methodologies. The following terms are essential philosophical assumptions and relevant methodologies applied in this study.

Postpositivist paradigm. According to Fitzpatrick, et al. (2011), postpositivists focused on quantitative methods as a better way to obtain objective information about causal relationships among the phenomena evaluators or researchers studied. They believed that evaluators should be focusing on the facts.

This evaluative study applied quantitative methods to collect and analyze the quantitative data using Chinese immersion instructional environment survey, meta-evaluation survey, and students' EOG test scores. The quantitative findings have substantiated the conclusion of the evaluation questions.

Constructivist paradigm. Based on Fitzpatrick, et al. (2011), "Constructivists were more concerned with describing different perspectives and with exploring and discovering new theories" (p. 118). Constructivists put more emphasis on understanding causal relationships than on establishing a definitive causal link between a program and its outcome. Constructivists favored qualitative measures, which include data collection methods such as interviews, focus groups, observations, and content analysis of existing documents. Finally, according to Fitzpatrick, et al. (2011) "Constructivists believed that evaluation is intended to provide understanding of a particular program and its context and is less concerned with generalibility and developing laws and theories for other settings" (p. 116).

This study applied qualitative method with semi-structured interviews to provide deep understanding CIP and its academic impact.

Mixed study methodology. In a mixed methods design format, the research brings together approaches that are included in both the quantitative and qualitative formats (Creswell & Clark, 2007). Even though the core beliefs of postpositivists and constructivists are incompatible, evaluative and methodological choices should not be based on paradigms or philosophical views but on practical characteristics of each specific evaluation and the concepts to be measured in that particular study.

This study used mixed study methodology to comprehensively evaluate CIP and its impact on the Chinese language immersion students.

Semi-structured interview. It is utilized when the questions are the same for each individual, but the evaluator may vary the questions or explore them in more detail, depending upon answers given by the participants (Lichtman, 2006).

Chinese language instructional environment. Foreign language immersion research has been mainly focusing on French and Spanish, less on Chinese (Chao, 1993; De Courcy, 1997); however, Chinese is markedly different from French or Spanish. In addition, the teaching philosophies of the native Chinese teachers are significantly different (Met, 2012). Therefore, the Chinese language immersion teaching pedagogy and strategies in the U.S. need to be studied in immersion classroom settings.

Meta-evaluation. According to Stufflebeam (2000d), "[i]t is formally defined as the process of delineating, obtaining, and applying descriptive information and judgmental information about the utility, feasibility, propriety, and accuracy of an evaluation in order to guide the evaluation and publicly report its strength and weakness"

(p. 458).

In this evaluation study, the advisory panel conducted a meta-evaluation survey to evaluate the evaluation process. The meta-evaluation survey was adapted from the Program Evaluation Meta-evaluation checklist (Stufflebeam, 1999) based on the CIP's needs.

Accountability models involved. The follow terms were designed for holding schools accountable for student success and were used for measuring the achievement level of a school and school district. The students' test data collected from CIP and three district comparable schools in this evaluation were 3-year's test results produced by the North Carolina's ABCs accountability model.

Adequate Yearly Progress. A measure identified by each state that is used to determine the achievement level of each school and school district for accountability purposes mandated by the No Child Left Behind Act of 2001 (Paige, 2002).

ABCs. The ABCs of public education is North Carolina's first school-level accountability system. It was first implemented in the 1996-97 school year at the 3rd-8th grade levels. It provided a means to hold schools "A"ccountable for student academic growth over the course of a school year. End Of Grade and End Of Course tests focused on "B"asic skills. Local "C"ontrol provided districts the flexibility to make management decisions that best meet the needs of their students (NCDPI, 2012).

READY. The READY initiative, which is being implemented in public schools in the 2012-13 school year, focuses not only on student proficiency in foundational subjects but on ensuring students are career- and college-ready when they graduate high school. The initiative is characterized by a new Standard Course of Study, assessments and accountability model (NCDPI, 2013).

Chapter 2: Literature Review

Theoretical Framework

The theoretical design of this study was built on language immersion theories, the CIPP evaluation model, the program theory, and mixed study methodology.

First, consistent findings have been obtained from French language immersion program evaluations that show, in early language immersion programs, students gain fluency and literacy in French at no apparent cost to their English academic skills (Campbell, Gray, Rhodes, & Snow, 1985; Curtain & Dahlberg, 2004; Genesee, 1987, 1994). Extensive research provides support to this conclusion and has been ongoing at least from the start of the Saint Lambert immersion project in Canada in 1965 (Cummins, 1981, 1987; Genesee, 1987). The Chinese language immersion program (CIP) in this study was designed based on the assumption that the French immersion model and pedagogy were transferrable to Chinese language immersion programs. Therefore, CIP replicated the early total French language immersion model with some modification. The full Chinese language immersion program served native speakers of English in an environment where Chinese was used exclusively by the Chinese language immersion teachers. The subjects, such as, math, science, social studies, and Chinese language arts, were delivered in Chinese. English Language Arts was introduced in Kindergarten. The students were expected to become bilingual, bi-literate, bicultural, and be equally proficient in both languages with near-native fluency in Chinese. The CIP's outcomes—the achievement in English reading, mathematics, and science—were expected to be at least at the same level as their peers in English programs.

Second, the program evaluation was designed to comprehensively evaluate CIP. A program evaluation is conducted to determine the merit and worth of the program

(Charles & Mertler, 2006; Fitzpatrick et al., 2011; Stufflebeam, 2003). According to Stufflebeam (2000a), 22 evaluation approaches have been divided into four categories. After comparing CIP's evaluative needs with the strength of the evaluation approaches, the CIPP evaluation model (Stufflebeam, 2003) was selected as the most appropriate method for use in this evaluation study. More details of selecting CIPP model for CIP's evaluation were introduced in Program Evaluation Design section of the chapter.

In addition, the Chinese immersion program was a new and complex phenomenon and was not well known by a majority of citizens and educators in the United States. The evaluation approach based on program theory was utilized for constructing the Comprehensive Chinese Language Immersion Program Sequence Model within the framework of the CIPP evaluation model (See Appendix B). This sequence model illustrated what a CIP was, what "evaluation guidelines" were, and how they could be replicated (Rogers, 2000).

Finally, the mixed study methodology was applied for the evaluation. Postpositivists' paradigm focuses on quantitative methods as a better way to obtain objective information about causal relationship among the phenomena the evaluator or researcher studies (Fitzpatrick, et al., 2011). Quantitative methods are the ones that yield numerical data, which include tests, surveys, and direct measures of certain quantitative constructs (Creswell, 2003, 2009, 2012). Constructivists are more concerned with describing different perspectives and with exploring and discovering new theories. Constructivists also play more emphasis on understanding causal relationships than on establishing a definitive causal link between a program and its outcome. Constructivists favor qualitative measures, which include data-collection methods, such as interviews, focus groups, observations, and content analysis of existing documents (Fitzpatrick, et al.,

2011). Pragmatists urge evaluators and researchers to look beyond ontological and epistemological arguments to consider what they are studying and the appropriate methods for studying the issues of concern (Fitzpatrick, et al., 2011). In this study of evaluation, the evaluator used both quantitative and qualitative methodology, which fit in the design of the CIPP evaluation model and was supported by many theorists (Collins, Onwuegbuzie, & Sutton, 2006; Creswell, 2003, 2009, 2012; Fitzpatrick, et al., 2011; Greene, 2006).

Use of Chinese Language

The use of the Chinese language became important to the U.S. as China has established itself as a world economic and political power. Increasing American students' intercultural awareness and supporting them to learn Chinese, a less commonly used language, are crucial for international prosperity and stability.

First, the efforts to increase student intercultural awareness and understanding are consistent with broader U.S. trends in international education. Sandell (2007), in her study regarding the impact of international education experience on undergraduate students, quoted U.N. Secretary-General Kofi Annan:

> Perhaps more than ever, international understanding is essential to world peace . . . Globalization, migration, economic integration, communication, and travel are bringing different races, cultures, and ethnicities into ever closer contact with each other . . . Combining the familiar with the foreign can be a source of powerful knowledge and insight. (p.12)

Among all the students who study foreign languages, only nine percent of them study the less commonly taught languages such as Arabic, Chinese, etc., spoken by the overwhelming majority of people around the world (National Council of Less Commonly

Taught Languages, 2012).

In addition, a congenial relationship between the United States and China is critical for global prosperity and stability. Preparing the young American leaders to be able to engage their Chinese counterparts on their own terms and in their own languages is a need. These young leaders and their Chinese counterparts will be stewards of a cooperative relationship going forward (Negroponte, 2012). Hagel (2012) stressed that the bilateral relationship between China and the United States has become more critical than ever in history, at least in modern history. He emphasized, "The United States and China don't have to agree on everything, but to develop a common ground which is essential to the world peace and prosperity" (C. Hagel, personal communication, April 12, 2012) (See Appendix A).

Furthermore, Fortune (2008) pointed out that Chinese language ability was of increasing importance to national security, economic competitiveness, delivery of health care, and law enforcement in the United States.

Research on Language Immersion Acquisition

This section primarily concentrated on six aspects of language immersion education in general, with a brief introduction of the initiation for Chinese language immersion programs first.

The studies of Chinese language immersion education (De Courcy, 2002; Liu, 1992; Tang, 1988) are comparatively fewer than those of French immersion (Curtain & Dahlberg, 2004; Genesee, 1987, 1994), and those of two-way Spanish immersion (Genesee, 1987; Snow, 1990; Thomas & Colliers, 2002). In the past decade, the need of learning the Chinese language has emerged and the Chinese language immersion program designers have replicated the French language immersion model for the Chinese language immersion programs.

In addition, 30 years worth of study on French language immersion has accumulated abundant findings of language immersion education, which were categorized into (a) history of language immersion, (b) academic impact of language immersion, (c) cognitive impact of language immersion, (d) linguistic impact of language immersion, (e) language immersion didactics and pedagogy, and (d) transferability from French to Chinese immersion. Each of those areas was examined individually.

The history of language immersion. Language immersion education experienced three developing stages in North America.

First, language immersion was originated long before French language immersion in St. Lambert in 1965. There is nothing new, of course, about using a second or foreign language as a medium of instruction (Johnson & Swain, 1997). Johnson and Swain pointed out, "Our claim is that the term 'immersion' can be legitimately and usefully applied beyond its purely historical origins in Canada to a wide range of programs despite differences in their aims, socioeconomic contexts, and manner of implementation" (p. 1). Johnson and Swain (1997) further stated:

> Throughout the history of formal education, the use of L2 medium has been the rule rather than the exception. Until the rise of nationalism, few languages other than those of great empires, religions, and civilizations were considered competent or worthy to carry content of a formal curriculum. Latin was the medium of religious and secular education in Europe for a thousand years after the fall of the Roman Empire. Classical Arabic is still widely used as the medium of instruction in Muslim countries where many different vernaculars are spoken. Each of the western imperial powers imposed its language upon the colonized,

and English, French, Spanish, and Portuguese are still widely used as media of instruction despite the ending of the colonial era. (p. 17)

Second, French language immersion established its pioneer position in foreign language education. With the focus of linguistic benefit, the launching of a St. Lambert French immersion program in 1965 as an experimental language program made the St. Lambert French immersion program a historical reference for foreign language immersion education. Genesee (1987) stated that the main goals of the immersion program in 1965 were for participating English-speaking children to achieve French proficiency in speaking and writing, to maintain English language development, to ensure academic achievement, and to promote understanding and appreciation of French Canadians and their culture.

Thereafter, two-way Spanish immersion, German immersion, Japanese immersion, and Chinese immersion began to emerge in the late 1990s. Met and Lorenz (1997) pointed out the following:

From modest beginning in the early 1970s, foreign language immersion programs in elementary schools in the United States have grown significantly. Today, there are 187 elementary immersion programs in twenty-five states and the District of Columbia, and their continued growth is testament to both their effectiveness and the resulting enthusiasm of educators and parents. The growth of immersion has been characterized by American's penchant for diversity. Although most immersion programs involve Spanish, there are programs in French, German, Japanese, and Chinese. About 60% of programs are early partial immersion and 40% are early total immersion. (p. 243)

Academic impact of language immersion. It was evident that the primary focus of language immersion education was academic achievement and very little data were available on the impact of the second language proficiency.

First, numerous studies on language immersion education repeated the same results: language immersion education has been generally found to be the most effective way to teach students a second language. Students gain fluency and literacy in French at no apparent cost to their English academic skills (Cummins, 1983, 1998; Curtain & Dahlberg, 2004; Genesee, 1987, 1994; Soderman, 2010). This was one of the fundamental findings that had laid the foundation for foreign language immersion education.

Second, several prominent scholars conducted methodical studies on French language immersion program models and their impacts on English academics, but very little data were available on the impact of the second language acquisition. Genesee (1987) concluded decades of research on English-speaking students of various academic abilities immersed in other languages showed that these learners were capable of achieving high levels of functional proficiency in the immersion language while at the same time achieving academically at or above their non-immersion peers on standardized tests administered in English.

According to Campbell et al. (1985), "Foreign language immersion programs are the most successful school based language learning program models currently available and immersion students typically achieve higher levels of proficiency when compared with students in non-immersion programs" (pp. 44-54).

Cummins (1983) conducted a comprehensive review of heritage language education in different cultural settings. He compared and contrasted the impact of the minority language programs on student academic and social development in Canada, the United States, and in Europe. He also noted, "because most program evaluations focus primarily on academic outcomes, little or no data are available on the impact of bilingual, or heritage language programs on the education system as a whole" (Cummins, 1983, p. 6). This view exposed a need to comprehensively evaluate the impact of the foreign language immersion program on both academic achievement and foreign language proficiency. The anticipated outcome of this study was to increase the body of knowledge in this context.

Cognitive impact of language immersion. Cognitive impact of language immersion was reviewed through the cognitive benefits of bilingualism in this section. Hence, (a) the relation of bilingualism and intelligence, (b) cognitive flexibility, (c) non-verbal problem-solving ability, (c) other cognitive benefits, for examples, bilinguals approaching cognitive tasks in truly analytic way and more attentive to structures and details, and (d) the correlation between cognitive benefits and fully proficient bilingualism were discussed respectively in the following texts.

First, Baker (1988) described the relation between bilingualism and intelligence and stated that, "Bilingualism is to intelligence as food to human fitness" (p. 1). Baker (1988) concluded the following:

> The relationship between the two is both central and controversial. Central, in that the disadvantages or advantages of being bilingual have been historically measured by reference to intelligence. Controversial, in that both terms are difficult to define, elusive to measure and evoke passions and prejudices. (p. 1)

In addition, Hakuta and Diaz (1985) provided a brief review of research about bilingualism and cognitive ability. According to Hakuta and Diaz (1985), in 1962, Peal and Lambert studied the relation of bilingualism and intelligence. The sample consisted of 75 monolinguals and 89 bilinguals who were 10-years-old and selected from the same school system in Montreal. Hakuta and Diaz (1985) stated:

> The results of the Peal and Lambert study showed that bilinguals performed significantly better than monolinguals on most of the cognitive tests and subtests, even when group differences in sex, age, and socioeconomic status were appropriately controlled. Bilingual children performed significantly higher than monolinguals on tests of both verbal and nonverbal abilities; the bilinguals' superiority in nonverbal tests was more clearly evident in those subtests that required mental manipulation and reorganization of visual stimuli, rather than mere perceptual abilities. A factor analysis of test scores indicated that bilinguals were superior to monolinguals in concept formation and in tasks that required a certain mental or symbolic flexibility. Overall, bilinguals were found to have a more diversified pattern of abilities than their monolingual peers. (p. 322)

Studies also showed that raising a child bilingually could result in numerous cognitive and linguistic benefits for the child, as Hakuta and Diaz (1985) concluded, "Recent research not only has replicated Peal and Lambert's positive findings regarding balanced bilingualism, but also has given empirical support for linguists' statements regarding the cognitive and linguistic advantages of raising a child bilingually" (p. 324).

Second, many researchers investigated how bilingualism related to cognitive flexibility. Cognitive flexibility is the ability to restructure knowledge in multiple ways depending on the changing situational demands (i.e. difficulty or complexity of the situation) (Spiro & Feltovich et al., 1995). Research finds evidence for greater cognitive flexibility in foreign language immersion students than monolingual students (Bruck,

Lambert, & Tucker, 1976).

Felderman and Shen (1971) did a test with 15 Spanish-English bilingual children and 15 unmatched monolingual children from the Head Start program. The 4-year-old to 6-year-old groups were tested for "object constancy." For example, a paper cup was crushed and placed with a cup identical to the original. Each child was given a task of selecting the object as initially shown. Ninety-five percent of the bilinguals answered correctly compared with 84% of monolinguals, a statistically significant difference.

Using six tests of linear measurement from Piaget (1952), Liedtke and Nelson (1968) found that bilinguals performed better on concept formation, and were more advanced on concept conservation, and on concept measurement. Their findings were based on 50 bilinguals and 50 monolinguals matched on sex, age, IQ, and socioeconomic level.

Duncan and DeAvila (1979) found out that the order of best performance on neo-Piagetian tests of conservation of identity, number, length, substance and distance was: Proficient Bilinguals, Monolinguals, Limited Bilinguals, Partial Bilinguals, and Later Language Learners, and the differences between proficient Bilinguals and Monolinguals were statistically significant.

Ben-Zeev (1977b) discovered that Bilinguals tended to give more classifications and were less inconsistent across the tests and gave more attention to the details. Though the results were mostly only marginally statistically significant, the trends were in favor of bilinguals. Ben-Zeev's findings were drawn from Piagetian classification and reclassification tests. An example of the stimuli in such a test was given in the diagram opposite. Sorting the objects into correct groups was required, taking into account shape, color, and size. A child might be asked to sort outside circles from outside squares, thus ignoring color and inside shape. The test administrator might request that the child separate red objects from white objects, thus ignoring a previous classification. The bilinguals, who are approximately equivalent in their abilities in L1 and L2, demonstrate better cognitive flexibility than the monolinguals on the condition that both groups are approximately matched for age, socioeconomic level, and other relevant variables (Hakuta & Diaz, 1985).

According to Lei and Moreira (2001), students face numerous demands to turn the unfamiliar into the familiar in the immersion learning environment, which indicates how students develop their cognitive skills in the language immersion learning environment. Cartwright (2008) stressed that knowledge-assembling tasks required children to pay greater attention to the context, interact flexibly with others, and decide over and over what was relevant and what was not. Soderman (2010) commented that, "Bilingual children are driven to higher levels of cognitive flexibility than are unilingual children in education settings. Learning a new language is greater than simply acquiring a vocabulary and workable syntax. It's problem-solving" (p. 57). Soderman (2010) also explained:

> We see our children in our program continuously juggling multiple mental representations in their attempts to choose the right word for the right context and right person. They are driven to reflect on their intended meaning as they respond to a speaker who doesn't share their primary language, and they must solve the problem of what it will take to have a peer or teacher understand what they are trying to say. Their day involves numerous demands to turn the unfamiliar to the familiar. (Lei & Moreira, 2001, p. 57)

Third, bilinguals demonstrated stronger non-verbal problem-solving ability than monolinguals. Bamford and Mizokawa (1991) pointed out that foreign language immersion students exhibited better nonverbal problem-solving abilities. Bamford and Mizokawa (1991) stressed, "the superior control of cognitive processing demonstrated by children in the early stages of additive bilingualism may enhance symbolic reasoning abilities. The developmental interdependence of L1 and L2 may allow additive-bilingual children to maintain normal native-language development" (p. 413). Bamford and Mizokawa (1991) further explained:

> The study examined the development of a Grade 2 additive-bilingual (Spanish-immersion) program class as compared to a monolingual classroom on measures of nonverbal problem-solving. The program was the independent variable in the comparison. Nonverbal problem-solving was the dependent variable, as measured by Raven's (1977) Coloured Progressive Matrices (CPM). As hypothesized, a repeated measures analysis of covariance (ANCOVA) of the results of fall and spring administrations of the CPM indicated significant differences in favor of the Spanish-immersion group, $F(1, 35)=5.85$, $p=.02$. (p. 413)

In 1988, Baker's study of issues of bilingualism and bilingual education found similar results that Bilinguals demonstrated superior ability in symbol substitution. Baker (1988) summarized the following:

> One test used by Ben-Zeev was the Symbol Substitution Test where a child expected to substitute one word for another (e.g. "macaroni" for "I" as in "Macaroni am warm"). To answer correctly, a child must be able to resist the interference of word substitution, to ignore word meaning and also sentence

framing. Bilinguals were found to be superior in symbol substitution not only with regard to meaning but also with regard to the grammatical rules of sentence construction. Having experienced two language systems with two different rules of construction, the bilinguals appear to be more flexible and analytical in language. (p. 30)

Fourth, bilinguals approached the cognitive tasks in a truly analytic manner. Ben-Zeev (1977a) pointed out that bilingual children seemed to approach the cognitive tasks in a truly analytic way. They also seemed more attentive to both the structure and details of the tasks administered, as well as more sensitive to feedback from the tasks and the testers. She argued that, in order to avoid linguistic interference, bilinguals had to develop a keen awareness of the structural similarities and differences between their two languages as well as a special sensitivity to linguistic feedback from the environment.

Furthermore, Fortune (2012) stated that, "There's a well-established positive relationship between basic thinking skills and being a fully proficient bilingual who maintains regular use of both languages. Fully proficient bilinguals outperform monolinguals in the areas of divergent thinking, pattern recognition, and problem solving" (p. 9). Cummins (1981) cautioned that there might be a certain threshold of second language proficiency necessary before cognitive benefits would develop. Fortune (2008) also pointed out, "Cognitive benefits accrue in relation to the level of second language proficiency attained" (p. 2).

Linguistic impact of language immersion. Language immersion students not only demonstrated stronger metalinguistic skills, but also exhibited fluency and confidence in speaking and reading using their second language.

First, bilinguals demonstrated perceptible metalinguistic skills. Vygotsky (1962) indicated that bilingualism enabled children "to see his language as one particular system among many, to view its phenomena under more general categories, and this leads to awareness of his linguistic operations" (p. 110). According to Hakuta (1985),

> There is an increasing correlation between the abilities of the children in the two languages over time. That is, when the students first entered the bilingual program, their abilities in Spanish and English were unrelated. However, by the end of three years, there were correlations as strong as $r = 0.70$ between the two languages. The pattern of correlations also suggested to us that children who came in with a strong base in their native language, Spanish, ended up with the strongest abilities in English. (p. 66)

Second, language immersion students exhibited fluency and confidence in using their second language. Genesee (1987) stated that native English-speaking immersion student displayed fluency and confidence in their second language and developed native like levels of comprehension, i.e., listening and reading skills, in their immersion language. This denoted a linguistic benefit of the immersion program.

Third, when it came to the linguistic benefit of language immersion, Fortune (2012) pointed out that:

> The immersion approach first gained traction in North America because educators believed in its potential to move students further towards bilingualism and bi-literacy. Immersion language programs took root in areas such as St. Lambert, Canada, and Miami, Florida, where educators felt that more than one language was necessary for children's future economic and social prosperity. Program designers wagered that making the second language the sole medium for teaching core subject content, instead of teaching the second language separately, would

result in more students reaching higher levels of proficiency. (p. 10)

In addition, regarding the initial concerns about the possible detriment to English language and literacy development, Fortune (2012) summarized that:

> English proficient immersion students typically achieve higher levels of minority (non-English) language proficiency when compared with students in other types of language programs (Campbell, R.N., Gray, T.C., Rhodes, N.C., and Snow, M.A., 2010) . . . Initial concerns about the possible detriment to English language and literacy development were eventually laid to rest. English-proficient immersion students who achieved relatively high levels of second-language proficiency also acquired higher levels of English language skills and metalinguistic awareness, an ability to think about how various parts of a language function. (p. 11)

Furthermore, to provide a child an opportunity to be able to speak, read, and write in more than one language was to present an invaluable gift to this child. Soderman (2010) concluded that:

> Bilingual children can be considered to be gifted children, because they're equipped with a skill that's considered an integral and necessary component in a truly educated person's portfolio . . . to be able to speak more than one language fluently . . . to be able to read and write fluently in more than one language, provides each of these children with treasures for the future. (p. 57)

Finally, research about the relationship between character-based and English literacy sub-skills continues to grow (Fortune, 2012). According to Gottardo, Yan, Siegel, and Wade-Woolley (2001), there is some evidence linking the transfer of phonological processing skills for native Chinese speakers who are learning English as a second language. However, "Much remains to be learned in these areas when it comes to English proficient children in Mandarin immersion programs who are acquiring literacy in Chinese and English" (Fortune, 2012, p. 11).

Didactical and pedagogy impact of Chinese language immersion. Chinese teachers teaching American students to learn Chinese in an immersion setting is a complicated process. The teaching methods and practices, as well as the underlying philosophical assumptions to which the Chinese teachers accustomed, were not necessarily the effective approaches for teaching American students.

First, Chinese language immersion students ought to learn and practice Chinese literacy specific skills. Studies revealed that immersion students who learn to read first in a language that was markedly different from English, such as Arabic or Chinese, would need to learn and practice literacy skills that were specific to each language (Kanagy & Hai, 2001; Met, 2000; Met, 2012; S. C. Wang, 2010; T. T. Wang, 2008).

Second, Chinese language is not an alphabet language but a logographic language, and there were significant differences between logographic language systems and alphabet language systems. Research found that Chinese used logographic script, and orthography-phonology mapping was largely unavailable (Xiao, 2009). Xiao further delineate that:

Unlike English, which uses an alphabet with a relatively transparent orthography-phonology mapping system, Chinese uses a logographic script with orthography-phonology mapping largely unavailable. In Chinese script, strokes are the basic spelling symbol, and characters are the basic analytical unit. Structurally, strokes form components, and components form characters. Based on their internal complexity, characters are classified as simple characters (about 18% percent of the total number of Chinese characters), which consist of a single un-analyzable component, and compound characters (about 82 percent of the total), which are comprised of two analyzable components with distinct functions: a semantic radical and phonetic element (Shu and Anderson 1999) . . . In principle, the phonetic element conveys the sound of the corresponding character, while the radical contains meaning bearing a semantic relationship with the corresponding character (p.116).

Therefore, according to Wang (2010), "an adequate infrastructure is essential for any field but especially for the introduction of a world language that is categorized by the Foreign Service Institute of the State Department as a Category Three language (meaning that it takes 2,200 hours to reach the same proficiency as 575-600 hours of instruction in Category One languages such as French or Spanish)" (p. 21).

Third, there are no direct didactical references from French to Chinese, except at the conceptual level, for example, using pictures to depict the meaning of the words. Therefore, Chinese language immersion teachers and program designers started from scratch for designing teaching materials and providing linguistic specific instructions. Genesee (1987) pointed out that the goal of language learning was not grammatical perfection but meaningful communication between students and teachers. However, situations in which the students were expected to develop original verbal utterances for the purposes of communication as a way to develop proficiency in alphabet languages did not really exist until they had at least mastered about 2,500 Chinese characters and had been immersed in Chinese language environment for at least 6 years. This was one fundamental difference between the logographic language and alphabet languages. The Chinese Tri-Input Model (See Appendix D) illustrated this concept, which has not been empirically tested in the field. However, it held its value in its current stage for Chinese immersion program curriculum design and program design.

Fourth, there are many different ways to teach Chinese characters to Chinese Foreign Learners (CFL) who typically have varied linguistic backgrounds (Xiao, 2009). Xiao (2009) recommended three field-tested teaching strategies, which consist of "(1) three step presentation of new characters, (2) methods to prevent orthographic errors, and (3) corrective measures to treat orthographic errors" (p. 116). Xiao (2009) further detailed the three steps presentation of new character:

> Step1: Present whole characters with color-coded radicals; elicit pronunciation and tones from students; model the pronunciation and tones of the target characters; explain the semantic relationship between the radical and the relevant character.
>
> Step 2: Present characters a second time with analyzable components further coded with different colors; analyze the configuration and stroke order.
>
> Step 3: Group characters with the same radicals together; contextualize the target character in phrases or sentences; have students write the target character and read aloud phrases or sentences containing the target character. (p. 116)

Finally, the culture that the teacher embraces impacts how language education actually takes place (Gudykunst, 1998). Finnamore (2006) pointed out that, "Chinese pedagogy tends to approach language as something to be possessed, emphasizing linguistic competence and correctness" (p. 55). He further poised that, "a traditional Chinese teacher is the authoritative source of knowledge that must never lose face" (Finnamore, 2006, p. 55). In addition, compounding this situation is the fact that Chinese immersion teachers were generally taught with the "4R's"—reception, repetition, review, and reproduction—and the "4M's"—meticulosity, memorization, mental activities, and mastery (Hu, 2002). They understandably favored traditional approaches to which they had grown accustomed, and they preferred maximum planning and control as opposed to more learner-centered, unpredictable approaches, such as the Communicative Language Teaching (CLT) approach, which approached language as something to be learned and used, emphasizing communicative competence and meaning (Finnamore, 2006).

The reviews above justified the need for examining the Chinese language immersion instructional strategies and environment in this study.

Transferability from French to Chinese immersion. As the Chinese language is character based, which is markedly different from French, an alphabet-based language (Kanagy & Hai, 2001; Met, 2000, 2012; S. C. Wang, 2010; T. T. Wang, 2008), the didactics of teaching the Chinese language in an immersion setting was different, so was the culture and teaching philosophy.

First, French immersion has pragmatically impacted the development of the Chinese language immersion programs due to the fact that there was little research on Chinese language immersion education in North America. Many Chinese immersion programs were modeled after French immersion programs in North America in the recent decade. But, what has worked for the Chinese language immersion programs? What were the similarities and differences between Chinese immersion programs and more commonly taught language immersion programs, such as French? How differently did the Chinese language immersion impact the students' academic outcomes and language proficiency? According to Met (2012),

> Chinese language immersion programs are conceptually similar to other language
> immersion programs (Spanish, French, etc.) and there are many commonalities

for setting proficiency targets, formative assessments, and curriculum design. There are however, some practical differences between Chinese and other language immersion programs that relate both to the special characteristics of the Chinese language and to the relatively short history of Chinese immersion. These differences include: a relative lack of engaging, high-quality materials; assessments; and language acquisition research specific to young learners of Chinese. (p. 20)

Consequently, Wang (2007) pointed out that there were many challenges in developing Chinese literacy compared to French, Spanish, or German literacy, which demanded more attention to the development of a language learning system for Chinese language acquisition in North America. In the same way, Met (2012) stressed that:

There are notable challenges related to the nature of the Chinese language; the most significant one involves the development of literacy in Chinese. Chinese writing is unique among world languages in its use of a character-based system that involves both phonetic and meaning elements—almost without exception, all other writing systems in use today rely exclusively on the phonetic. Developing literacy in Chinese simply takes longer than in any other languages, and the difficulty of learning to read and write Chinese is not confined to non-native speakers. It is also true of native Chinese speakers. (p. 20)

Second, it was challenging for program designers to determine when and how to introduce the Chinese phonetics, Pinyin, to the Chinese immersion students. Met (2012) poised:

There are different practices for whether and how to introduce pinyin, particularly for early learners who are also developing literacy in English. The bottom line is that for most students, Chinese literacy will proceed at a slower rate than it would in other languages, especially those languages that are relatively close to English such as Spanish, French, and German. (p. 21)

In addition, Met (2012) discussed the complexity and challenge of accumulating Chinese vocabulary. She commented that:

The final challenge related to the nature of Chinese language relates to vocabulary and expressions. Compared to languages like French and Spanish (or even Japanese), there are far fewer words that are cognate with English, and so accumulating new vocabulary is more difficult. Also, since Chinese has been written copiously for several thousand years, there is a vast number of expressions, classical and historical allusions, and other idioms and references to absorb in order to be truly literate. (p. 20)

To conclude, there were many linguistic differences between alphabetic languages, for example, French, Spanish, and German on the one side, and Chinese language on the other side. Therefore, transferring the research findings, didactical, and pedagogical theories developed for French, Spanish, and German immersion programs to Chinese immersion field without discerning the two very different language systems could jeopardize the quality and sustainability of the Chinese immersion programs in North America. Fortune (2012) stated that currently Chinese language immersion education was emerging rapidly, yet very limited research has been done in this field to support the growth of the Chinese language immersion programs. In addition, Wang (2010) pointed out that "through 1960s to the present time, the Chinese language field has built a foundation for the infrastructure, but this has proven to be too limited to adequately meet the sudden demands since 2004 . . . the strengthening and enhancement of this infrastructure is urgent and timely" (p. 21). It is time to think about how to sustain the Chinese immersion programs in the United States and how to ensure the accountability of the Chinese programs, which is a need that has surfaced and has to be addressed (National Chinese Language Conference, 2012). It was hoped that this comprehensive Chinese language immersion program evaluation could shed some light on this field.

Development of Chinese Pinyin Skill

Pinyin, the Chinese phonetic alphabets, held no parallel to alphabet languages. The descriptions and applications of Pinyin in the Chinese language system are reviewed in this section.

Descriptions of Pinyin. Chinese Pinyin is "an alphabet coding system that represents (i.e. spells) Chinese characters using both Roman alphabet letters and lexical tone transcriptions, in relation to word reading in Chinese, a logographic orthography" (Lin et al., in press). Lin et al. (in press) further stated that "Chinese Pinyin generally represents a syllable, and by convention, this syllable is dissected into onset, rime, and tone; simultaneously, each letter in Pinyin typically corresponds to a phoneme" (p. 12). Cheung & Ng (2003) stated that Pinyin was widely used as an aid to teach Chinese characters, that Pinyin was introduced in the beginning of first grade and was quickly mastered within a year. Lin et al. (in press) stated that:

> [A]lthough children's invented spelling has been demonstrated to be important for reading alphabetic languages (e.g., Quellette & Senechal, 2008), the case of Pinyin is particularly interesting because it is a phonological coding system created for and in Chinese, but it is only regarded as an aid to formal Chinese reading-its mastery does not constitute formal reading of Chinese itself. (p. 6)

Regarding the necessity of Pinyin mastery, Lin et al. (in press) pointed out that:

> [T]he extent to which early mastery of this coding system is beneficial for Chinese character reading itself is unclear. After all, Pinyin mastery implies understanding of a system of letters and tonal representations, which, on the face of it, have no direct correspondence to Chinese characters themselves. (p. 3)

In addition, Chinese Pinyin is conventionally made of 21 onsets, 35 rimes, and 4 lexical tone representations (Institute of Linguistics, Chinese Academy of Social Sciences, 2004). Lin et al. (in press) concluded:

> [T]here are 26 letters in the Pinyin alphabet, including almost all of the corresponding letters from the English alphabet except that there is no v but an additional Ü in the Pinyin system. Individual letter names are the same as the corresponding individual sounds. (p. 4)

Furthermore, Yiu, Van Hasselt, Williams, and Woo (1994) pointed out that lexical tone was an important component in Pinyin, with no clear parallel to English, that tone represented the pitch of the speech that was used to distinguish across syllables, and that there were four lexical tones in Mandarin Chinese, i.e., high, rising, falling-rising, and falling.

Applications of Pinyin. Pinyin practice can promote the mastery of Chinese character (Jordan, 1971; McBride-Chang, et al., 2005) in at least four ways. First, Shu, Chen, Anderson, Wu, and Xuan (2003) stated that it was reliable to directly use Pinyin to help with character pronunciation, which was particularly helpful given the unreliability of Chinese phonetic components within Chinese characters. Lin et al. (in press) stressed that, "Pinyin serves to represent the exact sound of a given character. It is reliable at the level of the onset, rime, and tone of the utterance . . . Chinese Pinyin can also function as a self-teaching tool for children to learn new Chinese characters" (p. 42). Second, as Lin et al. (in press) further stressed:

> Pinyin facilitates pronunciation and recognition of new characters through sub-lexical phonology, such as tone awareness, phoneme awareness, and syllable awareness, without assistance from teachers and parents (e.g., Dai & Lu, 1985; Huang & Hanley, 1997). For example, children who learn Chinese characters through the use of Pinyin have less difficulty analyzing speech into phonemes (Cheung, Chen, Lai, Wong, & Hill, 2001) and better awareness of phonetic radicals (Cheung, 2003), as compared to those who do not learn with the aid of Pinyin transcriptions. (p. 6)

Third, children who demonstrate mastery of Pinyin can greatly increase the chance of their self-learning of new Chinese characters either appearing in textbook or stories (Ku & Anderson, 2001). Finally, Pinyin practice might strengthen phonological awareness by increasing tone sensitivity or phoneme awareness. Fifth, Lin et al. (in press) found that the preschool children's invented Pinyin spelling skills could be used as longitudinal predictor of later Chinese word reading:

> [I]nvented Pinyin spelling allows children to manipulate different phonological units, including decomposing a syllable into onset, rime, tone, and phonemes, and then correspondingly, to reconnect them into a whole syllable. Thus, Pinyin itself may be an ideal measure for phonological awareness in Chinese. (p. 6)

Development of the Four Chinese Language Skills

Listening, speaking, reading, and writing skills are the four essential Chinese language skills. The following texts discussed listening and speaking, reading and writing respectively. The focus of this section was how different factors and processes of the Chinese language systems, including Chinese writing, impacted the development of Chinese reading skills.

Development of Chinese listening and speaking skills. The development of Chinese listening and speaking skills is briefly reviewed below. Even though Chinese listening and speaking skills are intertwined in the mode of interpersonal communication, from the perspective of psycholinguistics, listening and speaking are two different processes (Wen, 2009). Wen (2009) stressed the following:

> Listening is a decoding process that requires comprehension strategies. Speaking is a productive skill that maps concepts and ideas onto correct linguistic forms and appropriate pragmatic functions. Listening is a fundamental source of learning. The development of the listening skill precedes and empowers the speaking skill. Speaking derives from listening, and in turn, enhances the ability of comprehension. (p. 131)

Based on Wen (2009), the level of fluency of pronunciation is vital to speech processing, and comprehension. Cook (2001) commented, "pronunciation should be taken more seriously, not just for its own sake, but as the basis for speaking and comprehending" (p. 86). Cook (2001) also pointed out that how much one could remember depended on how fast one could repeat, and how fast the information circled.

Development of Chinese reading skills. Chinese reading is a complicated process and fundamentally different from alphabet-based languages. There are seven factors that impact one's Chinese reading skills: (a) metalinguistic skills, (b) phonological awareness, (c) syllable and tone awareness, (d) morphological awareness, (e) the process of other aspects of the Chinese language and writing system, (f) internal cues to pronunciation and phonetic principle, and (g) the insight of inter-substructure knowledge.

The seven factors and their impacts on the development of Chinese reading skills were discussed in the following texts.

First, generally speaking, learning to read is fundamentally metalinguistic (Nagy & Anderson, 1995), "and hence depends on the learner's cognitive and meta-cognitive development" (Li, Anderson, Nagy, & Zhang, 2002, p. 91). Shu (2003) pointed out that:

> To learn to read successfully, a child has to understand whether and how the print words represent phonemes, syllables, morphemes, and word. In the past two decades, one of the most important discoveries is that role of phonological awareness in learning to read alphabetic languages. Recent research has also supported that an understanding of the nature of the correspondence between print and sound, print and meaning is crucial in learning to read Chinese. (p. 46)

Second, phonological awareness plays an important role in reading Chinese. Li et al., (2002) pointed out:

> A couple of decades ago, at the dawn of research on the psycholinguistics of Chinese, there was theoretical speculation that in reading Chinese perhaps could go directly from printed characters to meaning with little or no phonological analysis and only incidental speech recoding. Pioneers such as Hung and Tzeng (1981) and Tzeng & Hung (1988) joined by Western psychologists such as Perfetti & Zhang (1991), have shown that contrary to the poorly informed speculation of some researchers, phonological processing is very important in reading Chinese. These pioneering researchers put forth a universal theory that emphasizes the importance of phonological processing in different writing systems. (p. 88)

Phonetic awareness could assist encode and remember the unknown characters.

Shu (2003) explained the process in the following way:

> School children in Beijing, Hong Kong, and Taiwan were found to read more accurately for regular characters than irregular characters (Shu, Anderson & Wu, 2000; Tzeng, Zhang, et al., 1995). The fact that the regularity effect was shown in both familiar and unfamiliar characters suggests that the phonetic awareness is important for encoding and remembering the pronunciations of unknown characters. (p. 46)

Third, syllable awareness and tone awareness impacted Chinese reading skills profoundly. Lin & McBride-Chang et al. (in press) stressed, "Unlike alphabetic reading, Chinese does not directly require phonemic-level processing to read because each character represents a syllable" (p. 3). Thus, measures of phonological sensitivity in Chinese, though correlated with Chinese literacy development (Cheung, 2003; Siok & Fletcher, 2001; Shu, Peng, & McBride-Chang et al., 2008), are not always independent markers of reading performance (McBride-Chang et al., 2005). Compared to alphabetic orthographies, Chinese was phonologically relatively simple, so traditional phonological awareness tasks, often focused on phoneme sensitivity might be inappropriate for capturing the full phonological sensitivity needed to read Chinese. More specifically, syllable awareness and tone awareness impacted Chinese reading skills profoundly, just as Li et al., (2002) stressed:

> A notable feature of Chinese is that it contains only about 400 syllables. Each syllable is further differentiated according to one of four tones making in all about 1, 200 distinct syllables . . . Phonological awareness in Chinese consists of the knowledge of onset, final, syllables, and tones . . . Syllable awareness is certain to be important for Chinese reading because Chinese characters are pronounced with

a single syllable . . . Tone awareness is another phonological insight that is implicated in learning to read Chinese. Because every syllable in Mandarin is differentiated with a tone, it is to be expected that a child who cannot or does not pay attention tone will often be confused. In fact, So and Siegel (1997) have reported a significant difference between poor and average readers in tone discrimination. (p. 89)

Fourth, morphological awareness also impacts Chinese reading (Chan & Nunes, 1998; Shu & Anderson, 1997; Li et al., 2002). Li et al. (2002) commented:

Morphological awareness in Chinese consists of three facets: Morpheme awareness, homograph awareness, and radical awareness. Morpheme awareness is the understanding that words with the same pronunciation may have different meanings. The morphemically aware child will be alert for any morphological or contextual clues that may help distinguish meanings. Morpheme awareness can develop to some extent apart from experience with the writing system . . . Homograph awareness is the understanding that the same character may have different meanings. It is indexed by the ability to distinguish on the basis of context words in which a character is used with the same meaning from those in which a character has different meanings. Both morpheme awareness and homograph awareness both involve making judgments about identity or non-identity of meaning. Radical awareness concerns the understanding the role of radicals in the Chinese writing system. A radical usually gives information about the meaning of a character. However, the semantic information represented by radicals is from reasonably obvious to relatively subtle or misleading. (p. 90)

Fifth, the processing of other aspects of the Chinese language and writing system also impacts Chinese reading, as Li et al., (2002) stressed, "The rules of Chinese word formation are potentially of great importance in learning to read" (p. 89).

Sixth, there are internal cues to pronunciation, and children presumably acquire the phonetic principle gradually as they learn to read increasing numbers of characters, according to Shu et al., (2003), and they further stated the following:

> The corpus analysis showed that about 72% of the characters children learn in primary school contain internal cues to pronunciation, in which 23% of the compound characters are fully regular and 42% are semi-regular. The proportion of regular and semi-regular characters children learn through the textbooks steadily increases as the frequency of characters decreases. Children who are aware of the phonetic principle are able to organize the lexicon efficiently and able to learn and remember characters in a systematic fashion. Children who are unaware have to encode characters as a whole and memorize their pronunciations one by one. Even though there are many semi-regular characters in which the phonetic of a character provides, only partial information of the research has revealed that children can make use of partial information in learning and memorizing new characters. (p. 47)

Seventh, the insight of inter-substructure knowledge of characters is important in children reading and writing, as Shu (2003) further stressed,

> The vocabulary of Chinese is represented with a vast number of visually complex characters. Research reported that children of all grades made false response for non-characters (components in impossible positions) less than for pseudo-characters (components in possible positions). The rate of false response for ill-formed component pseudo-characters decreased over the school years (Cheng and

Huang, 1995; Shu & Anderson, 1998). Children were able to be aware of components position information at early stage, and the internal structure of components, positional frequency relatively later (Li, Fu & Lin, 2000; Peng & Li, 1995). The findings suggested that children decomposed characters into sublexical units. (p. 46)

Furthermore, a study with first and fourth grade children showed that both morphological and phonological awareness contributed to reading proficiency, in which the role of morphological awareness was relatively larger than that of phonological awareness (Li et al., 2002).

Shu (2003) pointed out that reading difficulty for poor readers was mainly in character and word levels. Poor readers were found to process much slower in accessing to phonology and semantics than good readers in on-line tasks. Their poor performance might reflect the poor quality and organization of their orthographic and phonological representations and access.

Chinese reading fluency threshold. In order to read Chinese fluently, one ought to master approximately 3,500 frequently used Chinese characters and learn more than 10,000 Chinese characters (Institute of Linguistics, Chinese Academy of Social Sciences, 2004). This index served as a guide for CIP Chinese curriculum design.

Chinese curricula types. He and Jiao (2010) discussed existing types of Chinese curricula, which were summarized in the following texts:

(1) Unity type, emphasizing the unity of all aspects of Chinese language learning; (2) delay type, avoiding teaching the students any Chinese characters for a prolonged period of time, or even at all during the entire first year, with all instructional needs relying on phonetic symbols such as Pinyin; and (3) lag type,

emphasizing the oral-aural skills with a temporary lag in character-learning and a stronger emphasis on speaking more and writing less. The underlying feature affecting the learning process and curriculum design of all three of these types is character learning, specifically the writing characters. (p. 219)

Learning Chinese and brain activation. Learning Chinese activates a different part of the brain in comparing learning alphabetic languages, just as Chu (2003) points out that:

The study on the language representation in Chinese-English bilinguals' brain found that in the orthographic task, besides the overlapped brain areas induced by both Chinese and English, the left posterior middle temporal gyrus and the anterior cingulated gyrus was activated by Chinese stimuli only, while the bilateral parietal inferior lobe and supramarginal gyrus by English only. In the semantic task, the left middle and posterior temporal lobe and the fusiform gyrus are activated by both Chinese and English stimuli. (p. 48)

In addition, brain-imaging research in Chinese processing reported the possibility that phonology was automatically generated when reading, even when attention was not directed to the words (Peng & Xu, et al., 2003).

In summary, the four essential Chinese language skills are interdependent and consequently impact the Chinese language proficiency collectively. Therefore, CIP applied the Unity-Type Chinese curriculum.

Chinese Language Immersion Program Development

Chinese language immersion programs have a comparably short history and lacked research for alternative Chinese language immersion models and studies on Chinese language immersion curriculum, instruction, and assessment design. The sound

Chinese immersion model and curriculum design relied on a deep understanding on the development of the four essential Chinese language skills, Pinyin and lexical tones, which were reviewed in the previous two sections. In this section, (a) a brief introduction of Chinese language immersion research, (b) Chinese curriculum design, (c) Chinese teacher selection and training, and (d) administrative and collegial support were viewed respectively.

Limited Chinese language immersion research. Chinese language immersion education has a relatively short history and lacked Chinese language acquisition research in North America. Met (2012) stressed:

> Chinese language immersion programs are conceptually similar to other language immersion programs (Spanish, French, etc.) and there are many commonalities for setting proficiency targets, formative assessments, and curriculum design. There are however, some practical differences between Chinese and other language immersion programs that relate both to the special characteristics of the Chinese language and to the relatively short history of Chinese immersion. These differences include: a relative lack of engaging, high-quality materials; assessments; and language acquisition research specific to young learners of Chinese. (p. 20)

Nevertheless, the development of Chinese language immersion program benefited from three dimensions of the studies in language acquisition. First, teaching Chinese as a second language (TCSL) started in China in the 1950s and eight domains of interests have generally been understood as research focuses in this field since (Zhu, 2010, p. 36). The findings from the eight domains of research have impacted Chinese language education, including Chinese language immersion education, in China and the United

States. Second, Chinese as a foreign language had experienced a slow growth in the United Stated from the 1960s to 2000, with a rapid expansion from 2004 to present (Wang, 2010), which consequently established research platforms for Chinese language acquisition. Finally, the research conducted for French immersion programs since 1965 has accumulated abundant information in the domain of program model alternatives and language immersion didactics, and pedagogies.

In addition, several Chinese language immersion forerunners have provided their insights for the field. He and Jiao (2010) pointed out, "the popularity of learning Chinese is growing in the United States. According to Asian Society, a nonprofit institution dedicated to educating Americans about Asian, the number of the Chinese program in K-12 grade in the United States has grown by almost 200% since 2004" (p. 218). According to He and Jiao (2010),

> [B]ecause the United States is so culturally and linguistically different from China, it may seem that Chinese may be extremely difficult to learn. Because of the characteristics in the pronunciation and writing systems, Chinese is very different from English and is considered one of the most difficult foreign languages for English speakers in America. When learning a character, students have to deal with five different tasks—pronunciation, meaning, shape of the character, strokes and structure of the character, and even more difficult, reproduction of the character stroke by stroke in the right order and right position. (p. 218)

Wang (2010) also stated that, "in formal foreign language education, Chinese is a newcomer as opposed to commonly-taught European languages, such as French, German, or Spanish" (p. 15). Only limited research studies have been conducted in the design of the Chinese language immersion programs in the United States in the 1990s (Chao, 1993; De Courcy, 1997).

In 1993, Chao did a case study of learning Chinese in a summer immersion program at a university. Two undergraduate students participated in his study. The focus of his study was students' experiences in the Chinese language immersion program, and the finding was that teaching and learning Chinese as a foreign language in general was not yet a developed field. The curriculum was textbooks, and instructional approach was drill-based direct instruction. According to Chao (1993), immersion programs were a trend in teaching Chinese at the college and university level in the early 1990s. In 1997, Kubler, et al., investigated possible approaches to learning Chinese more quickly, in comparison to learning Chinese in the traditional approach.

Furthermore, Kubler, et al. (1997) stated, "a foundation in listening, speaking, and reading should be established before taking up writing. At the basic level, reading should be emphasized over writing" (p. 10). Kubler, et al. (1997) continued by explaining that, "[s]ome characters should be taught for both production and recognition, [and] others for recognition only. Learners at this level do not necessarily need to know the characters for everything they can say" (p. 10). Since 2004, Chinese has become an expanding field as a foreign language, however, lacking of capacity for supporting early Chinese language learners in the United States is observed (Wang, 2010).

Comparably, more studies have been conducted on the design of French immersion programs (Swain & Lapkin, 1981; Genesee, 1984, 1985), less in Chinese language immersion programs (Chao, 1993; De Courcy, 1997; Fortune, 2012; Kubler, 1997; Met, 2012; Wang, 2010), which could endanger the quality of rapidly expanded Chinese language immersion programs.

Program model alternatives. The most critical step in language immersion program design is to select the immersion model (Fortune, 2008). However, as of this study, were no studies on Chinese language immersion model alternatives. Therefore, the existing French language immersion model alternatives and relevant impacts were reviewed in this section.

Fortune (2008) stated that immersion programs in Canada and the United States have followed a number of different models, which could be defined with reference to two factors, the grade level in which the second language was used for instruction (early, delayed, late) and the amount of content instruction time in the second language (total or partial); and that the first immersion program, implemented in St. Lambert, Canada, followed the early total immersion model. The following section discusses (a) the early total immersion program, (b) partial immersion program model, (c) the difference between the early total immersion and partial immersion program models, (d) the delayed immersion model, (e) late immersion model, and (f) the double immersion model.

An early total immersion program is characterized by 100% of the instruction being given in French in kindergarten and the first grade. Starting in the 2nd grade, about 80% of the instruction day is in French, and for the remaining time English is taught. At the 5th grade, from 60% to 80% of the instruction time is conducted in French and the remaining time in English. At sixth grade, English instruction is increased to 50% to 60%, and at 7th grade, half of the instruction is in French and half in English (Swain & Lapkin, 1981).

Early partial immersion model offers instruction in the second language in early grades only 50% of the total instructional time (Fortune, 2008).

The early partial model differs from the early total model in second language instruction time and in the introduction of English literacy instruction. In the early total immersion program, the second language instructional time decreases as the student progresses through the grades; in early partial immersion programs, the second language instruction time remains constant throughout the grades. The second difference between the two models is the introduction of literacy instruction. In a total immersion program, English reading is introduced only after students are taught reading in the second language. In early partial immersion, participants are taught reading in both languages simultaneously, beginning in the first grade (Genesee, 1987).

In the delayed-immersion model, instruction in the second language begins in the later elementary grades (i.e., 4th or 5th grade). First language literacy is developed before the introduction of second language literacy. The instruction time for the second language is typically 80% during the first three years (i.e., 4th, 5th, and 6th grades), then gradually decreases to about 40% from the 9th to 12th grade (Fortune, 2008).

In the late immersion model, second language instruction occurs at the beginning of secondary school. All or most of the curriculum is taught in the second language, either for 1 or 2 years. Prior to entrance to the late-immersion program, students usually have received core second language instruction throughout the elementary grades or special second language preparatory courses (Genesee, 1984).

The double immersion model provides instruction in two non-native languages during the elementary grades. According to Genesee (1985), French-Hebrew immersion programs exist in Canada, and an English-Spanish-French tri-lingual immersion program exists in Washington, DC. However, only one type of double immersion program (Hebrew and French) is documented.

The outcomes of all the types of language immersion programs in the K-5 settings reveal that the early total immersion program has provided the most benefits to the 2nd language acquisition without apparent cost to the English academic success (Genesee, 1987).

Was the early total French immersion program an effective Chinese language immersion program model for the diverse American public student population? It was hoped that the comprehensive CIP program evaluation would offer some answer for this question. Furthermore, CIP adopted the early total French immersion model with a modification that the introduction of English was in kindergarten; and the Chinese language immersion program (CIPL), which was chosen as a comparable program for this study, adopted the early total French immersion model.

Chinese curriculum design. The Chinese language curriculum was by no means equivalent to a textbook or set of textbooks. CIP has implemented a Chinese curriculum designed from scratch, based on NCSCOS, World Language Standards, and guidelines of *International Curriculum for Chinese Language Education,* and *Chinese Language Proficiency Scales for Speakers of Other Languages*.

First, commonality between Chinese language and others was reviewed. Generally speaking, the Chinese character is morphosyllabic, which represents both morphemes and syllables. Perfetti (2003) pointed out that, "Chinese characters correspond not to an abstract formless piece of meaning, but usually to a spoken Chinese syllable that is also a morpheme" (p. 7). According to Perfetti (2003), the most important universal property of reading is the universal language constraint: All writing systems represent spoken language or writing systems encode spoken language, which applies to Chinese. Perfetti (2003) further stressed the following:

Reading is embedded in two interrelated systems: the Language System and the

Writing System. The relationship between the first and the second is variable but persistent. There are no writing systems currently in use that bypass language to erect an independent system of signs. (p. 5)

Chinese character can be read to a corresponding a meaning, to a spoken word, or both. Perfetti (2003) further reasoned:

Because Chinese does not have graphic elements that correspond to phonemes, it is not alphabetic. But the writing unit does correspond to a meaning-bearing spoken language unit-the syllable. Thus Chinese writing system maps its language system. (p. 8)

Second, Chinese is significantly different from other languages, and its uniqueness has to be studied and addressed in Chinese language immersion settings. There was limited literature about Chinese language immersion curriculum design when CIP was started, therefore, the findings about the learning languages in general, especially the findings about learning Chinese language and developing the Chinese Pinyin, listening, speaking, reading, and writing skills have served as core guidelines for designing the CIP Chinese language curriculum. The development of Chinese literacy comprised the acquisition of Pinyin, listening, speaking, reading, and writing skills, and those elements were examined previously in the sections of Development of the Chinese Pinyin Skills and Development of the Four Chinese Language Skills.

Teacher selection and training. Teacher selection and training is a critical component of developing Chinese language immersion programs (Anderson, Lindholm-Leary, Wilhelm, Zeigler, & Bourdreaux, 2005).

First, the teachers were required to be native Chinese speakers for the Chinese language immersion programs, based on the selected language immersion model. This requirement imposed a major challenge to the development of the program. The native speakers grew up in China or Taiwan and were educated in China. Their education experiences defined their teaching philosophies. Firmly rooted in the traditional teaching approach, native Chinese teachers deem the practice of rote learning appropriate (Jin & Cortazzi, 1998). Influenced by Confucian teaching philosophy, past and present Chinese teachers enjoy their prestigious status as transmitters of knowledge and cultivators for the young generation.

Second, research showed that the foreign teachers might not be well prepared for teaching in the American classrooms. Kissau, Yon, and Algozzine (2012) pointed out that, "in response to the shortage of foreign language (L2) teachers in the United States, many school districts employ individuals from other countries. Despite the benefits offered by such teachers, there is growing concern that they may not be adequately prepared for teaching in American schools" (p. 1). Kissau et al. (2012) further analyzed,

> Survey results indicated that international L2 teachers hold many of the same core beliefs related to L2 teaching as do their American-born peers. Interview data, however, suggested the existence of differing beliefs among sub-groups of international L2 teachers that often lead to problems with classroom management. These problems seem to be aggravated by the extent of the cultural differences between the L2 teacher's native land and the country where the instruction is taking place. Recommendations for improvement of practice including having international L2 teachers observe American-born L2 teachers, offering more professional development, and providing greater administrative support. (p. 1)

Therefore, to be an effective language immersion teacher in an American classroom, the native Chinese teachers not only needed classroom management trainings but also Chinese immersion didactical and pedagogical trainings (Anderson et al., 2005). In addition, Chinese language is markedly different from French or English (Kanagy & Hai, 2001; Met, 2000, 2012; S. C. Wang, 2010; T. T. Wang, 2008). Therefore, studying how to better support Chinese teachers to be effective in the American classrooms and evaluating Chinese language immersion instructional environments were immediate needs.

Administrative and collegial support. Continuous support from school administrators and colleagues in the learning communities was needed for any new programs and the learning organization was an optimal environment for fostering CIP.

First, providing professional trainings for the Chinese language immersion teachers and ensuring that they were adequately prepared for working with the diverse student population and that they clearly understood their responsibilities was vital. Kissau et al. (2012) recommended that international L2 teachers observe American-born L2 teachers, participate in more professional development, and obtain greater administrative support. Second, Pettigrew (1973) stated, "Leading change is also complex and situation specific . . . It requires building a climate accepting of change within the firm . . . " (p. 172). Placing a Chinese language immersion program in the matured language immersion school organization was a strategic change, while the acceptance of the new program, including new teachers and their significantly different cultures were critical. Pettigrew (1973) further stressed, "It is vital to regard human resources as both assets and liabilities . . . and to take appropriate action. The organization's members must provide the knowledge base for learning, but it is also necessary to undertake 'unlearning' when the established conceptions and skills are no longer appropriate" (p. 173).

Second, a functional school system ought to be a learning organization, which would be an optimal environment for building CIP. Senge (1992) pointed out that, "In the present-day complex world, organizations must be able to learn how to cope with continuous change in order to be successful: They have to become learning organizations" (p. 179). Among the five disciplines Senge proposed for organizations to practice in order to become learning organizations, the third discipline, which concerns the building of a shared vision for the organization and its members of the future that they wish to create is relevant and the value driven nature of excellence in an organization lays the foundation for success in school. The fourth discipline is team learning. Senge (1992) defined it more as an open dialogue of cooperation in groups than a turf battle and only then could the intelligence of the team exceed that of its members rather than reduce it drastically. Administrative and collegial support were carried out by providing an optimal environment for a new program to take off, grow, mature, and produce, and for staff to adapt, learn, unlearn, improve, excel, and contribute in the learning organization.

In this study, the Chinese language immersion instructional environment survey was designed to collect Chinese teachers' perceptions in this context.

Program Evaluation Design

Program evaluation is a process of a study designed and conducted to assist some audience to assess an object's merit and worth (Stufflebeam, 2000c, 2003).

First, program evaluation is a critical component of program development, and evaluation uses inquiry and judgment methods. According to Stufflebeam (2003), program evaluation includes: (a) determining the criteria and standards for judging quality and deciding whether those standards should be relative or absolute, (b) collecting relevant information, and (c) applying the standards to determine value, quality, utility, effectiveness or significance. It leads to recommendations intended to optimize the evaluation object in relation to its intended purposes (Fitzpatrick et al., 2011).

Second, the approach recommended by the Joint Committee on Standards for Educational Evaluation (Stufflebeam, 1999) is to evaluate the program based upon the four components of utility, feasibility, propriety, and accuracy. In consideration of these components, the Joint committee on the Standards for Education Evaluation highly recommended the CIPP model for use in conducting program evaluation (Fitzpatrick et al., 2004, 2011; Stufflebeam, 2003).

In addition, CIP was a complex system and a program sequence model depicted what CIP was, guided the evaluation subsequently, and provided a framework for replication (Rogers, 2000).

Program evaluation standards. The Standards for Evaluations of Educational Programs, Projects, and Materials, consisting of a set of 30 standards designed to guide the conduct of evaluation and to judge the soundness of such evaluation, were issued in 1980 by the Joint Committee and published in 1981 by the McGraw-Hill Company (Stufflebeam & Madaus, 1983). Stufflebeam (2000c) posited that, "evaluations of U.S. education programs should be conducted in accordance with these standards in general" (p. 282). The Joint Committee groups the 30 standards according to the four attributes of an evaluation into (a) utility, which establishes the expectation that the evaluation will serve the information needs of the users; (b) feasibility, which establishes the expectation that the evaluation will be realistic, prudent, diplomatic, and frugal; (c) propriety, which establishes the expectation that the evaluation will be conducted legally, ethically, and with regard to all stakeholders; and (d) accuracy, which establishes the expectation that the evaluation will contain and convey adequate information to enable stakeholders to determine the worth and merit of the identified program. The overall rating of an evaluation against 10 accuracy standards is an index of the evaluation's overall validity (Stufflebeam & Madaus, 1983).

In CIP program evaluation, the evaluator utilized each of the standards for the meta-evaluation using a meta-evaluation survey (See Appendix E), which was adapted from the Program Evaluation Meta-evaluation Checklist (Stufflebeam, 1999).

Four categories of evaluation models. Based upon the definition of program evaluation, 22 evaluation approaches have been divided into four categories (Stufflebeam, 2000a), and they are:

1. Pseudo-evaluation oriented, which fails to produce and report to all right-to-know audiences valid assessments of merit and worth. The evaluators and clients are sometimes tempted to shade, selectively release, or even falsify findings.

2. Improvement/accountability oriented, which focuses on the identification and provision of informational needs for decision-makers. The CIPP evaluation model is classified as improvement/accountability oriented.

3. Social mission/advocacy oriented, which seeks to ensure that all segments of society have equal access to educational and social opportunities and services.

4. Questions/methods oriented, which address specified questions, answers to which may or may not be sufficient to assess a program's merit and worth and /or use some preferred methods.

Whether the questions and methodology are appropriate for developing and supporting value claims is a secondary consideration. The one endorsed with the strongest rating among the 22 program evaluation approaches is improvement/accountability oriented (Stufflebeam, 2000a).

CIPP evaluation model. The root term for the CIPP evaluation model is *value*. The value provides the foundation for deriving the particular evaluative criteria. The criteria, along with questions of stakeholders, dictate information needs. These will provide the directions for selecting the evaluation instruments and interpretation standards (Stufflebeam, 2000c).

According to Stufflebeam (2000c), there are seven levels of values and criteria, which are basic societal values, criteria inherent in the definition of evaluation, the criteria in the definition of Context, Input, Process, and Product evaluation, institutional values, pertinent technical standards, duties of personnel, and idiosyncratic criteria (the ground-level criteria). Thus, according to Stufflebeam (2000c), "Evaluators should consider all seven levels of criteria to assure comprehensiveness in their evaluation" (p. 308).

The CIPP evaluation model is a comprehensive framework for conducting and reporting evaluations. Stufflebeam (2000c) stated the following:

> CIPP model's core concepts are Context, Input, Process, and Product evaluation. Context evaluations assess needs, problems, and opportunities as bases for defining goals and priorities and judging the significance of outcomes. Input evaluation assesses alternative approaches to meeting needs as a means of planning programs and allocating resources. Process evaluations assess the implementation of plans to guide activities and later to help explain outcomes. Product evaluations identify intended and unintended outcomes both to help keep the process on track and determine effectiveness. (p. 279)

The purpose of employing four interrelated types of evaluation is to allow evaluators to conduct or contract evaluations and to help initiate, develop, and install sound programs (Stufflebeam, 2000a).

The CIPP is categorized as an improvement/accountability oriented evaluation model. It also reflects an objectivist orientation. Stufflebeam (2000c) posited, "Objectivist evaluations are firmly grounded in ethical principles . . . Fundamentally, objectivist evaluations are intended, over time, to lead to conclusions that are correct—not correct or incorrect relative to an evaluator's or other party's predilections, position, preferences, standing, or point of view" (p. 281).

The CIPP model by its design intends to provide both formative evaluation and summative evaluation, which serves strategies for improving and proving (Stufflebeam, 2000c, 2003). According to Stufflebeam (2003), "The CIPP evaluations are formative when they proactively key the collection and reporting of information to improvement. They are summative when they look back on completed project or program activities or performances of services, pull together and sum up the value meanings of relevant information, and focus on accountability." (pp. 34-35) Because the model provides a systematic process for defining explicit criteria seeking accurate information, the model allows an evaluator to objectively explore and measure viable alternatives to determine if those alternatives may strengthen the program (Stufflebeam, 2003).

Use of the CIPP model provided the evaluator assistance in generating numerous key questions in order to examine and identify recommendations for revising and improving all aspects of a program (Stufflebeam, 2003). Four different decisions can be made using the CIPP model. First, by identifying needs and defining objectives integral to the program, decisions regarding planning can be made. Second, by identifying available resources and effective strategies, decisions regarding structuring can be made. Third, by identifying how well the program is being conducted, including any barriers that may exist and possible revisions for strengthening the program, implementation decisions can be made. Fourth, by evaluating obtained results, recognizing the degree to which these results impact the needs of stakeholders, and determining whether the program should be continued, decisions regarding cessation or continuation of the program can be made (Stufflebeam, 2003).

Collectively, all these aspects contributed to the application of the CIPP evaluation model being selected for CIP evaluation.

Program theory. Program theory has two essential elements: an explicit model of the program and an evaluation, which is guided by this model (Rogers, 2000). Evaluators have used it for three quite different purposes: (a) certain types of summative evaluation which focus on answering the question, "Does the program cause the intended outcome?" (Bickman, 1996); (b) formative evaluations which are intended to suggest how the program can be improved (Clarke, 1995); and (c) ongoing program monitoring, which provides continuous indicators of program performance (Funnel, 1997). When the program is very complex, a program logic model can be used to depict what the program is and subsequently guide the replication of the program (Rogers, 2000).

In this study, CIP was a very complex, new program; therefore, a program sequence model designed with the guide of program theory assisted the description and replication of CIP program.

Mixed study methodology in program evaluation. Finally, the program evaluation was conducted with a mixed study design comprising both quantitative and qualitative data. The qualitative data were collected through semi-structured interviews. The semi-structured interview is utilized when questions are the same for each individual, but the evaluator may vary the questions or explore them in more detail, depending upon answers given by the participant (Lichtman, 2006; Roybal, 2011). Also semi-structured interviews can provide the evaluator with comparable data for each participant (McNeil, Newman, & Steinhauser, 2005; Vengraf, 2001).

These views collectively lent support to gather in-depth data from the three individuals who initially planned and implemented CIP. The quantitative data were collected through surveys and student academic assessments. An advisory panel, using a meta-evaluation survey, determined the overall quality of the evaluation process.

Summary. In almost all the studies in a language immersion setting, the foci are on the academic performance, not on the target language acquisition (Cummins, 1983). In this study, not only was the CIP's academic effectiveness evaluated both quantitatively and qualitatively, but also the target language acquisition was examined both qualitatively and quantitatively so as to gain more in-depth understanding of this Chinese language immersion program in the less-researched field.

In addition, as Chinese is a fundamentally different language from the alphabet-based languages, such as, English or French (Kanagy, 2001; Met, 2000, 2012; S. C. Wang, 2010; T. T. Wang, 2008), effective teaching strategies in the immersion classroom, especially for reading and writing, needed to be investigated. In this study, the Chinese language immersion instructional environment survey was designed to assess the CIP's effectiveness of the Chinese language instruction.

Finally, in spite of so little research done in this field, Chinese language immersion programs have grown rapidly in the K-12 schools and colleges in the United States (National Chinese Language Conference, 2012), and many stakeholders wanted to know how the Chinese language immersion programs were doing; many administrators were thinking about how to implement Chinese language immersion programs.

Therefore, a comprehensive evaluation of a Chinese language immersion program using the CIPP model provided a holistic reference for the stakeholders and decision makers (Stufflebeam, 2003). In addition, the program sequence model served as a reference model for replication (Rogers, 2000). Furthermore, mixed study methodology was utilized to collect both qualitative and quantitative data in this evaluation

Purpose Statement

The purpose of this study was to evaluate the effectiveness of the K-5 CIP developed and implemented at a school that served a diversified population in the school district. To accomplish this purpose, the study employed Stufflebeam's (2003) revised CIPP design. Stufflebeam's (2003) model divides the program that is being evaluated into four separate components: Context, Input, Process, and Product. This program evaluation utilized all four components of the model. The criteria of the evaluation were based on the North Carolina Standard Course of Studies for math, English language arts, world languages, and the CIP Chinese curriculum.

Evaluation Questions

Based on the CIP's needs, the evaluator's experience in the language immersion field, and after reviewing numerous models of evaluation, the Context Input Process Product (CIPP) evaluation model (Stufflebeam, 2003) was selected for evaluating CIP. The intention was to examine the four components of the CIPP model in relationship to the CIP's implementation in order to make data-driven recommendations concerning the CIP's effectiveness.

The following questions were categorized based upon the four components of the CIPP model.

1. To what extent did the program goals reflect the assessed needs (Context)?

2. To what extent were the selected approaches and plans feasible, compatible, potentially successful, and cost effective for meeting the assessed needs (Input)?

3. To what extent was the program implemented as designed (Process)?

4. To what extent was there a difference in the academic performance of the immersion students when compared to similar students (Product)?

5. To what extent did the students perform differently in English reading and mathematics (Product)?

6. To what extent did the students of the program perform differently in Chinese compared to the students in the similar program in Minnesota (Product)?

Chapter 3: Methodology

Statement of the Problem

The Chinese immersion program (CIP) was implemented at an urban school in North Carolina in 2006. Yet, it had not been evaluated. It was not known how and to what extent CIP met the needs of immersion students. This study was designed to answer the evaluation questions by obtaining substantial data from the school district and the school. The criteria for evaluating the Chinese immersion program were based on the North Carolina Standard Course of Studies for math, English language arts, science, world language guidelines, and CIP Chinese curriculum.

Statement of the Purpose of the Study

The purpose of this study was to evaluate the effectiveness of the K-5 CIP developed and implemented at a school that served a diverse population in the school district. To accomplish this purpose, the study employed Stufflebeam's (2003) revised CIPP design. Stufflebeam's (2003) model divides the program being evaluated into four separate components: Context, Input, Process, and Product. This program evaluation utilized all four components of the model. The checklist provided by Stufflebeam (2002) was used for each component of the evaluation. The Context, Input, Process, and Product components were analyzed, using quantitative and qualitative data analysis methods, to address the following: the concerns addressed by the program; the values, mission, goals, and priorities of the program; what strategies were implemented and why; which resources were utilized; who were the participants; whether resources were used effectively; the degree of implementation with fidelity; and how concerns and ideas for improvement were handled (Stufflebeam, 2003). More specifically, a semi-structured interview for three program planners and the Chinese Immersion Instructional

Environment Survey from the Chinese immersion team were used to collect qualitative data (Creswell, 2009; Creswell, 2012). Qualitative data analysis involves preparing the data for analysis, conducting different analyses, and moving deeper and deeper into understanding the data (Creswell, 2009; Creswell, 2012). Creswell (2009) stressed that "[T]he process of data (qualitative) analysis involves making sense out of text and image data" (p. 183). A survey for the Chinese language immersion team and a survey for the advisory panel members were used for collecting quantitative data (Creswell, 2009, 2012). Students' academic performance data were used to analyze the CIP outcomes with comparative statistics. The comparative statistical analysis was to determine how CIP impacts student English academic performance and how differently the Chinese immersion program impacted CIP student English reading, math, and science. In addition, the CIP students' 2012-2013 YCT test data were used for examining CIP's effectiveness in promoting Chinese language and culture. Descriptive statistics were used to indicate general tendencies in the YCT test data and the spread of the YCT test scores. Furthermore, a comparative statistical analysis was utilized to examine how CIP program model and instructional environment impacted students' YCT test results (Creswell, 2012).

Evaluation Questions

The following evaluation questions were categorized based upon the four components of the CIPP model:

1. To what extent did the program goals reflect the assessed needs (Context)?
2. To what extent were the selected approach and plans feasible, compatible, potentially successful, and cost effective for meeting the assessed needs (Input)?

3. To what extent was the program implemented as designed (Process)?

4. To what extent was there a difference in the academic performance of the immersion students when compared to similar students (Product)?

5. To what extent did the students perform differently in English reading and mathematics (Product)?

6. To what extent did the students of the program perform differently in Chinese compared to the students in the similar program in Minnesota (Product)?

The Chinese Language Immersion Program Evaluation Plan (See Table 4) was developed to summarize important elements of this evaluative study that were relevant to the evaluation (Fitzpatrick et al., 2011).

Table 4

Chinese Language Immersion Program Evaluation Plan

Part I: Interpretation Procedures and Criteria for Evaluation Question 1					
Evaluation Question 1: To what extent did the program goals reflect the assessed needs (Context)?					
Information Required	Method for Collecting Information	Information Source	When	Analysis Procedures	Interpretation Procedures and Criteria
Opinions from the program planners	Interview	Three Program Planners	August, 2013	General consensus against assessed needs	At least 2/3 of program planners would agree that the goals met the addressed needs.
Opinion from Chinese team	Survey	Chinese team	August, 2013	Scale analysis	At least 2/3 of the teachers would agree that the program goals met the addressed needs.
Opinions from the Advisory Panel	Survey	Advisory panel	October, 2013	Scale analysis	At least 2/3 of advisory panel member would give the program evaluation process a score of at least 80% for utility, feasibility, propriety, and accuracy of the process.

(Continued)

Part II: Interpretation Procedures and Criteria for Evaluation Question 2

Evaluation Question 2: To what extent were the selected approaches and plans feasible, compatible, potentially successful, and cost effective for meeting the assessed needs (Input)?

Information Required	Method for Collecting Information	Information Source	When	Analysis Procedures	Interpretation Procedures and Criteria
Opinions from the program planners	Interview	Three Program Planners	August, 2013	General consensus against assessed needs	At least 2/3 of the people would agree that the selected approach and plans were feasible, compatible, potentially successful, and cost effective for meeting the assessed needs
Opinion from Chinese team	Survey	Chinese team	August, 2013	Scale analysis	At least 2/3 of the teachers would agree that they utilized research-based Chinese language instructional strategies, and that placed the Chinese language immersion program in a matured language immersion environment was feasible, successful, and cost effective for the Chinese program.
Opinions from the Advisory Panel	Survey	Advisory panel	October, 2013	Scale analysis	At least 2/3 of advisory panel member would give the program evaluation process a score of at least 80% for utility, feasibility, propriety, and accuracy of the process.

(Continued)

Part III: Interpretation Procedures and Criteria for Evaluation Question 3
Evaluation Question 3: To what extent was the program implemented as designed (Process)?

Information Required	Method for Collecting Information	Information Source	When	Analysis Procedures	Interpretation Procedures and Criteria
Opinions from the program planners	Interview	Three Program Planners	August, 2013	General consensus against assessed needs	At least 2/3 of the people would agree the program was implemented as designed
Opinion from Chinese team	Survey	Chinese team	August, 2013	Scale analysis	At least 2/3 of the teachers would acknowledge the selected Chinese language immersion model, Chinese literacy model, and the Chinese curriculum articulation, and would agree that the models and curriculum were implemented with fidelity.
Opinions from the Advisory Panel	Survey	Advisory panel	October, 2013	Scale analysis	At least 2/3 of advisory panel member would give the program evaluation process a score of at least 80% for utility, feasibility, propriety, and accuracy of the process.

(Continued)

Part IV: Interpretation Procedures and Criteria for Evaluation Question 4

Evaluation Question 4: To what extent was there a difference in the academic performance of the immersion students when compared to similar students (Product)?

Information Required	Method for Collecting Information	Information Source	When	Analysis Procedures	Interpretation Procedures and Criteria
Test scores for math, English reading, and science from CIP and all the comparison schools in the same district	EOG scores from 2009-2010; 2010-2011; and 2011-2012	All the CIP Chinese language students and the sample students in each of the comparison schools in the same school district	August, 2013	Distributive statistics and *t*-tests	There would be no significant difference in English reading performance between the Chinese immersion students and their grade level peers in the comparable schools (NSS and MSS) and the same expected results would hold true for math and science. The NSL students would be expected to score significantly higher than the CIP students by all measures.
Opinion from Chinese team	Survey	Chinese team	August, 2013	Scale analysis	At least 2/3 of the teachers would agree that learning Chinese improved students' math and problem solving skills.
Opinions from the Advisory Panel	Survey	Advisory panel	October, 2013	Scale analysis	At least 2/3 of advisory panel member would give the program evaluation process a score of at least 80% for utility, feasibility, propriety, and accuracy of the process.

(Continued)

Part V: Interpretation Procedures and Criteria for Evaluation Question 5

Evaluation Question 5: To what extent did students perform differently in English reading and mathematics (Product)?

Information Required	Method for Collecting Information	Information Source	When	Analysis Procedures	Interpretation Procedures and Criteria
Test scores for math and English from the program and school NSL in the same district	EOG scores from 2009-2010; 2010-2011; and 2011-2012	All the Chinese immersion students and sample students from NSL	August, 2013	Distributive statistics and *t*-tests	There would be a significant difference between the CIP students' performance in math and English reading and CIP students would perform better in math than English reading, while such a difference would not be evident in school NSL.
Opinion from Chinese team	Survey	Chinese team	August, 2013	Scale analysis	At least 2/3 of the Chinese teachers would agree that the CIP students should perform better in math than English reading.
Opinions from the Advisory Panel	Survey	Advisory panel	October, 2013	Scale analysis	At least 2/3 of advisory panel member would give the program evaluation process a score of at least 80% for utility, feasibility, propriety, and accuracy of the process.

(Continued)

Part VI: Interpretation Procedures and Criteria for Evaluation Question 6

Evaluation Question 6: To what extent did the students of the program perform differently in Chinese compared to the students in the similar program in Minnesota (Product)?

Information Required	Method for Collecting Information	Information Source	When	Analysis Procedures	Interpretation Procedures and Criteria
YCT test scores from the program and comparable Chinese program in Minnesota	2012-2013 and YCT Level III and Level IV test results	The 2nd and 3rd grade Chinese language students from CIP and CIPL in Minnesota	June, 2013	Frequency Distributive analysis Distributive analysis and t-tests	There would not be a significant statistical difference in YCT test scores between the CIP Chinese immersion students and their grade level peers in the comparable program in Minnesota.
Opinion from Chinese team	Survey	Chinese team	August, 2013	Scale analysis	At least 2/3 of the Chinese teachers would agree that the CIP Chinese language students should score at least the same level in the YCT tests as their peers in CIPL in Minnesota.
Opinions from the Advisory Panel	Survey	Advisory panel	October, 2013	Scale analysis	At least 2/3 of advisory panel member would give the program evaluation process a score of at least 80% for utility, feasibility, propriety, and accuracy of the process.

Note. The criteria for evaluation question 6 were determined before more details about the comparison Chinese immersion program's student demographics and setting were identified. Due to its less diverse student population and more in-class Chinese instruction hours for its students, it was expected that the students in the comparison program would score significantly higher than CIP students in the YCT test by all measures. This expected result was incorporated in this study.

Evaluation Methodology

A mixed methodology was used in this evaluation study. The evaluation questions were incorporated with the CIPP (Stufflebeam, 2003) evaluation model, which includes Context, Input, Process, and Product component.

Context component. The evaluation question for this component was as follows: To what extent did the program goals reflect the assessed needs (Context)?

Input component. The evaluation question for this component was as follows: To what extent were the selected approach and plans feasible, compatible, potentially successful, and cost effective for meeting the assessed needs (Input)?

Process component. The evaluation question for this component was as follows: To what extent was the program implemented as designed (Process)?

Product component. The evaluation questions for this component were as follows: To what extent was there a difference in the academic performance of the immersion students when compared to similar students? To what extent did the students perform differently in English reading and math? And to what extent did the students of the program perform differently in Chinese compared to the students in the similar program in Minnesota?

Evaluation Sequence Model

A Comprehensive Chinese Language Immersion Program Sequence Model (See Appendix B) was developed to portray what CIP was and to align the Chinese language immersion program development components with the CIPP evaluation model. The Chinese language immersion program development components were (a) Chinese immersion teacher preparation; (b) Chinese language immersion curriculum design, which included Chinese language goals and objectives, Chinese instructional content and materials, as well as Chinese instruction and assessment; (c) administrative and collegial support; (d) Chinese language specific teaching strategies; and (e) CIP output.

This research study utilized mixed methods in the program evaluation. The mixed methodology provided the evaluator with the opportunity to analyze and compare both qualitative content and quantitative performance data. The purpose of this study design was to incorporate the inherent strengths of each approach, as noted by several prominent researchers (Collins et al., 2006; Creswell, 2003, 2009, 2012; Greene, 2006).

The incorporation of qualitative methods provided both depth and richness to this evaluative study that could only have been acquired through the inclusion of narrative language (Fitzpatrick et al., 2011). The use of qualitative methods allowed for elaboration and clarification of results to support and develop the findings acquired through the analysis of quantitative data, including students' EOG test data and survey data in this study. Validity doesn't carry the same connotations in qualitative research as it does in quantitative research, nor is it a companion of reliability or generalizability (Creswell, 2009). Qualitative validity means that the researcher checks for the accuracy of the findings by employing certain procedures, while qualitative reliability indicates that the researcher's approach is consistent across different researchers and different projects (Gibbs, 2007). Creswell (2003, 2009) emphasized that qualitative research was interpretative, while a mixed study design used numerical data to justify implications derived through the analysis and interpretation of qualitative data.

Furthermore, to increase the validity of the evaluative outcomes, triangulation of the data was incorporated in this study. This approach enabled the evaluator to cross validate data sources for the purpose of comparing and contrasting patterns surfacing in the data (McMillan & Schumacher, 2006). These collective reasons provided confidence that the purpose of the study achieved, and the findings contributed to improved practices in this evaluation setting.

Procedures

This study began with an examination of factors, both national and local, affecting the effectiveness of the Chinese language immersion school practices in the setting. This was followed by a comparative analysis of trends in the literature, which provided the opportunity for the evaluator to develop a keen discernment of the meaning and implications regarding data that were collected (Duvall, 2011). Creswell (2012) emphasized the value of applying the findings from literature review to analyze the collected data: "literature review provides an explanation for the results at the end of the study by citing other studies and by returning to the theoretical predication" (p. 104).

Procedures involved the use of interview questions (See Appendix F) to gather information about CIP's Context, Input, Process, and Product components. This instrument was designed to collect qualitative data from the director of the magnet office, the school principal, and a Chinese immersion teacher who was selected for planning CIP. These individuals were knowledgeable and experienced in planning CIP.

The semi-structured interview was conducted in May 2013, on the condition that the evaluator had obtained the Institutional Review Board (IRB) approval prior to that date. The analysis and interpretation of the interview was completed in May 2013 (See Appendix G).

Procedures also included the use of a survey to gain insights about the CIP instructional environment. This survey included questions on a five-point Likert scale and rooms for comments. This instrument was designed to collect quantitative data and qualitative data from 15 CIP Chinese teachers and teachers' assistants. Through comparing CIP teacher frequently-used strategies with recommended strategies from literature, conclusions of the effectiveness of the Chinese immersion instructional environment were reached and possible recommendations were made for CIP. This survey collected data concerning how well the teachers had implemented the selected language immersion model and Chinese curriculum. In addition, this survey collected information about the CIP teachers' experiences and observations of the CIP implementation and outcomes.

The Chinese Immersion Instructional Environment Survey (See Appendix H) was conducted in May 2013, on the condition that the evaluator had obtained IRB approval prior to that date. The analysis and interpretation of the survey was completed in May 2013 (See Appendix G).

A meta-evaluation, designed to collect quantitative data, was administered to the members of the advisory panel as the final data collection. The meta-evaluation survey (See Appendix E) was derived from the program evaluation standards within the areas of merit, feasibility, propriety, and utility (Stufflebeam, 1999). The meta-evaluation survey was completed in August 2013, on the condition that the evaluator had obtained IRB approval prior to that date. The analysis and interpretation of the interview was fulfilled in August 2013 (See Appendix G).

Students' academic performance was measured by the End Of Grade (EOG) test scores in English reading, math, and science and by the 2012-2013 YCT Chinese test scores. The 3rd, 4th, and 5th grade CIP students' EOG test scores in English reading, math, and science were collected, and so were their peers' in three comparable schools in the same school district. These schools were: (a) A neighborhood school with a similar percentage of economically disadvantaged students (NSS), (b) a higher academically performing magnet school with a similar percentage of economically disadvantaged students (MSS); and (c) a highly achieving neighborhood school with a lower percentage of economically disadvantaged students (NSL). The English reading, math, and science EOG test scores were compared between the CIP students and the students from each comparable school. The independent *t*-tests were conducted to determine if there were statistically significant differences between the academic success in English reading between the CIP students and each comparable school students. The same analysis applied for math and science EOG test results. An independent *t*-test analysis was conducted to determine if there was a statistically significant difference between the CIP students' EOG test scores in English and math, and the same analyses were applied for the high performing neighborhood school (NSL) (See Appendix I).

In order to determine how CIP impacted the student Chinese language proficiency, a comparison Chinese language immersion program (CIPL) with a similar program setting but a lower percentage of economically disadvantaged students was selected. CIPL was implemented in Minnesota in 2007 and its Chinese language immersion setting qualified CIPL as a comparable program for CIP in this study. The comparison was designed to assess how differently the CIP students performed on the 2012-2013 YCT Chinese test based on the differences of Chinese immersion instructional hours and the student socioeconomic and demographic backgrounds between the two Chinese language immersion programs.

The CIP students' Chinese language proficiency was measured by the YCT Chinese test scores. The 2012-2013 2nd and 3rd grade students' YCT test scores were compared between CIP and CIPL using both descriptive and inferential statistical analyses (See Appendix I).

The 2009-2010, 2010-2011, and 2011-2012 EOG test results were collected for the CIP students and each comparable school students from the accountability department of the school district in May after the IRB approval from the university and the approval from the North Carolina school district. The 2012-2013 YCT Chinese test scores were collect for the CIP students and for the CIPL students in July 2013 after the IRB approval from the university and the approval from the Minnesota school district. The various SPSS tests and interpretation of the results were completed in August 2013 (See Appendix G).

Participants

The semi-structured interview. Three people who were central to CIP planning at the initial stage participated in the program evaluation. These were (a) the director of the magnet office; (b) the school principal, as the primary administrator; and (c) the Chinese immersion teacher. The three educators were between 40 and 60 years of age. Ethnicities and ages of these individuals were considered irrelevant to the evaluation design. The selection was solely based on their roles in the school and school districts, and their participation was on a voluntary basis.

The Chinese Immersion Instructional Environment Survey. The 12 CIP Chinese immersion teachers and three teachers' assistants were invited to participate in the CIP Chinese Immersion Instructional Environment Survey. The anticipated participants were from 25 to 60 years of age (See Table 1); 100% were females; and all were born in China or Taiwan. Twelve teachers possessed at least a 4-year college degree from China, with one teacher having graduated from elementary school in China and later having earned her 4-year degree in the U.S. In addition, 11 of the teachers were certified K-6 teachers in North Carolina; one was a VIF teacher; and three were teacher's assistants (See Table 5).

Table 5

Chinese Language Immersion Teacher Education Profile

Country of Education	Elementary (Graduated)	College (Graduated)	Graduate School (Graduated)	Lateral Entry Camp Training	Chinese Immersion 101 Training
China	1	14	1		
United States		1	6	12	5

Note. There were 14 staff members in the Chinese language immersion team, 12 of whom were certified teachers and three of whom were teachers' assistants.

The age range of the teachers was between 25-60 years. Ethnicities and ages of the individuals were considered irrelevant to the evaluation design. The selection was solely based on their roles in the school and school districts, and their participation was on a voluntary basis.

The advisory panel. An advisory panel, consisting of two members from within the local school district and one member from the school district in Minnesota, was created. The members included an English facilitator, a language immersion facilitator, and a department coordinator of Assessment, Evaluation, and Research in Minnesota. The age range of panel members was between 40-65 years. Ethnicities and ages of the individuals were considered irrelevant to the evaluation design. The selection was solely based on their roles in the school and school districts, and their participation was on a voluntary basis.

Student participants. CIP was a full K-5 Chinese language immersion program that provided all students with at least 65% of instruction in Chinese, with English instruction provided at each grade level in one session lasting 45-60 minutes, beginning in Kindergarten. This school was part of the school district that served approximately 133,600 students. It was the second largest school district in North Carolina. There were 1,209 students in this school, which included 780 K-5 students in German, French, Japanese, and Chinese language-immersion programs. It was a county-wide magnet school. The proportion of children from the immediate neighborhood who were interested in attending the school was relatively low. There were 42% white, 25% African American, 19% Hispanic, 5% Asian, and 9% Multiracial students (See Table 3). In addition, 33% of K-8 students qualified for free or reduced lunch. The CIP students were very diverse and came from different socioeconomic backgrounds. One comparable English magnet school and two neighborhood schools in the same school district were selected.

School NSS had similar student socioeconomic makeup, including 34.8% white, 57.7% African American, 2.8% Hispanic, 1.9% Asian, and 2.8% Multiracial (See Table 3). At NSS, 34.1% of the students qualified for free or reduced lunch.

School MSS was a higher academically performing school based on the North Carolina ABC report, with 60.8% white, 31.7% African American, 3.1% Hispanic, 1.8% Asian, and 2.6% Multiracial students (See Table 3). At MSS, 24.8% of the students qualified for free or reduced lunch.

School NSL was a higher academically performing neighborhood school, with 77.4% white, 15% African American, 5.8% Hispanic, 3.4% Asian, and 2.4% Multiracial students (See Table 3), and 16.6% of the students qualified for free or reduced lunch.

The comparable Chinese language immersion program (CIPL) was implemented in 2007 in Minnesota. CIPL had the similar program setting, which made it a comparable program for CIP in this evaluation. There were 62.6% white, 6.7% African American,

2.1% Hispanic, 27.6% Asian, and 1.1% Multiracial in CIPL (See Table 3).

As mentioned in the earlier section, CIP was implemented in August of 2006. The first group of Chinese immersion students took the EOG test in May of 2010. By May of 2012, 3 years of EOG data were collected for the 3rd grade CIP students, 2 years EOG data for the 4th grade CIP students, and year of EOG data for the 5th grade CIP students.

Due to the full implementation of Common Core State Standards and Common Core Essential Standards in the 2012-2013 school years, the North Carolina Public Schools have endured dramatic changes in curriculum, instruction, and assessment. As part of the curricular changes, the North Carolina ABC accountability model was replaced with the North Carolina READY accountability model. In order to maintain the consistency of the assessment data for this study, the 2012-2013 student assessment data was excluded from this study. There were 272 CIP students when the study was conducted (including the 6th grade Chinese immersion students).

All the 3rd, 4th, and 5th grade CIP students' EOG test data, except that of the 2012-2013 school year, were retrieved for this study. More specifically, three groups of the 3rd grade CIP student EOG test results were gathered for this study: the 27 3rd grade CIP students' EOG test results in 2009-2010 school year (Class06), 28 3rd grade CIP students' EOG test results in 2011-2012 school year (Class07), and 27 3rd grade CIP students' EOG test results in 2011-2012 school year (Class08) were collected (See Table 6).

Table 6

CIP Class Participants

Classes	2006-07	2007-08	2008-09	2009-10	2010-11	2011-12
Class06	K	1st grade	2nd grade	3rd grade	4th grade	5th grade
Class07		K	1st grade	2nd grade	3rd grade	4th grade
Class08			K	1st grade	2nd grade	3rd grade

Note. K = Kindergarten

The student participants in the comparison non-immersion schools in the same school district were selected within the same time frame as CIP student participants were (See Table 7). In addition, 30 3rd grade students were randomly selected from each of the comparison schools and their 3rd, 4th, and 5th grade EOG test data were collected for this study (See Table 7).

Table 7

District Comparable Class Participants

CCP	2006-07	2007-08	2008-09	2009-10	2010-11	2011-12
CCP06	K	1st grade	2nd grade	3rd grade	4th grade	5th grade
CCP07		K	1st grade	2nd grade	3rd grade	4th grade
CCP08			K	1st grade	2nd grade	3rd grade

Note. CCP = Comparable class participants; K = Kindergarten

The 2012-2013 2nd and 3rd grade CIP students' YCT test results were collected for the study. The same procedure applied for the CIPL students. In addition, in the 2012-2013 school year, there were 44 2nd grade students and 34 3rd grade students in CIP; at the same time, there were 47 2nd grade and 44 3rd grade students in CIPL (See Table 8).

Table 8

YCT Chinese Immersion Program Participants

School	CIP	CIPL	CIP	CIPL
Grade Level	2nd grade	2nd grade	3rd grade	3rd grade
2012-2013	Class10YCT3	MN10YCT3	Class09YCT4	MN09YCT4
No. of Students	44	34	47	44

Note. Class10YCT3 = Class 2010-2011 Youth Chinese Test level 3; Class09YCT4 = Class 2008-2009 Youth Chinese Test level 4; MNY10CT3 = Minnesota 2010-2011 Youth Chinese Test level 3; MN09YCT4 = Minnesota 2008-2009 Youth Chinese Test Level 4.

Furthermore, the CIP class participants were classified into short-term, medium-term, and long-term participants for evaluation (See Table 9). There were three short-term participant groups, two medium-term participant groups, and one long-term participant group (See Appendix I).

Table 9

Short-term, Medium-term, and Long-term Class Participants

3rd Grades (Short-term) (Math & English)		4th Grades (Medium-term) (Math & English)		5th Grades (Long-term) (Math & English)	
Class06	CCP06				
Class07	CCP07	Class06	CCP06		
Class08	CCP08	Class07	CCP07	Class06	CCP06

Note. CCP = Comparable class participants

Instrumentation

The evaluation questions were used to guide the design of the instrumentation and collection of data.

A semi-structured interview was conducted with three people: the director of the magnet office, the school principal, and the Chinese immersion teacher. The benefit of using semi-structured interviews was that it provided the evaluator with comparable data for each participant (McNeil et al., 2005) and allowed for additional probing when appropriate or necessary. The director of the magnet office, the school principal and the Chinese immersion teacher were interviewed with the same set of interview questions (See Appendix F). These questions were adapted from a doctoral study, a summative program evaluation of a comprehensive 9th grade transition (Roybal, 2011). Moreover, these interview questions were originally adapted from Stufflebeam's (2003) checklist for summative evaluation. The questions were open-ended questions and qualitative in nature.

A survey with 50 questions was used to collect quantitative data and qualitative data from 15 CIP Chinese language immersion teachers and teachers' assistants. This survey included questions on a 5-point Likert scale: Strongly Agree (1), Agree (2), Neutral (3), Disagree (4), Strongly Disagree (5). The data were tabulated, and the internal consistency estimate of reliability of test scores were measured using Cronbach's alpha. The CIP Chinese teacher frequently-used strategies were compared with the recommended strategies for the same topic from the literature in order for a conclusion of the effectiveness of the Chinese language instructional environment to be reached. In addition, this survey was used to determine how well the CIP program model and Chinese curriculum was implemented. The evaluator designed the Chinese immersion instructional environment survey, but a pilot study was not feasible due to the limited availability of Chinese staff members.

A meta-evaluation survey regarding the integral procedures of CIP evaluation were conducted with the advisory panel members. This anonymous data collection reflected evaluation standards developed by members of the Joint Committee on Standards for Education Evaluation (Stufflebeam, 1999). The instrument was designed to examine the integral quality and processes of the program evaluation. Responses were used to substantiate recommendations for the CIP revision and improvement and for subsequent use in other similar programs.

The meta-evaluation survey was derived from the program evaluation standards within the areas of utility, feasibility, propriety, and accuracy (Stufflebeam, 1999). The instrument contains 40 items to be rated as 0-1 (poor), 2-3 (fair), 4 (good), 5 (very good), or 6 (excellent). The instrument was administered at the conclusion of the final meeting occurring between the evaluator and panel members. Responses were not used to answer the evaluation questions, but to evaluate the integral procedures of the program evaluation and substantiating recommendations for the CIP revision and improvement and for subsequent use in other similar programs.

The 2009-2010 3rd grade CIP student' EOG test data, the 2010-2011 3rd and 4th grade CIP students' EOG test data, and the 2011-2012 3rd, 4th, and 5th grade CIP students' EOG test data were collected. The same procedure was applied for each comparable school in the same school district.

The 2012-2013 2nd and 3rd grade YCT Chinese test data were collected in July 2013 from CIP and CIPL with the approval of the IRB approval from the university and the approval from the Minnesota school district prior to that date (See Appendix G). This design was intended to determine how differently the CIP students performed in the YCT Chinese test compared to the CIPL students.

The validity of the findings was increased by the regular participation of members serving on the advisory panel and by cross-checking the overall themes of qualitative data through having outsiders transcribe the audio recordings. The methodology of semi-structured interviews, which was used for the three program planners, and meta-evaluation, which was used in the survey for the advisory panel members, were used by the evaluator and are commonly used in qualitative studies (Creswell, 2012). These methods enhanced the reliability of the qualitative study results in this evaluation. The validity and reliability of the quantitative study were tested by various *t*-tests and Cronbach's alpha.

Data Collection Procedure

Procedures for collecting data began with acquiring approval to implement the evaluation study from the Institutional Review Board (IRB) of the university and school district. Approvals required the completion of detailed forms clearly depicting how the right of participants and confidentiality of data were to be protected. Additional topics included procedures involving (a) recruiting participants; (b) conducting interviews with three people–the director of the magnet office, the school principal, and the Chinese immersion teacher; conducting surveys with the Chinese language immersion team; and conducting surveys with the advisory panel members; (c) analyzing data collection instruments; and (d) acquiring and analyzing academic data. Each procedure was described in detail within the following text.

Recruitment of participants. After receiving IRB approval from the university and the school district, the evaluator scheduled an individual meeting with the director of the magnet office, the school principal, and the Chinese immersion teacher. After describing the problem, purpose, evaluation questions, and the expected outcomes of the program evaluation, each individual's role in the evaluation was explained. In the end, the process of informed consent was discussed and the informed consent form (See

Appendix J) was provided for the participants.

The evaluator met with the Chinese language immersion teachers and assistants during the Chinese staff meeting after receiving IRB approval from the university and the approval from Minnesota school district for conducting the program evaluation. The problem, purpose, evaluation questions, and the expected outcomes of the program evaluation were described. It was emphasized that each person would fill out a survey regarding the participant's perceptions and observations of CIP instructional environment. In the end, the process of informed consent was discussed and the informed consent form (See Appendix J) was provided for the participants.

The evaluator collected the CIP students' EOG test results and that of each comparable school from the accountability department in the school district. The evaluator contacted the district coordinator in Minnesota on the subject of collecting the 2nd and 3rd grade CIPL students' YCT test data after receiving IRB approval for conducting the program evaluation. The problem, purpose, evaluation questions, and expected outcomes of the program evaluation were described to the district coordinator in Minnesota. It was emphasized that the academic data collected for this study were protected with all and any identification information removed. In the end, the process of informed consent was discussed and the informed consent form (See Appendix J) was provided for the participants.

The evaluator met with the local advisory panel members in person and contacted the panel member in Minnesota by email after receiving IRB approval for conducting the program evaluation. The problem, purpose, evaluation questions, and expected outcomes of the program evaluation were described. The evaluator explained that each member of the advisory panel was expected to (a) meet twice in this process either in person or via emails, (b) provide ongoing guidance throughout the evaluation period, (c) assist in interpreting integral results and findings, and (d) complete a meta-evaluation survey of the collective processes involved in the program evaluation. In the end, the process of informed consent was discussed, and the informed consent form (See Appendix J) was provided for the participants.

Administration Data Collection Instruments

Semi-structured interviews. The semi-structured interviews were conducted for the director of the magnet office, the school principal, and the Chinese immersion teacher.

1. Director of the magnet office. Semi-structured interview was conducted immediately after receiving approval from the dissertation committee and members of the IRB for conducting the program evaluation.

2. School principal. Semi-structured interview was conducted immediately after receiving approval from the dissertation committee and members of the IRB for conducting the program evaluation.

3. Chinese immersion teacher. Semi-structured interview was conducted immediately after receiving approval from the dissertation committee and members of the IRB for conducting the program evaluation.

Chinese Immersion Instructional Environment Survey. The survey was conducted immediately after receiving approval from the dissertation committee and members of the IRB for conducting the program evaluation.

Members of the advisory panel. Panel members completed the meta-evaluation survey regarding the integral procedures of the program evaluation at the conclusion of the final meeting occurring with the evaluator. Each panel member returned the completed instrument to the evaluator's school mailbox in a sealed envelope, without identification.

Acquiring academic data. The CIP students' EOG test data and that of each comparable school were obtained from the accountability department in the school district. The 2009-2010 3rd grade English reading, and math EOG scores, the 2010-2011 3rd and 4th grade students' English reading and math EOG test scores, and the 2011-2012 3rd, 4th, and 5th grade students' English reading, math, and science EOG test scores were requested (See Appendix I). In addition, the 2012-2013 2nd and 3rd grade CIP students' YCT test results and that of CIPL were obtained in July 2013 after IRB approval.

Data Analysis and Expected Outcomes

Data analysis. The qualitative data analysis methods were conducted to get a general sense of the data from semi-structured interview data, as well as the data from the Chinese Immersion Instructional Environment Survey and then to determine coding descriptions and themes. The object of the coding process was to "make sense of the text data, divide it into text, label the segments with codes, examine the codes for overlap and redundancy, and collapse these codes into broad themes" (Creswell, 2005, p. 237). The themes of the semi-structured interview data and the Chinese Immersion Instructional Environment Survey data were described by "answering the major research questions and forming an in depth understanding of the central phenomenon description and thematic development" (Creswell, 2005, p. 241).

The findings of the qualitative analysis were cross-checked by an outsider to determine the overall themes and commonalities. The audio recorded interviews were transcribed by an outsider to cross-check the collected data. The results were displayed in a narrative discussion format.

In summary, both qualitative and quantitative data were collected in this evaluative study. The primary qualitative data were collected by the semi-structured interviews and by the Chinese immersion instructional environment survey. The three primary types of quantitative data were collected; these involved one survey from the Chinese team, one survey from the advisory panel, and one from 3 years of students' EOG test results.

Various procedures were used to analyze each data source. Validity of the findings was increased by the regular participation of members serving on the advisory panel and by cross-checking the overall themes of qualitative data by outsiders and transcribing the audio recordings by outsiders. The methodologies of semi-structured interviews, which were used by the three program planners, and meta-evaluation, which was used in the survey for the advisory panel members, are commonly used by researchers in qualitative studies (Creswell, 2012). These same methodologies enhanced the reliability of the qualitative study results in this evaluation.

Semi-structured interviews. To analyze the responses from the semi-structured interviews, the evaluator transcribed the recorded interviews and followed Strauss and Corbin's (1988) approach to read repeatedly until themes were constructed. This methodology helped to obtain insights into the interviewees' emerging thoughts in CIP's implementation and outcomes (Fung King Lee, 2001). Members of the advisory panel analyzed this system for sufficiency. Based on the patterns of processes and topics identified in responses, with the assistance of the advisory panel, interpretation was made, which was used to answer the questions regarding the evaluation of Context, Input, Process, and Product components of the CIPP model.

Chinese Immersion Instructional Environment Survey. This survey included questions on a five-point Likert scale and offered the opportunity for comments (See Appendix H). The instrument was designed to collect quantitative and qualitative data from 15 CIP Chinese teachers and teachers' assistants. The data were tabulated, and the internal consistency estimate of the reliability of test scores was measured using Cronbach's alpha. By comparing the CIP Chinese teacher frequently-used strategies to the recommended strategies for the same topic from the literature, conclusions of the level of the effectiveness of the Chinese immersion instructional environment and how well the program model and Chinese curriculum were implemented were determined. Possible recommendations were then made for CIP improvement.

Meta-evaluation. The survey included questions on a five point Likert scale (See Appendix E). The instrument was designed to evaluate the integral processes of the program evaluation within the area of utility, feasibility, propriety, and accuracy (Stufflebeam, 1999). Survey results were used in both the evaluation of integral procedures of the CIP evaluation and the CIP revision and improvement.

Student academic performance. Student academic performance was examined by answering the evaluation question 4, 5, and 6. Evaluation question 4 was answered by analyzing and comparing students' EOG test results in English reading, math, and science between CIP and each comparable school in the same school district. Evaluation question 5 was answered by analyzing and comparing CIP students' EOG test results between English reading and math. The same statistical analysis applied to the highly achieving neighborhood school (NSL). Evaluation question 6 was answered by analyzing and comparing 2012-2013 2nd and 3rd grade YCT test scores between the CIP students and CIPL students.

1. Student performance in English reading, math, and science. Two analyses were conducted in order to examine the student performance in English reading, math, and science. First, the evaluator acquired de-identified EOG English reading, math, and science EOG test scores for 2009-2010, 2010-2011, and 2011-2012 school years. The English reading, math, and science EOG test scores included 3 sets for the 3rd grade, 2 sets for 4th grade, and 1 set for the 5th grade. The first analysis identified the means and standard deviation for each data set. The second analysis compared the group means between the CIP students' EOG scores and that of each comparable school in the same school district. Four sets of de-identified EOG test scores for each grade level were used for this analysis: one data set was from CIP, and the other three were from the three comparable schools in the same school district. The four sets of EOG test scores were compared using SPSS independent t-test to determine if a statistically significant difference existed between the group means. This design was intended to examine the evaluation criteria for evaluation question 4.

2. Student performance differences between English reading and math. It had been noted that students reach similar proficiency levels in English reading and mathematics in non-immersion schools. Therefore, this test was used to examine if the similarity between English reading and math was evident in the Chinese immersion setting. Two de-identified data sets of EOG for each grade level were used for this analysis. One data set was collected from CIP and the other was collected from the higher academically performing neighborhood school (NSL) in the same school district. The independent t-test analysis was performed between math EOG test score and English reading EOG test score for each school

respectively. This design was intended to answer the evaluation question 5.

3. Student performance in Chinese language arts. First, the evaluator collected the de-identified 2012-2013 2nd and 3rd grade YCT Chinese test scores from CIP and CIPL. The first analysis identified how many students demonstrated expected Chinese language proficiency using frequency distribution analysis. The second analysis compared the group means. The two sets of YCT test scores were compared, using SPSS independent *t*-test, to determine if a statistically significant difference existed between the group means. This design was intended to examine the evaluation criteria for evaluation question 6.

Expected outcomes. The expected outcomes were illustrated as follows: (a) At least 2/3 of the program planners and the Chinese team would agree that the goals met the addressed needs; the academic performance analysis would substantiate this consensus as well; (b) at least 2/3 of the program planners and the Chinese team would agree that the selected approach and plans were feasible, compatible, successful, and cost effective; and at least 2/3 of the teachers would agree that they had provided research-based Chinese language instructional strategies for the students; at least 2/3 of the teachers would agree that they had participated in the articulation of the Chinese curriculum and implemented it with fidelity; (c) at least 2/3 of the program planners and the Chinese team would agree that CIP was implemented as designed, that concerns and ideas for improvement were handled efficiently, and that negative side effects were analyzed and minimized; and at least 2/3 of the teachers would agree that they had utilized research-based Chinese language instructional strategies and implemented the selected program model and Chinese curriculum with fidelity; (d) It was expected that the CIP students would perform at least at the same level in English academics as their peers in school NSS and school MSS, that the NSL students would perform significantly higher than that of the CIP students, and that the CIPL students would perform significantly higher in Chinese language proficiency than that of the CIP students. In addition, it was expected that at least 2/3 of the program planners and the Chinese team would agree that Chinese student academic achievement were satisfactory.

More specifically, there would be no significant difference in students' English academic performance between CIP and school NSS and school MSS in the same district, with CIP students performing better in math. But there would be significant difference in students' English academic performance between CIP and school NSL, and the NSL students would score significantly higher than the CIP students. There would be some level of differences between the CIP students' EOG test scores between English reading and math, and there would be no significant difference between NSL students' English reading scores and math scores. In addition, it was expected that at least 2/3 of the program planners and the Chinese team would agree that Chinese student academic achievement were satisfactory. Finally, it was expected that at least 2/3 of the advisory panel members would give the program evaluation process a score of at least 80% for the utility, feasibility, propriety, and accuracy of the process.

Summary. CIP was implemented at an urban school in North Carolina in 2006, yet had not been evaluated. It was not known how and to what extent this Chinese immersion program met the needs of immersion students. This study was designed to answer the evaluation questions by obtaining substantial data from CIP, the three comparable schools in the same school district, and CIPL from Minnesota. The criteria of the evaluation were based on the North Carolina Standard Course of Studies for math, English language arts, science, world languages, and the CIP Chinese curriculum. The purpose of this study was to comprehensively evaluate CIP's effectiveness. Participants included the director of the magnet office, the school principal, the Chinese immersion teacher, the Chinese language immersion team, and an advisory panel. In addition, the participants included the 3rd to 5th grade CIP students, students of the three comparable schools at the same school district, and the 2nd and 3rd grade CIP students and CIPL students. The evaluation study provided the opportunity to examine CIP with the four components of the CIPP model using six evaluation questions, with one question addressing Context, Input, and Process components of the CIPP model respectively, and three evaluation questions addressing the Product of the CIPP model.

Both qualitative data and quantitative data were used to examine Context, Input, Process, and Product components of the CIPP model. The program missions, objectives, and priorities, such as immersion model selection, teacher selection, identifying training programs for the Chinese language immersion teachers, and identifying effective Chinese language immersion specific teaching strategies, were examined through this effort. Specifically, semi-structured interviews were utilized to collect qualitative data. Chinese language teaching environment surveys were used to collect quantitative data and qualitative data from the Chinese team. Quantitative data regarding CIP students' EOG and YCT test data were analyzed. A meta-evaluation survey was used to collect quantitative data from the advisory panel to ensure the integral procedures of the program evaluation.

Mixed methods were utilized in the program evaluation, providing the evaluator the opportunity to analyze and compare both qualitative content and quantitative performance data. The design was identified for the purpose of incorporating the inherent strengths of each approach, as noted by several prominent researchers (Creswell,

2003, 2012; McMillan & Schumacher, 2006). To minimize potential weaknesses and to increase the validity of outcomes, triangulation of the data was incorporated in this study. Creswell (2012) pointed out, "Triangulation is the process of corroborating evidence from different individuals, types of data, or methods of data collection in descriptions and themes in qualitative research" (p. 259). This study was validated by the use of triangulation among different evidence, which enabled the evaluator to cross-validate data sources for the purpose of comparing and contrasting patterns that surfaced (McMillan & Schumacher, 2006). According to Creswell (2012), "This ensures that the study will be accurate because the information draws on multiple sources of information, individuals, or processes. In this way, it encourages the author to develop a report that is both accurate and credible" (p. 259).

Procedures were carefully followed throughout the implementation to ensure ethical performance. The data collection involved the use of a semi-structured interview, two surveys, and quantitative students' EOG test data regarding the areas of academic performance. Through both triangulation and a thorough literature review, the dimensions and scope of findings were reliable and applicable for consideration in determining decisions regarding CIP's effectiveness.

Assumptions

1. All the participants would report information on the interviews and surveys accurately.
2. The program goals and objectives had been implemented consistently and with integrity.

Limitations

This study has the following limitations:

1. The pilot study for the Chinese Teaching Environment Survey was not available for this evaluation.
2. The school was a magnet school that brought in students who would not otherwise have attended this school; as high-level learners, they might have had an impact on the data.
3. Outside factors that might affect student performance (e.g., family support and individual intelligence) were not addressed in this study.
4. The students being studied were not randomly selected from a large group of Chinese language immersion students in the setting. Rather, only two schools with specific characteristics were selected for the Chinese language immersion program evaluation, for convenience and accessibility.
5. The findings of the YCT test results might have had some limitations since it was a pilot YCT test for the CIP students.
6. The internal validity might have been limited by the maturation, experiences, emotions, judgments, and preferences of the respondents.
7. The generalizability might have been limited by the fact that both the teacher and student populations involved in this study might have been unique when compared to the general population throughout the geographical area. However, generalizability might exist for Chinese language immersion program settings.

Delimitations

The basis for selecting this school was that this school implemented the Chinese language immersion program 7 years ago. This program appeared to be very effective in promoting Chinese language skills and cultural awareness, while at the same time demonstrating evident academic success every year, as indicated by ABC status. In addition, this school had a highly diverse student population with different social and economic backgrounds. A program evaluation of such a school could provide useful information for decision makers and other schools.

Chapter 4: Results

This chapter presents two major sections of the results. Initially the findings from the semi-structured interview and Chinese Immersion Instructional Environment Survey are presented. The data collected through the two instruments mentioned above are used for answering all the evaluation questions in this study. More specifically, the frequency distribution tendency of the quantitative data from the Chinese Immersion Instructional Environment Survey and the narrative discussion of the qualitative data from both the semi-structured interviews and the Chinese Immersion Instructional Environment Survey were incorporated within each of the evaluation questions. Following this, the statistical analyses were then organized by evaluation questions. Particularly, this chapter presents the analyses of the EOG test scores and the related findings in evaluation question 4 and 5, as the EOG test scores were collected to answer evaluation question 4 and 5. This chapter presents the analyses of the YCT test scores and the related findings in evaluation question 6, as the YCT test scores were collected to answer evaluation question 6. Finally, this chapter presents the meta-evaluation results at the end of this chapter.

Based on the Context, Input, Process, and Product of the Stufflebeam's CIPP program evaluation model, this study categorized six evaluation questions as follows:

1. To what extent did the program goals reflect the assessed needs (Context)?
2. To what extent were the selected approaches and plans feasible, compatible, potentially successful, and cost effective for meeting the assessed needs (Input)?
3. To what extent was the program implemented as designed (Process)?
4. To what extent was there a difference in the academic performance of the immersion students when compared to similar students (Product)?
5. To what extent did the students perform differently in English reading and

mathematics (Product)?

6. To what extent did the students of the program perform differently in Chinese compared to the students in the similar program in Minnesota (Product)?

Semi-Structured Interview Analysis

The semi-structured interviews with the three program planners were aimed to investigate in-depth information about the Chinese program implementation, development, and outcomes. The interviews were recorded and transcribed for various data analyses. The interview data were read repeatedly, following Strauss and Corbin's (1988) approach, until themes were constructed to obtain insights into the program planners' emerging themes about the Chinese program implementation and development.

The qualitative data collected by semi-structured interview were codified as "funding and resources," "program model selection," "making teaching materials," "recruiting and preparing Chinese teachers," "supports from the principal and colleagues in the building," "Chinese language is very different," "Chinese culture and cultural gaps," "cultural shocks and cultural adaptation," "handling behavioral issues in classrooms of American schools," "trainings and national conferences," "academic and linguistic benefits." To analyze the data effectively, the codes were categorized into eight themes: (a) program funding and resources, (b) program model implementation, (c) curriculum implementation, (d) professional development, (f) administrative and collegial support, (f) classroom management, (g) Chinese instructional environment, and (h) Chinese program output. The narrative analyses of the eight emerged themes were presented within each evaluation question correspondingly.

Chinese Instructional Environment Analysis

Fourteen members of the Chinese immersion program studied participated in this survey. There were 16 members in the Chinese team with one on long-term medical leave and one being exempted from the participation of this survey due to the role of this member at the time the survey was distributed. Therefore, the participation rate of the Chinese team in the program under study was 100%.

The quantitative data collected from the Chinese instructional survey were tabulated. The internal consistency estimate of reliability of scale scores was measured by Cronbach's alpha. Cronbach's alpha for program funding and resources was 0.892, that for program model implementation was 0.399, that for curriculum implementation was 0.839, that for professional development was 0.318, that for administrative and collegial support was 0.733, that for classroom management was 0.767, that for Chinese instructional environment was 0.841, that for Chinese immersion program output was 0.788, and that for the entire survey was 0.926

The score of Cronbach's alpha for the entire survey (0.926) indicated that the test items were inter-related for the Chinese Immersion Instructional Environment Survey. For the eight subtopics, six of them were reliable based their Cronbach's Alpha, two of them were less than 0.70, which indicated that the items under both subtopics were not interrelated.

Table 10, Chinese Immersion Instructional Environment Survey Results, shows the findings from the Chinese instructional staff in the program. All the questions were categorized on eight dimensions: (a) program funding and resources, (b) program model implementation, (c) curriculum implementation, (d) professional development, (f) administrative and collegial support, (f) classroom management, (g) Chinese instructional environment, and (h) Chinese immersion program output.

The mean for the questions ranged from 0.363 to 1.477 (See Table 10).

Table 10

Chinese Immersion Instructional Environment Survey Results

Funding and Resources	n	Mean	Std. dev.
1. I have teaching materials needed for my students to learn Chinese.	14	1.64	0.842
2. My class has the technologies needed to promote effective teaching and learning in Chinese.	14	1.86	1.099
3. My students were provided resources for cultural activities, such as, Chinese calligraphy instructions, Chinese New Year celebrations, etc.	14	1.86	1.167

Program Model Implementation	n	Mean	Std. dev.
4. I use Chinese most of the time and English only when needed. I am a _____ teacher (please indicate your grade level).	14	1.86	1.292
5. I use Chinese only.	14	3.21	1.251
6. I allow mixture of language use by the students.	14	2.43	0.852
7. It is helpful for me to observe my language immersion colleagues in Japanese, French, or German teaching students in the same building.	14	1.93	1.269
8. I can get immediate support from the experienced Japanese, French or German language immersion colleagues in the same building.	14	2.14	1.099

Curriculum Implementation	n	Mean	Std. dev.
9. I teach my students subject contents based on NCSCOS and world language standards	14	1.64	1.008
10. I participated in the discussion of what I should teach at my grade Level.	14	1.64	1.277
11. I teach my students based on what I should teach at my grade level.	14	1.21	0.426

(Continued)

Curriculum Implementation	n	Mean	Std. dev.
12. I know the articulation of the Chinese curriculum across K-5 levels.	14	2.21	1.477
13. Chinese team has discussed and revised the Chinese curriculum annually.	14	2.21	1.251
14. The concerns and ideas for improvement have been handled satisfactorily.	14	1.93	1.072
15. The Chinese teachers share teaching materials at the same grade level.	14	2.00	0.961

Professional Development	n	Mean	Std. dev.
16. I am satisfied with the professional development opportunities.	14	2.21	1.051
17. CMS lateral entry training camp was useful for me to start my teaching practice in CMS.	14	2.93	1.072
18. Chinese immersion 101 or National Chinese Conference is informative for me to teach Chinese in language immersion settings.	14	2.50	0.855

Administrative and Collegial Support	n	Mean	Std. dev.
19. I know what my principal expect of me.	14	1.64	0.842
20. I feel respected and supported by school administration regarding promoting Chinese language and cultural.	14	1.86	0.949
21. I feel supported by administration regarding behavioral challenges.	14	1.50	0.941
22. The people I work with care about each other on a personal level.	14	1.86	0.770
23. I feel that people around me are collaborative.	14	1.79	0.802

Classroom Management	n	Mean	Std. dev.
24. My students learn rules and expectations in the first day of the school.	14	1.14	0.363
25. My classroom management plan was implemented with fidelity.	14	1.14	0.363
26. My students follow their daily routines.	14	1.43	0.938

(Continued)

Classroom Management	n	Mean	Std. dev.
27. My students observe the rewarding and consequence system in my class.	14	1.14	0.535

Chinese Instructional Strategies	n	Mean	Std. dev.
28. I use teacher-fronted and student-centered instructional strategy.	14	1.43	0.646
29. Mastery of Pinyin and tone at the 1st and 2nd grades is critical for students to develop their phonological awareness.	14	1.50	0.941
30. I use real objects or pictures to introduce new characters or new concepts, use Pinyin to help them pronounce the new characters with accurate tone.	14	1.43	0.646
31. I read aloud corresponding character prints to facilitate character recognition.	14	1.21	0.579
32. I use body language to assist students understand my input in Chinese.	14	1.21	0.579
33. I use context clues to help students understand the story.	14	1.21	0.579
34. I make connection to students' lives	14	1.29	0.611
35. I make repetitive comprehension check.	14	1.43	0.756
36. I ask students to read aloud for enhancing their pronunciation.	14	1.21	0.426
37. I ask students to read aloud for enhancing reading fluency.	14	1.14	0.363
38. I ask students to read aloud for developing reading comprehension.	14	1.21	0.426
39. I teach students the basic writing rule for composing the Chinese characters: from top to bottom, from left to right.	14	1.21	0.426
40. I ask students to practice the characters with its pinyin, tones, radicals, stroke orders, and stroke numbers.	14	1.50	0.760
41. I instruct students to identify the radical.	14	1.71	1.069
42. I ask students to practice the formation and pronunciation of the new characters, phrases, sentences and summary of the passages.	14	1.29	0.469
43. I ask students to demonstrate their comprehension of the characters by making phrases related to the characters and using them in sentences for meaningful communication.	14	1.36	0.633

(Continued)

Chinese Immersion Output	n	Mean	Std. dev.
44. I allocated time for students to act out what they read from the textbook.	14	1.14	0.535
45. I allocated time for students to share their group Chinese projects findings.	14	1.36	0.745
46. All my students reached the grade level bench mark in Chinese.	14	2.57	1.222
47. All my students reached the grade level benchmark in English and math.	14	3.07	1.269
48. I observed that studying Chinese improves students' mathematic skills and problem solving skills.	14	2.07	1.072
49. I observed that my students are responsive to Chinese cultural nuances.	14	1.71	0.825
50. I observed that my students appreciate Chinese culture.	14	1.71	0.825

In addition, the frequency distribution findings from the Chinese immersion instructional environment survey were illustrated in Table 11, Chinese Immersion Instructional Environment Frequency Distribution. Among all the items, the questions on classroom management, Chinese instructional strategies, and Chinese curriculum implementation received the highest ratings. Thirteen out of 14 teachers (94.75%) agreed that their classroom management plan was implemented with fidelity and being effective. Thirteen out of the 14 teachers (91.39%) agreed that they used the instructional strategies listed in the survey in their classrooms. Eleven out of 14 teachers (79%) agreed that they have instructional materials, instructional technologies to support their Chinese language instructional needs, and cultural activities in their classrooms. Eleven out of 14 teachers (78.4%) agreed that they got administrative and collegial support. Ten out of 14 teachers (77.43%) agreed that Chinese language immersion program was implemented with fidelity and the problems and concerns regarding the implementation were handled satisfactorily. Nine out of the 14 teachers (67.4%) agreed that the program model was implemented as designed. The majority of the Chinese teachers (94.75%) believed that the full Chinese language immersion model was very effective for teaching students to learn Chinese. One teacher specifically stated that, "I strongly feel that using 90/10 or 80/20 for K-2 is appropriate. However, due to the amount of testing conducted in grades 3-5, I feel the need to use both English and Chinese is vital." The two items that received the lowest ratings were student learning outcomes and professional development. Eight out of 14 teachers (57%) agreed that the students met the grade-level benchmark in reading, math, and Chinese, and that the Chinese immersion program improved students' mathematical and problem solving skills. Three perspectives surfaced in this subtopic. Firstly, the Chinese immersion program focused on the development of students' academic ability across all content areas, including Chinese, English, math, and Chinese culture. For an example, a teacher commented that the Chinese immersion program worked to build the students' academic ability in all respects, Chinese, English, and mathematics. She further stated that her students appreciated Chinese culture, and that they enjoyed the cultural activities planned for them throughout the year, like the Chinese New Year celebration. This teacher's comment represented the majority of the Chinese teachers' experiences and observations. Secondly, English proficiency level was an indicator of success in Chinese language acquisition and mathematical skill development. Just as a teacher pointed out that those who could not reach the English grade level benchmark were the ones who struggled in Chinese and Math. This perception also represented the majority of the Chinese teachers' perspectives. Lastly, struggling Chinese learners, even with tremendous tutoring and support, were not able to make noticeable progress expected by the teachers. For examples, one teacher noted that many of her students have done well and have reached the grade-level benchmark in Chinese; unfortunately, some students were unable to do so despite extra help and attention. This teacher offered another common observation in the program. Another teacher indicated that she did not agree that studying Chinese could improve a student's mathematic skills and problem solving skills for the low academic achievement students.

Six out of the 14 teachers (43.00%) agreed that professional development has enhanced their effectiveness of instruction in the Chinese language immersion setting. The teachers' comments in this subtopic could be classified into three perspectives. Firstly, the Chinese team offered some professional development opportunities that were effective for the instruction. One teacher commented that, "the Chinese department offers many professional development opportunities for its teachers, and I believe that these are useful and informative in helping teachers align their teaching methods to national standards." Secondly, the professional development at the national level was very informative and should be available for the teachers. For example, one teacher mentioned that the National Chinese Conference and Language Immersion 101 Training at the University of Minnesota were very informative, and she wished that she could get trained again. This teacher's point of view represented the great part of the Chinese teachers' opinions. Finally, the teachers agreed that the district lateral entry training was not worth the time. For instance, one commented that the lateral entry training camp provided by the school district was not helpful, nor practical, an opinion noted by many teachers (See Tables 10-11).

Table 11

Chinese Instructional Environment Frequency Distribution

Funding and Resources	Agree (%)	Neutral (%)	Disagree (%)
1. I have teaching materials needed for my students to learn Chinese.	79	21	0
2. My class has the technologies needed to promote effective teaching and learning in Chinese.	79	7	14
3. My students were provided resources for cultural activities, such as, Chinese calligraphy instructions, Chinese New Year celebrations, etc.	79	14	7
Mean (%)	79	14	7
Program Model Implementation	Agree (%)	Neutral (%)	Disagree (%)
4. I use Chinese most of the time and English only when needed. I am a _____ teacher (please indicate your grade level).	79	21	0
5. I use Chinese only.	43	14	43
6. I allow mixture of language use by the students.	64	22	14
7. It is helpful for me to observe my language immersion colleagues in Japanese, French, or German teaching students in the same building.	79	7	14
8. I can get immediate support from the experienced Japanese, French or German language immersion colleagues in the same building.	72	21	7
Mean (%)	67.4	17	15.6
Curriculum Implementation	Agree (%)	Neutral (%)	Disagree (%)
9. I teach my students subject contents based on NCSCOS.	79	14	7
10. I participated in the discussion of what I should teach at my grade Level.	86	7	7
11. I teach my students based on what I should teach at my grade level.	100	0	0

(Continued)

Curriculum Implementation	Agree (%)	Neutral (%)	Disagree (%)
12. I know the articulation of the Chinese curriculum across K-5 levels.	77	0	23
13. Chinese team has discussed and revised the Chinese curriculum annually.	64	21	14
14. The concerns and ideas for improvement have been handled satisfactorily.	64	29	7
15. The Chinese teachers share teaching materials at the same grade level.	72	21	7
Mean (%)	77.43	13.14	9.29

Professional Development	Agree (%)	Neutral (%)	Disagree (%)
16. I am satisfied with the professional development opportunities available to me.	50	43	7
17. CMS lateral entry training camp was useful for me to start my teaching practice in CMS.	36	36	28
18. Chinese immersion 101 or National Chinese Conference is informative for me to teach Chinese in language immersion settings.	43	50	7
Mean (%)	43	43	14

Administrative and Collegial Support	Agree (%)	Neutral (%)	Disagree (%)
19. I know what my principal expect of me.	79	21	0
20 I feel respected and supported by school administration regarding promoting Chinese language and cultural.	69	31	0
21 I feel supported by administration regarding behavioral challenges.	86	7	7
22 The people I work with care about each other on a personal level.	79	21	0
23 I feel that people around me are collaborative.	79	21	0
Mean (%)	78.4	20.2	1.4

Classroom Management	Agree (%)	Neutral (%)	Disagree (%)
24 My students learn the classroom rules and expectations from the first day of the school.	100	0	0
25 My classroom management plan was implemented with fidelity.	100	0	0
26 My students follow their daily routines.	86	7	7
27 My students observe the rewarding and consequence system in my class.	93	7	0

(Continued)

Chinese Instructional Strategies	Agree (%)	Neutral (%)	Disagree (%)
28 I use teacher-fronted and student-centered instructional strategy.	93	7	0
29 Mastery of Pinyin and tone at the 1st and 2nd grades is critical for students to develop their phonological awareness.	86	7	7
30 I use real objects or pictures to introduce new characters or new concepts, use Pinyin to help them pronounce the new characters with accurate tone.	93	7	0
31 I read aloud corresponding character prints to facilitate character recognition.	79	21	0
32 I use body language to assist students understand my input in Chinese.	93	7	0
33 I use context clues to help students understand the story.	93	7	0
34 I make connection to students' lives	93	7	0
35 I make repetitive comprehension check.	86	14	0
36 I ask students to read aloud for pronunciation.	100	0	0
37 I ask students to read aloud for enhancing reading fluency.	100	0	0
38 I ask students to read aloud for developing reading comprehension.	100	0	0
39 I teach students the basic writing rule for composing the Chinese characters: from top to bottom, from left to right.	100	0	0
40 I ask students to practice the characters with its pinyin, tones, radicals, stroke orders, and stroke numbers.	86	14	0
41 I instruct students to identify the radical.	71	29	0
42 I ask students to practice the formation and pronunciation of the new characters, phrases, sentences and summary of the passages.	100	0	0
43 I ask students to demonstrate their comprehension of the characters by making phrases related to the characters and using them in sentences for meaningful communication.	93	7	0
44 I allocated time for students to act out what they read from the textbook.	93	7	0

(Continued)

Chinese Instructional Strategies	Agree (%)	Neutral (%)	Disagree (%)
45 I allocated time for students to share their group Chinese projects findings with the class.	86	14	0
Mean (%)	91.39	8.17	0.39

Chinese Immersion Output	Agree (%)	Neutral (%)	Disagree (%)
46 All my students reached the grade level bench mark in Chinese.	50	29	21
47 All my students reached the grade level benchmark in English and math.	28	36	36
48 I observed that studying Chinese improves students' mathematic skills and problem solving skills.	57	36	7
49 I observed that my students are responsive to Chinese cultural nuances.	71	29	0
50 I observed that my students appreciate Chinese culture.	79	21	0
Mean (%)	57	30.20	12.80

Analysis for Evaluation Question 1

Evaluation Question 1: To what extent did the program goals reflect the assessed needs (Context)? For answering this question, the qualitative data collected from semi-structured interviews and the Chinese Immersion Instructional Environment Survey were transcribed and analyzed following Strauss and Corbin's (1988) approach. The internal reliability was tested for the Chinese Immersion Instructional Environment Survey and its subtopics using Cronbach's alpha. The triangulation of the collected data from various tools was used for answering the evaluation question 1.

From both the interviews and the survey, the assessed need in the community in 2005 was that the students should learn the Chinese language and culture in order to be prepared for the world economy when they are ready to get out in the workplace. China, as one of the new emerging countries, has demonstrated its rapid economic growth since 1995, which has attracted attention from the western world. The global economy and competition impact people's daily lives, including the people of United States. The director of the magnet office commented, "The communities across the United States of America realized that there is a big wide world out there besides United States of America. This is especially true after September 11, 2001. We'd better learn how to prepare our children to live in the world that is basically a flat world" (Director of the Magnet Office, personal communication, June 14, 2013). *The World is Flat*, published in 2005, clearly presented the context of the world at that time. The director of the magnet office stated that, "There was a recognition that Chinese economy was going to have significant role in the world. We want our students to have opportunities to learn the language and to be prepared for the world economy when they are ready to go out in the work place." (Director of the Magnet Office, personal communication, June 14, 2013)

The key local educational leaders responded to this global environment promptly and started investigating the need of adding a Chinese program in the school district and searching for the solutions. According to the director of the magnet office, there were initial discussions about adding a Chinese program to the world language selection as early as 2003-2004. The magnet office team started meeting the members of community as early as 2005. The school principal indicated that, "Dr. Frances Haithcock's granddaughter was in a Spanish immersion program in California. She went to China in 2005 and visited Chinese schools, which helped her make the link between learning Chinese and using language immersion model. She said that we need Chinese immersion after she came back from the trip in China" (Principal, personal communication, June 27, 2013).

According to the director of the magnet office (Director of the Magnet Office, personal communication, June 14, 2013), the previous director of the magnet office,

Robbie Kale was very much a proponent of global education before global education had become a familiar term and perceived a need of providing Chinese language for the students in the school district after her team gathered data from local communities. Under her leadership, the magnet office also identified a need to provide Chinese language and culture for the adopted Chinese children in the community.

As a result, the Chinese immersion program was started in the 2005-2006 school year to address these needs, with the un-wavering support from the superintendent, Dr. Frances Haithcock, and director of the magnet office at that time, Robbie Kale and her staff, and the school principal. The CIP's goal was to establish an optimal Chinese immersion environment so that students could become proficient in the Chinese language and develop increased cultural awareness while reaching at least the same level of academic achievement as their peers in the English programs. More specifically, the goal was that the students would learn all their content subjects in Chinese and become proficient in Chinese language and culture while demonstrating their mastery on the subject contents defined by NCSCOS.

The optimal Chinese immersion environment can be measured with eight factors: (a) program funding and resources, (b) program model implementation, (c) curriculum implementation, (d) professional development, (f) administrative and collegial support, (f) classroom management, (g) Chinese instructional strategies, and (h) Chinese program outcomes (Anderson et al., 2005; Cheung, 2003; Finnamore, 2006; Genesee, 1987; Gudykunst, 1998; He & Jiao, 2010; Kissau et al., 2012; Pugh & Hickson, 2007; Senge, 1992; Smith, 2007; Xiao, 2009).

The Chinese Immersion Instructional Environment Survey was designed and used to collect both quantitative and qualitative data from the Chinese teachers for this analysis. Based on the scale analysis of the survey results, eleven out of fourteen teachers (75.91%) agreed that the program goals addressed the assessed needs.

The findings from the interview with the director of the magnet office and the school principal indicated that the language immersion program has been the most effective way of learning a second language and that the Chinese program goal, to a great extent, addressed the assessed needs. The findings from the Chinese teachers also concurred with that of the director of the magnet office and the school principal.

Summary. Findings from qualitative data collected from the three program planners showed that three out of three program planners (100%) agreed that the program goals addressed the assessed needs. Eleven out of fourteen Chinese teachers (75.91%) agreed that the program goals addressed the assessed needs.

Analysis for Evaluation Question 2

Evaluation Question 2: To what extent were the selected approaches and plans feasible, compatible, potentially successful, and cost effective for meeting the assessed needs (Input)? For answering this question, the qualitative data collected from semi-structured interviews and the Chinese Immersion Instructional Environment Survey were transcribed and analyzed following Strauss and Corbin's (1988) approach. The internal reliability was tested for the Chinese Immersion Instructional Environment Survey and its subtopics using Cronbach's alpha. The triangulation of the collected data from various tools was used for answering the evaluation question 2.

The selection of Chinese immersion program model, the Chinese literacy model, the Chinese curricular type, and the school environment for CIP were critical program inputs and were analyzed as represented in the following information.

Selecting the program model. At the initial planning stage at district level, a dual Chinese language immersion model was the option. The dual Chinese immersion program at Chapel Hill, North Carolina could have served as a model for the Chinese immersion program at that time. According to the director of the magnet office, selecting the program model that was suitable for the needs of the students was challenging. Being flexible and being able to make critical changes based on the assessed needs were always crucial for implementing a new program, especially for implementing a new Chinese immersion program. He further stated,

> Initially, we planned to have a dual Chinese language program, and that was one of the reasons that we were interacting with the Chinese community in such a high level. We want to have a 50/50 mixed Chinese speakers and non-Chinese speakers. We attempted the first three years in our recruitment through our magnet fair to establish that dual immersion program. But it was a challenge. We have to make some modification to a full immersion program when we saw that we could not recruit the native Chinese speaker to the program (Director of the Magnet Office, personal communication, June 14, 2013).

At the school level, intensive research and investigation has been conducted for selecting the program model. According to the interview with the school principal, the school principal and three other teachers visited California Association of Independent Schools (CAIS) and Cupertino school in the 2005-2006 school year. Both schools were using a 50/50 model with more Chinese instruction introduced in Kindergarten and 1st grade where about 90% of the instruction in Chinese and 10% in English were introduced to the Kindergarten and 1st grade students. The school principal stated, in the interview, that they then decided to create a full Chinese immersion program with a 80/20 model, offering English literacy at the beginning in Kindergarten but continuing the rest of the program as much full immersion as possible.

In addition, all the existing language immersion programs in the school used the full language immersion model. The selected CIP Chinese immersion program model was a natural fit in the school environment as well as the CIP Chinese immersion student population based on their demographic backgrounds.

Selecting the Chinese literacy model. The school principal further stated that it was not very clear that which Chinese literacy model would be appropriate for the Chinese immersion program when it was started, but a major decision was made to use simplified Chinese characters instead of traditional characters, and to use Zhuyin instead of Pinyin. One year later, the school principal and the Chinese team made a critical modification for the Chinese literacy model, which was to use Pinyin as the Chinese phonetic base instead of Zhuyin.

Selecting of Chinese curricula type. After visiting CAIS and Cupertino Chinese immersion programs, the Chinese teachers and school principal determined to use the traditional Chinese teaching approach, which is to develop student's speaking, listening, reading, and writing skills in the Chinese immersion program, with different language skill foci at each grade level (See Appendix C).

The process of selecting the Chinese immersion program model, the Chinese literacy model, and the Chinese curricula type were complicated and situation-dependent. The expertise of the school principal and teachers were major contributing factors in this process. As the director of the magnet office summarized,

> The school principal has so much experience with establishing world language programs. She understands the different models. We rely a great deal on her

expertise to look at how the program to best be implemented at the school level. She knew that so well that we have to trust and rely on her experience. The success of the school has obtained with other languages that have been implemented was very clear that they know what they are doing. They have the knowledge, skills, and expertise to bring in another language and get it started . . . The success of the school has achieved and the expertise of the staff at school, and the culture of the school that school has established which was very international culture and very embracing different background of cultures. It seems a natural fit to locate Chinese in an environment that already supports this kind of goals (Director of the Magnet Office, personal communication, June 14, 2013).

Selecting the program location. To place the Chinese program in the language immersion school was an easy decision to make, according to the director of magnet office, and it was a natural fit for the program in this international environment of the school. The findings of the semi-structured interviews showed that the principal of the school and the panel Chinese teacher both agreed that the international environment of the school was open to the professionals of different ethnicities, beliefs, cultures, and languages, and that the Chinese program has thrived in this environment.

Also, the findings of the Chinese Immersion Instructional Environment Survey from the Chinese teachers permitted the same conclusion. The Chinese Immersion Instructional Environment Survey was designed with multiple measures for this analysis: (a) It is helpful for me to observe my language immersion colleagues in Japanese, French, or German teaching students in the same building, (b) I can get immediate support from the experienced Japanese, French, or German language immersion colleagues in the same building, (c) I feel respected and supported by school administration regarding promoting

Chinese language and cultural in the program, (d) the people I work with care about each other on a personal level, (e) I feel that people around me are collaborative, and (f) I utilize research-based Chinese language instructional strategies in my teaching. Based on the scale analysis, 11 out of 14 Chinese teachers (79%) agreed that it was helpful for them to observe their language immersion colleagues in Japanese, French, or German teaching students in the same building. Ten out of 14 Chinese teachers (72%) agreed that they could get immediate support from their experienced Japanese, French, or German language immersion colleagues in the same building. One of the Chinese teachers commented in her survey that she felt that her colleagues in other language departments have been very helpful in offering support and sharing insight. She further pointed out that the other language programs, such as the 10-year-old Japanese program, were mature and a lot of the teachers of these programs were more experienced and always willing to offer tips. Ten out of 14 teachers (69%) agreed that they felt respected and supported by school administration regarding promoting Chinese language and cultural in the program. Eleven out of 14 teachers (79%) agreed that the people they worked with care about each other on a personal level. Eleven out of 14 teachers (79%) agreed that they felt that people around them were collaborative. Thirteen out of 14 teachers (91.39%) agreed that they utilized research-based Chinese language instructional strategies in their teaching. In addition, 13 out of 14 teachers (93.39%) agreed that they applied the balanced Chinese teaching approach in their practices.

Twelve out of 14 teachers (83.50%) agreed that that they utilized research-based Chinese language instructional strategies and that placing the Chinese language immersion program in a matured language immersion environment was feasible, successful, and cost effective for the implementing and growing the Chinese immersion program.

Summary. Three out of three program planners (100%) agreed that the selected Chinese immersion model, modified Chinese literacy model, Chinese curricula type, and the plan of placing this new Chinese immersion program in a mature language immersion school was practical, compatible, and very successful, and cost effective. Twelve out of 14 Chinese teachers (83.50%) agreed that that they utilized research-based Chinese language instructional strategies and that placing the Chinese language immersion program in a mature language immersion environment was feasible, successful, and cost effective for the implementing and growing the Chinese immersion program.

Analysis for Evaluation Question 3

Evaluation Question 3: To what extent was the program implemented as designed (Process)? For answering this question, the qualitative data collected from semi-structured interviews and the Chinese Immersion Instructional Environment Survey were transcribed and analyzed following Strauss and Corbin's (1988) approach. The internal reliability was tested for the Chinese Immersion Instructional Environment Survey and its subtopics using Cronbach's alpha. The triangulation of the collected data from various tools was used for answering the evaluation question 3.

The qualitative data collected from semi-structured interviews and the Chinese Immersion Instructional Environment Survey were analyzed following Strauss and Corbin's (1988) approach, and quantitative data collected from the Chinese Immersion Instructional Environment Survey were analyzed with both descriptive and frequency distributive statistics for answering this question.

The program implementation, leadership roles in the program implementation, making adjustments based on the assessed needs, and the challenges for the Chinese program were the major process factors that stood out from the semi-structured interview and the Chinese Immersion Instructional Environment Survey.

The director of magnet office stated that, "it [the program implementation] was about flawless" (Director of the Magnet Office, personal communication, June 14, 2013). He further elaborated that the staff and the administration certainly have the passion and commitment to make sure that the program would be implemented at the same standards that other excellent programs at the school have been implemented. The Chinese immersion teachers concurred with the perception of the director of magnet office. The scale analysis results showed that 10 out of 14 Chinese teachers (67%) agreed that the Chinese immersion program model was implemented with fidelity. Eleven out of 14 teachers (77.43%) agreed that the Chinese curriculum was implemented with fidelity. And 13 out of 14 teachers (91.39%) agreed that they utilized research-based Chinese language instructional strategies in their teaching.

Findings from the interview with the school principal showed that leadership has played a critical role in this process:

> The Superintendent, Dr. Frances Haithcock, had the opportunity to go on the first North Carolina trip to China in 2005 and she got to visit schools. She got it [learning Chinese and learning Chinese in an immersion setting] from seeing what her granddaughter could do [her granddaughter was in a Spanish immersion program in California]. That was the piece where she said that we need Chinese immersion. So in 2005-2006, CMS provided funding through the magnet office to identify teachers. We hired two teachers in January to begin setting up the program. (Principal, personal communication, June 27, 2013)

Findings from the interview with the director of the magnet office and school principal showed that there was a quick change to the program model for the Chinese immersion program at the very beginning of the first school year. The initial plan was to establish a 50/50 dual immersion program, but it did not take off at the first school year as there were not enough native Chinese speakers registered into the Chinese immersion program. The program was started as a full Chinese immersion program based on the actual participants of the student demographic background, and it turned out to be a very effective change. This was due to the knowledge of the school administrator and flexibility demonstrated by the magnet office in the process. The full immersion program model was deemed as the most effective language immersion for the Chinese immersion program, based on the nature of the student population, by the magnet office, the Chinese immersion school principal, and Chinese immersion teachers, as it was compatible with that of other language immersion programs at the school.

According to the school principal and the panel Chinese teacher, the modification of the Chinese literacy model was very critical, practical, cost effective, and a successful change to the Chinese immersion program. Because of this change, the teachers could access a majority of the Chinese teaching materials on the market, saved a great amount of time, and were able to enhance the student Chinese learning experience and outcomes.

In addition, based on information from the director of the magnet office, program model selection was a big challenge, retaining the teacher designed Chinese immersion teaching materials was the second challenge, and recruiting native Chinese speakers and getting them licensed was the third challenge. In order to implement the program plan and model with fidelity, all these challenges needed to be addressed efficiently, and have been addressed successfully, based on the director of magnet office (Director of the

Magnet Office, personal communication, June 14, 2013). All the teachers in the Chinese immersion program are native speakers, the Chinese immersion model is a full language immersion program currently, and the authentic Chinese teaching materials have been created by the teachers and shared among the Chinese team. The findings from interviews with the panel Chinese teacher also agreed with the findings from both the director of the magnet office and the principal of the school.

Summary. Three out of three program planners (100%) agreed that the program was implemented as designed. In addition, about 11 out of 14 teachers (78.61%) recognized that the selected immersion model, Chinese curricular model, and the curriculum articulation were implemented with fidelity.

Analysis for Evaluation Question 4

Evaluation Question 4: To what extent is there a difference in the academic performance of the immersion students when compared to similar students (Product)? For answering this question, the EOG test scores in reading, math, and science in the 3rd, 4th, and 5th grades of the Chinese program and of the comparable schools were analyzed with descriptive and inferential statistics. The qualitative data collected from semi-structured interviews and the Chinese Immersion Instructional Environment Survey were transcribed and analyzed following Strauss and Corbin's (1988) approach. The internal reliability was tested for the Chinese Immersion Instructional Environment Survey and its subtopics using Cronbach's alpha. The triangulation of the collected data from various tools was used for answering the evaluation question 4.

The following sections presented student demographic description, student participant description, descriptive and inferential analysis results for combined grades, short-term impact, medium-term impact, and long-term impact consequently.

In addition, based on the student socioeconomic and demographic backgrounds (See Table 3), it was expected that there was no significant difference between the CIP students' test score and that of school NSS and school MSS, and it was also expected that the NSL students score significantly higher than the CIP students.

The findings showed that the CIP student scored significantly higher than the NSS students and the MSS students. It also showed that the CIP students scored significantly higher in math and science than the NSL students, and scored higher in reading in all the grade levels than NSL students and significantly higher in the 4th grade reading.

Student participant description. The participating schools were selected based on the economic disadvantaged students index (EDS). Based on the district-published EDS, the three comparable schools were selected (See Table 3).

All the 3rd, 4th, and 5th grades in the 2009-2010, 2010-2011, and 2011-2012 school years participated in this study. Specifically, 82 3rd grade CIP students participated in this study, 27 of which took their End Of Grade (EOG) test in 2009-2010, 28 in 2010-2011, and 27 in 2011-2012 school years. Their reading, math, and science EOG scores in their 3rd, 4th, and 5th grade were extracted for this study. At the same time, 90 3rd grade students, 30 from 2009-2010, 30 from 2010-2011, and 30 from 2011-2012 were randomly picked from each school respectively. Their EOG scores in their 3rd, 4th, and 5th grades were extracted from each comparable school for this study (See Table 12).

Table 12

Reading, Math, and Science EOG Participants

School Year	Participants	3rd Grade Students	4th Grade Students	5th Grade Students
2009-2010	CIP	27		
	NSS	30		
	MSS	30		
	NSL	30		
2010-2011	CIP	28	28	
	NSS	30	27	
	MSS	30	30	
	NSL	30	28	
2011-2012	CIP	27	27	27
	NSS	30	28	26
	MSS	30	30	29
	NSL	30	30	29

All the participants from the comparable schools were randomly selected from the 3rd grade classes in the schools. The 4th and 5th grade EOG test scores were extracted from the same group of the students who were randomly selected from the 3rd grade classes. Some cognitively challenged students were picked among the participants (See Table 13).

Table 13

Reading, Math, and Science EOG NCEXTEND I Participants

School Year	Participants	3rd Grade Students	4th Grade Students	5th Grade Students
2009-2010	CIP	0	0	0
	NSS	1	0	1
	MSS	0	0	0
	NSL	0	0	0
2010-2011	CIP	0	0	
	NSS	2	2	
	MSS	0	0	
	NSL	1	1	
2011-2012	CIP	0		
	NSS	2		
	MSS	0		
	NSL	0		

Because the scores were coded differently for the NCEXTEND I students (NCDPI, 2011) from the rest of student population, in order to ensure the validity of the study and satisfy the requirement of the statistical tests, the NXEXTEND I scores must be converted into the same scores using student achievement level as the reference key. In the randomly sampled data, eight counts of test scores were included in School NSS, and four in school NSL. All test scores were converted based on the NCEXTEND I Reading, Math, and Science Scale Score Conversion table (See Table 14).

Table 14

NCEXTEND I Reading, Math, and Science Scale Score Conversion

Grade Level	School	Reading Score	Converted Reading Score	Math Score	Converted Math Score	Science Score	Converted Science Score
3rd Grade	NSS	16	337	14	333		
3rd Grade	NSS	18	338	20	339		
3rd Grade	NSS	24	344	20	339		
3rd Grade	NSS	24	344	22	341		
3rd Grade	NSS	25	345	23	342		
3rd Grade	NSL	28	350	20	339		
4th Grade	NSS	22	345	14	343		
4th Grade	NSS	28	354	16	345		
4th Grade	NSL	28	354	28	362		
5th Grade	NSS	22	355	26	363	20	158

Descriptive analysis on reading, math, and science scores. The CIP students scored higher than that of all the comparable schools in reading, math, and science. Also, it was evident that the CIP students scored higher in math than in reading across 3rd, 4th, and 5th grade levels, which was not evident in school NSL, the neighborhood school, based on descriptive analysis (See Tables 15-18).

Table 15

Combined Grades Mean Scores and Standard Deviations for All Measures

Me	N	M	SD	n	M	SD	n	M	SD	N	M	SD
Pr		CIP			NSS			MSS			NSL	
Re	163	348.8	10.8	171	340.5	20.5	179	340.9	21.1	177	342.7	25.3
Ma	163	358.1	8.3	171	334.2	54.4	179	344.6	32.9	177	340.2	47.7
Sc	27	163.2	7.0	26	157.0	8.2	28	155.5	9.1	29	155.9	8.4

Note. Eight converted NCEXTENDED I scores were in NSS, and 2 in NSL (See Table 14); n = sample size; M = group mean; SD = Standard deviation; Pr = Program; Me = Measures; Re = Reading; Ma = Math; Sc = Science.

Table 16

Grade 3 Mean Scores and Standard Deviations for All Measures

Me	N	M	SD	n	M	SD	n	M	SD	n	M	SD
Pr		CIP			NSS			MSS			NSL	
Re	82	345.2	11.1	90	338.9	16.4	90	338.4	19.5	90	339.2	39.4
Ma	82	356.1	7.6	90	329.0	55.2	90	339.9	35.0	90	340.6	41.0

Note. Five converted NCEXTENDED I scores were in school NSS, and one in school NSL (See Table 14); n = sample size; M = group mean; SD = Standard deviation; Pr = Program; Me = Measures; Re = Reading; Ma = Math; Sc = Science.

Table 17

Grade 4 Mean Scores and Standard Deviations for All Measures

Me	N	M	SD	n	M	SD	n	M	SD	N	M	SD
Pr		CIP			NSS			MSS			NSL	
Re	54	349.5	9.6	55	340.1	24.6	60	339.6	26.2	58	339.9	29.8
Ma	54	357.8	8.6	55	342.2	46.0	60	344.3	35.6	57	337.4	54.5

Note. Two converted NCEXTENDED I scores were in school NSS, and one in school NSL (See Table 14); n = sample size; M = group mean; SD = Standard deviation; Pr = Program; Me = Measures; Re = Reading; Ma = Math; Sc = Science.

Table 18

Grade 5 Mean Scores and Standard Deviations for All Measures

Me	N	M	SD	n	M	SD	N	M	SD	N	M	SD
Pr		CIP			NSS			MSS			NSL	
Re	27	358.0	5.5	26	347.2	22.9	29	351.0	7.6	29	348.0	26.9
Ma	27	365.0	6.2	26	335.3	67.0	29	357.5	9.2	29	344.6	53.7
Sc	27	163.2	7.0	26	157.0	8.2	28	155.5	9.1	29	155.9	8.4

Note. One NCEXTEND I score was converted in school NSS for the *t*-test (See Table 14). One student in school MSS did not take the science test, which was not counted for the test. n = sample size; M = group mean; SD = Standard deviation; Pr = Program; Me = Measures; Re = Reading; Ma = Math; Sc = Science.

Inferential analysis for combined grade reading and math scores. The students scored significantly higher in aggregated reading scores of the 3rd, 4th, and 5th grades than that of the comparable schools and the same finding applied for math (See Table 19 and Tables 20-25). An independent samples *t*-test found that there was a statistical difference between the aggregated reading scores of the 3rd, 4th, and 5th grades in CIP and that of each comparable school, and the CIP students scored significantly higher than all the comparable schools. It also found that there was a statistically significant difference between the aggregated math score of the 3rd, 4th, and 5th grade in CIP and that of each comparable school, and the CIP students scored significantly higher than each comparable school.

Table 19

Summary of t-test for Combined Grades

	Reading		Math	
	t-stat	p	t-stat	P
CIP and NSS	4.63	0.00000566	5.67	0.000000056
CIP and MSS	4.41	0.000015	5.32	0.00000027
CIP and NSL	2.93	0.004	4.92	0.00000185

An independent samples *t*-test was used to check the difference of the reading scores of the combined grades between CIP and school NSS, $t(261) = 4.63$, $p = 0.00000566$, therefore, a statistically significant difference between the reading scores of CIP and that of school NSS was found, and the CIP students scored significantly higher (See Table 20).

Table 20

Combined Grades t-test Results for CIP and School NSS in Reading

	CIP Reading	NSS Reading
Mean	348.7791411	340.5380117
Variance	116.9262289	418.0382525
Observations	163	171
Hypothesized Mean Difference	0	
Df	261	
t Stat	4.634525993	
P(T<=t) one-tail	2.82763E-06	
t Critical one-tail	1.650712727	
P(T<=t) two-tail	5.65526E-06	
t Critical two-tail	1.969094724	

Note. Eight NCEXTEND I test scores in school NSS were converted for the *t*-test (See Table 14).

An independent samples *t*-test was used to check the difference of the reading scores of the combined grades between CIP and school MSS, $t(270) = 4.41$, $p =$

0.0000148. Therefore, a statistically significant difference between the reading scores was found and the CIP students scored significantly higher (See Table 21).

Table 21

Combined Grades t-test Results for CIP and School MSS in Reading

	CIP Reading	MSS Reading
Mean	348.7791411	340.8715084
Variance	116.9262289	446.6294646
Observations	163	179
Hypothesized Mean Difference	0	
Df	270	
t Stat	4.411909322	
P(T<=t) one-tail	7.40935E-06	
t Critical one-tail	1.650516748	
P(T<=t) two-tail	1.48187E-05	
t Critical two-tail	1.968789022	

An independent samples *t*-test was used to check the difference of the reading scores of the combined grades between CIP and school NSL, $t(243) = 2.93$, $p = 0.004$; therefore, a statistically significant difference between the reading score of CIP and that of school MSS was found, and the CIP students scored significantly higher (See Table 22).

Table 22

Combined Grades t-test Results for CIP and School NSL in Reading

	CIP Reading	NSL Reading
Mean	348.7791411	342.6723164
Variance	116.9262289	638.1079224
Observations	163	177
Hypothesized Mean Difference	0	
Df	243	
t Stat	2.937308383	
P(T<=t) one-tail	0.001814441	
t Critical one-tail	1.651148402	
P(T<=t) two-tail	0.003628881	
t Critical two-tail	1.969774395	

Note. Two NCEXTEND I test scores in school NSL were converted for the *t*-test (See Table 14).

An independent samples *t*-test was used to check the difference of the math scores of the combined grades between CIP and school NSS, $t(178) = 5.67$, p= 0.0000000555; therefore, a statistically significant difference between the math score of CIP and that of school NSS was found, and the CIP students scored significantly higher (See Table 23).

Table 23

Combined Grades t-test Results for CIP and School NSS in Math

	CIP Math	NSS Math
Mean	358.1104294	334.2046784
Variance	69.33340907	2962.128449
Observations	163	171
Hypothesized Mean Difference	0	
Df	178	
t Stat	5.67454154	
P(T<=t) one-tail	2.77342E-08	
t Critical one-tail	1.653459126	
P(T<=t) two-tail	5.54685E-08	
t Critical two-tail	1.973380889	

Note. Eight NCEXTEND I test scores in School NSS were converted for the *t*-test (See Table 14).

An independent samples *t*-test was used to check the difference of the math scores of the combined grades between CIP and school MSS, $t(203) = 5.32$, p = 0.000000270. Therefore, a statistically significant difference between the math scores was found and the CIP students scored significantly higher (See Table 24).

Table 24

Combined Grades t-test Results for CIP and School MSS in Math

	CIP Math	MSS Math
Mean	358.1104294	344.5642458
Variance	69.33340907	1083.460737
Observations	163	179
Hypothesized Mean Difference	0	
Df	203	
t Stat	5.322177977	
P(T<=t) one-tail	1.35128E-07	
t Critical one-tail	1.65239446	
P(T<=t) two-tail	2.70256E-07	
t Critical two-tail	1.971718848	

An independent samples *t*-test was used to check the difference of the math scores of the combined grades between CIP and school NSL, t(188) = 4.92, p = 0.00000185. Therefore, a statistically significant difference between the math scores was found and the CIP students scored significantly higher (See Table 25).

Table 25

Combined Grades t-test Results for CIP and School NSL in Math

	CIP Math	NSL Math
Mean	358.1104294	340.1638418
Variance	69.33340907	2275.490049
Observations	163	177
Hypothesized Mean Difference	0	
Df	188	
t Stat	4.924505928	
P(T<=t) one-tail	9.22808E-07	
t Critical one-tail	1.652999113	
P(T<=t) two-tail	1.84562E-06	
t Critical two-tail	1.972662692	

Note. Two NCEXTEND I test scores in school NSL were converted for the *t*-test (See Table 14).

The short-term, medium-term, and long-term English academic impact of the program were analyzed in the following three sections. All the 3rd grade EOG test scores in the 3 school years (See Tables 6-7) were tested to determine the short-term English academic impact. The CIP students scored significantly higher in math than the students of each comparable school and the same finding applied for English reading, except English reading in school SNL. The CIP students scored higher in English reading, but not significantly higher, than the NSL students (See Table 26 and Tables 27-32). All the 4th grade EOG test scores in the 3 school years (See Tables 6-7) were tested to determine the medium-term English academic impact. The CIP students scored significantly higher in math than the students of each comparable school and the same finding applied for English reading (See Table 26 and Tables 33-38). All the 5th grade EOG test scores in the 3 school years (See Tables 6-7) were tested to determine the long-term English academic impact. The CIP students scored significantly higher in math than the students of each comparable school. The same findings applied for science and English reading, except English reading in SNL. The CIP students scored higher in reading, but not significantly higher, than the NSL students (See Table 26 and Tables 39-47).

Table 26

Summary of t-test Results for Different Terms

Programs	Short-Term (3rd Grade)		Medium-Term (4th Grade)		Long-Term (5th Grade)	
	t-stat	p	t-stat	P	t-stat	P
Reading						
CIP and NSS	3.00	0.0031	2.65	0.009	2.34	0.026
CIP and MSS	2.83	0.005	2.74	0.0076	3.998	0.0002
CIP and NSL	0.98	0.329	2.34	0.022	1.967	0.058
Math						
CIP and NSS	5.57	4.41E-05	2.46	0.0166	2.25	0.033
CIP and MSS	4.28	2.70E-07	2.63	0.01	3.57	0.0008
CIP and NSL	3.53	0.0006	2.81	0.006	2.03	0.051
Science						
CIP and NSS					2.96	0.004
CIP and MSS					3.51	0.0009
CIP and NSL					3.54	0.0008

Inferential analysis for short-term impact on reading and math scores. All the 3rd grade EOG test scores in the 3 school years (See Tables 6-7) were tested to determine the short-term English academic impact. The CIP students scored significantly higher in math than the students of each comparable school. The CIP students also scored significantly higher in all comparisons in English reading except for the NSL students and there was no statistically significant difference between the CIP students' English reading score and that of NSL students (See Table 26 and Tables 27-32).

An independent samples *t*-test was used to check the difference of short-term impact on reading scores between CIP and school NSS, $t(157) = 3.00$, $p = 0.003$. Therefore, a statistically significant difference between the short-term impact on the CIP students' reading score and that of school NSS was found, and the CIP students scored significantly higher (See Table 27).

Table 27

t-test Results for CIP and School NSS Short-Term Impact on Reading

	CIP 3rd Grade Reading	NSS 3rd Grade Reading
Mean	345.2317073	338.8888889
Variance	122.5012045	267.2009988
Observations	82	90
Hypothesized Mean Difference	0	
Df	157	
t Stat	3.002463485	
P(T<=t) one-tail	0.001558457	
t Critical one-tail	1.654617035	
P(T<=t) two-tail	0.003116915	
t Critical two-tail	1.975189163	

Note. Five NCEXTEND I test scores in school NSS were converted for the *t*-test (See Table 14).

An independent samples *t*-test was used to check the difference of short-term impact on reading scores between CIP and school MSS, $t(143) = 2.83$, $p = 0.005$. Therefore, a statistically significant difference in the short-term impact on the students' reading score between CIP and that of school MSS was found, and the CIP students scored significantly higher (See Table 28).

Table 28

t-test Results for CIP and School MSS Short-Term Impact on Reading

	CIP 3rd Grade Reading	MSS 3rd Grade Reading
Mean	345.2317073	338.4444444
Variance	122.5012045	381.6204744
Observations	82	90
Hypothesized Mean Difference	0	
Df	143	
t Stat	2.834394841	
P(T<=t) one-tail	0.002628151	
t Critical one-tail	1.655579143	
P(T<=t) two-tail	0.005256302	
t Critical two-tail	1.976692198	

An independent samples *t*-test was used to check the difference of short-term impact on reading scores between CIP and school NSL, t(136) = 0.98, p = 0.33. Therefore, no statistically significant difference between the short-term impact on the CIP students' reading score and that of school NSL was found, though CIP students scored higher (See Table 29).

Table 29

t-test Results for CIP and School NSL Short-Term Impact on Reading

	CIP 3rd Grade Reading	NSL 3rd Grade Reading
Mean	345.2317073	342.7333333
Variance	122.5012045	453.2314607
Observations	82	90
Hypothesized Mean Difference	0	
Df	136	
t Stat	0.977702598	
P(T<=t) one-tail	0.16497869	
t Critical one-tail	1.656134988	
P(T<=t) two-tail	0.32995738	
t Critical two-tail	1.977560777	

Note. One NCEXTEND I test scores in school NSL was converted for the *t*-test (See Table 14).

An independent samples *t*-test was used to check the difference of short-term impact on math scores between CIP and school NSS, $t(113) = 5.57$, $p = 0.00000017$. Therefore, a statistically significant difference was found and the CIP students scored significantly higher (See Table 30).

Table 30

t-test Results for CIP and School NSS Short-Term Impact on Math

	CIP 3rd Grade Math	NSS 3rd Grade Math
Mean	356.0853659	342.7333333
Variance	58.30126468	453.2314607
Observations	82	90
Hypothesized Mean Difference	0	
Df	113	
t Stat	5.569685935	
P(T<=t) one-tail	8.7453E-08	
t Critical one-tail	1.658450216	
P(T<=t) two-tail	1.74906E-07	
t Critical two-tail	1.981180359	

Note. Five NCEXTEND I test scores in School NSS were converted for the *t*-test (See Table 14).

An independent samples *t*-test was used to check the difference of short-term impact on math scores between CIP and school MSS, $t(98) = 4.28$, $p = 0.000044$. Therefore, a statistically significant difference in the short-term impact on the students' math score between CIP and that of school MSS was found, and the CIP students scored significantly higher (See Table 31).

Table 31

t-test Results for CIP and School MSS Short-Term Impact on Math

	CIP 3rd Grade Math	MSS 3rd Grade Math
Mean	356.0853659	339.9111111
Variance	58.30126468	1223.295381
Observations	82	90
Hypothesized Mean Difference	0	
Df	98	
t Stat	4.276694727	
P(T<=t) one-tail	2.20562E-05	
t Critical one-tail	1.660551217	
P(T<=t) two-tail	4.41123E-05	
t Critical two-tail	1.984467455	

An independent samples *t*-test was used to check the difference of short-term impact on math scores between CIP and school NSL, $t(96) = 3.53$, $p = 0.00065$.

Therefore, a statistically significant difference in the short-term impact on the students' math score between CIP and that of school MSS was found, and the CIP students scored significantly higher (See Table 32).

Table 32

t-test Results for CIP and School NSL Short-Term Impact on Math

	CIP 3rd Grade Math	NSL 3rd Grade Math
Mean	356.0853659	340.5555556
Variance	58.30126468	1680.833958
Observations	82	90
Hypothesized Mean Difference	0	
Df	96	
t Stat	3.527050663	
P(T<=t) one-tail	0.000323191	
t Critical one-tail	1.66088144	
P(T<=t) two-tail	0.000646383	
t Critical two-tail	1.984984312	

Note. One NCEXTEND 1 test score in school NSL was converted for the *t*-test (See Table 14).

Inferential analysis for medium-term impact on reading and math scores. All the 4th grade EOG test scores in the 3 school years (See Tables 6-7) were tested to determine the medium-term English academic impact. The CIP students scored significantly higher in math than the students of each comparable school. The same finding applied for medium-term English reading (See Table 26 and Tables 33-38).

An independent samples *t*-test was used to check the difference of medium-term impact on reading scores between CIP and school NSS, $t(70) = 2.65$, $p = 0.0099$. Therefore, a statistically significant difference between the medium-term impact on the CIP students' reading score and that of school NSS was found, and the CIP students scored significantly higher (See Table 33).

Table 33

t-test Results for CIP and school NSS Medium-Term Impact on Reading

	CIP 4th Grade Reading	NSS 4th Grade Reading
Mean	349.537037	340.0727273
Variance	91.46086653	606.6983165
Observations	54	55
Hypothesized Mean Difference	0	
Df	70	
t Stat	2.653181173	
P(T<=t) one-tail	0.004929662	
t Critical one-tail	1.666914479	
P(T<=t) two-tail	0.009859324	
t Critical two-tail	1.994437112	

Note. Two NCEXTEND I test scores in School NSS were converted for the *t*-test (See Table 14).

An independent samples *t*-test was used to check the difference of medium-term impact on reading scores between CIP and school MSS, $t(76) = 2.74$, $p = 0.0076$. Therefore, a statistically significant difference was found and the CIP students scored significantly higher (See Table 34).

Table 34

t-test Results for CIP and School MSS Medium-Term Impact on Reading

	CIP 4th Grade Reading	MSS 4th Grade Reading
Mean	349.537037	339.6166667
Variance	91.46086653	683.7319209
Observations	54	60
Hypothesized Mean Difference	0	
Df	76	
t Stat	2.742019102	
P(T<=t) one-tail	0.003805151	
t Critical one-tail	1.665151353	
P(T<=t) two-tail	0.007610301	
t Critical two-tail	1.99167261	

An independent samples *t*-test was used to check the difference of medium-term impact on reading scores between CIP and school NSL, t(69) = 2.34, p = 0.022. Therefore, a statistically significant difference between the medium-term impact on the CIP students' reading score and that of school NSL was found, and the CIP students scored significantly higher (See Table 35).

Table 35

t-test Results for CIP and School NSL Medium-Term Impact on Reading

	CIP 4th Grade Reading	NSL 4th Grade Reading
Mean	349.537037	339.9137931
Variance	91.46086653	885.7292801
Observations	54	58
Hypothesized Mean Difference	0	
Df	69	
t Stat	2.33639173	
P(T<=t) one-tail	0.011190856	
t Critical one-tail	1.667238549	
P(T<=t) two-tail	0.022381713	
t Critical two-tail	1.994945415	

Note. One NCEXTEND I test score in school NSL was converted for the *t*-test (See Table 14).

An independent samples *t*-test was used to check the difference of medium-term impact on math scores between CIP and school NSS, t(58) = 2.46, p = 0.017. Therefore, a statistically significant difference between the medium-term impact on the CIP students' math score and that of school NSS was found, and the CIP students scored significantly higher (See Table 36).

Table 36

t-test Results for CIP and School NSS Medium-Term Impact on Math

	CIP 4th grade Math	NSS 4th Grade Math
Mean	357.7592593	342.2181818
Variance	73.62019567	2111.914478
Observations	54	55
Hypothesized Mean Difference	0	
Df	58	
t Stat	2.46460999	
P(T<=t) one-tail	0.008349902	
t Critical one-tail	1.671552762	
P(T<=t) two-tail	0.016699804	
t Critical two-tail	2.001717484	

Note. Two NCEXTEND I test scores in school NSS were converted for the *t*-test (See Table 14).

An independent samples *t*-test was used to check the difference of medium-term impact on math scores between CIP and school MSS, $t(67) = 2.63$, $p = 0.011$. Therefore, a statistically significant difference was found and the CIP students scored significantly higher (See Table 37).

Table 37

t-test Results for CIP and School MSS Medium-Term Impact on Math

	CIP 4th Grade Math	MSS 4th Grade Math
Mean	357.7592593	345.2833333
Variance	73.62019567	1267.15565
Observations	54	60
Hypothesized Mean Difference	0	
Df	67	
t Stat	2.631173837	
P(T<=t) one-tail	0.005274677	
t Critical one-tail	1.667916114	
P(T<=t) two-tail	0.010549354	
t Critical two-tail	1.996008354	

An independent samples *t*-test was used to check the difference of medium-term impact on math scores between CIP and school NSL, $t(60) = 2.81$, $p = 0.0066$.

Therefore, a statistically significant difference between the medium-term impact on the CIP students' math score and that of School NSL was found, and the CIP students scored significantly higher (See Table 38).

Table 38

t-test Results for CIP and School NSL Medium-Term Impact on Math

	CIP 4th Grade Math	NSL 4th Grade Math
Mean	357.7592593	337.362069
Variance	73.62019567	2966.620992
Observations	54	58
Hypothesized Mean Difference	0	
Df	60	
t Stat	2.814758714	
P(T<=t) one-tail	0.003296598	
t Critical one-tail	1.670648865	
P(T<=t) two-tail	0.006593197	
t Critical two-tail	2.000297822	

Note. One NCEXTEND I test score in school NSL was converted for the *t*-test (See Table 14).

Inferential analysis for long-term impact on reading, math, and science scores. All the 5th grade EOG test scores in the 3 school years (See Tables 6-7) were tested to determine the long-term English academic impact. The CIP students scored significantly higher in math than the students of each comparable school. The same findings applied for science and English reading, except English reading in SNL. The CIP students scored higher in reading, but not significantly higher, than the NSL students (See Table 26 and Tables 39-47).

An independent samples *t*-test was used to check the difference of long-term impact on reading scores between CIP and school NSS, $t(28) = 2.34$, $p = 0.027$. Therefore, a statistically significant difference between the long-term impact on the CIP students' reading score and that of school NSS was found, and the CIP students scored significantly higher (See Table 39).

Table 39

t-test Results for CIP and School NSS Long-Term Impact on Reading

	CIP 5th Grade Reading	NSS 5th Grade Reading
Mean	358.037037	347.2307692
Variance	30.57549858	524.1046154
Observations	27	26
Hypothesized Mean Difference	0	
Df	28	
t Stat	2.341989155	
P(T<=t) one-tail	0.013261223	
t Critical one-tail	1.701130934	
P(T<=t) two-tail	0.026522446	
t Critical two-tail	2.048407142	

Note. One NCEXTEND I test scores in school NSS was converted for the *t*-test (See Table 14).

An independent samples *t*-test was used to check the difference of long-term impact on reading scores between CIP and school MSS, t(51) = 4.00, p = 0.00021. Therefore, a statistically significant difference in the long-term impact on the students' reading score between CIP and that of school MSS was found, and the CIP students scored significantly higher (See Table 40).

Table 40

t-test Results for CIP and School MSS Long-Term Impact on Reading

	CIP 5th Grade Reading	MSS 5th Grade Reading
Mean	358.037037	351
Variance	30.57549858	57
Observations	27	29
Hypothesized Mean Difference	0	
Df	51	
t Stat	3.998095074	
P(T<=t) one-tail	0.000103191	
t Critical one-tail	1.67528495	
P(T<=t) two-tail	0.000206382	
t Critical two-tail	2.00758377	

An independent samples *t*-test was used to check the difference of long-term impact on reading scores between CIP and school NSL, t(31) = 1.97, p = 0.058. Therefore, a statistically significant difference between the long-term impact on the CIP students' reading score and that of school NSL was found, and the CIP students scored significantly higher (See Table 41).

Table 41

t-test Results for CIP and School NSL Long-Term Impact on Reading

	CIP 5th Grade Reading	NSL 5th Grade Reading
Mean	358.037037	348
Variance	30.57549858	722.0714286
Observations	27	29
Hypothesized Mean Difference	0	
Df	31	
t Stat	1.967235826	
P(T<=t) one-tail	0.029080178	
t Critical one-tail	1.695518783	
P(T<=t) two-tail	0.058160356	
t Critical two-tail	2.039513446	

An independent samples *t*-test was used to check the difference of long-term impact on math scores between CIP and school NSS, t(25) = 2.25, p = 0.033. Therefore, a statistically significant difference between the long-term impact on the CIP students' math score and that of school NSS was found, and the CIP students scored significantly higher (See Table 42).

Table 42

t-test Results for CIP and School NSS Long-Term Impact on Math

	CIP 5th Grade Math	NSS 5th Grade Math
Mean	364.962963	335.2692308
Variance	38.34472934	4486.284615
Observations	27	26
Hypothesized Mean Difference	0	
Df	25	
t Stat	2.251272807	
P(T<=t) one-tail	0.016702572	
t Critical one-tail	1.708140761	
P(T<=t) two-tail	0.033405143	
t Critical two-tail	2.059538553	

Note. One NCEXTEND I test score in school NSS was converted for the *t*-test (See Table 14).

An independent samples *t*-test was used to check the difference of long-term impact on math scores between CIP and school MSS, $t(49) = 3.57$, $p = 0.00081$. Therefore, a statistically significant difference in the long-term impact on the students' math score between CIP and that of school MSS was found, and the CIP students scored significantly higher (See Table 43).

Table 43

t-test Results for CIP and School MSS Long-Term Impact on Math

	CIP 5th Grade Math	MSS 5th Grade Math
Mean	364.962963	357.5172414
Variance	38.34472934	84.83004926
Observations	27	29
Hypothesized Mean Difference	0	
Df	49	
t Stat	3.571860159	
P(T<=t) one-tail	0.000403291	
t Critical one-tail	1.676550893	
P(T<=t) two-tail	0.000806581	
t Critical two-tail	2.009575237	

An independent samples *t*-test was used to check the difference of long-term impact on math scores between CIP and school NSL, t(29) = 2.03, p = 0.051. Therefore, a statistically significant difference between the long-term impact on the CIP students' math score and that of School NSL was found, and the CIP students scored significantly higher (See Table 44).

Table 44

t-test Results for CIP and School NSL Long-Term Impact on Math

	CIP 5th Grade Math	NSL 5th Grade Math
Mean	364.962963	344.5517241
Variance	38.34472934	2884.541872
Observations	27	29
Hypothesized Mean Difference	0	
Df	29	
t Stat	2.032129905	
P(T<=t) one-tail	0.025694918	
t Critical one-tail	1.699127027	
P(T<=t) two-tail	0.051389836	
t Critical two-tail	2.045229642	

An independent samples *t*-test was used to check the difference of long-term impact on Science scores between CIP and school NSS, t(49) = 2.96, p = 0.0047. Therefore, a statistically significant difference between the long-term impact on the CIP students' science score and that of school NSS was found, and the CIP students scored significantly higher (See Table 45).

Table 45

t-test Results for CIP and School NSS Long-Term Impact on Science

	CIP Science	NSS Science
Mean	163.1481481	156.9615385
Variance	48.28490028	66.99846154
Observations	27	26
Hypothesized Mean Difference	0	
Df	49	
t Stat	2.961085619	
P(T<=t) one-tail	0.002357819	
t Critical one-tail	1.676550893	
P(T<=t) two-tail	0.004715637	
t Critical two-tail	2.009575237	

Note. One NCEXTEND I test score in school NSS was converted for the *t*-test (See Table 14).

An independent samples *t*-test was used to check the difference of long-term impact on Science scores between CIP and school MSS, $t(50) = 3.51$, $p = 0.00095$. Therefore, a statistically significant difference in the long-term impact on the students' science score between CIP and that of school MSS was found, and the CIP students scored significantly higher (See Table 46).

Table 46

t-test Results for CIP and School MSS Long-Term Impact on Science

	CIP Science	MSS Science
Mean	163.1481481	155.5
Variance	48.28490028	82.7037037
Observations	27	28
Hypothesized Mean Difference	0	
Df	50	
t Stat	3.512157555	
P(T<=t) one-tail	0.000476292	
t Critical one-tail	1.675905025	
P(T<=t) two-tail	0.000952584	
t Critical two-tail	2.008559112	

An independent samples *t*-test was used to check the difference of long-term impact on Science scores between CIP and school NSL, t(53) = 3.54, p = 0.00084. Therefore, a statistically significant difference between the long-term impact on the CIP students' science score and that of School NSL was found, and the CIP students scored significantly higher (See Table 47).

Table 47

t-test Results for CIP and School NSL Long-Term Impact on Science

	CIP Science	NSL Science
Mean	163.1481481	155.862069
Variance	48.28490028	70.908867
Observations	27	29
Hypothesized Mean Difference	0	
Df	53	
t Stat	3.541163697	
P(T<=t) one-tail	0.000419793	
t Critical one-tail	1.674116237	
P(T<=t) two-tail	0.000839586	
t Critical two-tail	2.005745995	

In summary, the *t*-test analyses showed that (a) the CIP students scored significantly higher by all measures than the students of school NSS, a neighborhood school with EDS of 34.1%; (b) the CIP students scored significantly higher by all measures than the students of school MSS, a magnet school with EDS of 28.6%; (c) the CIP students scored significantly higher than the students of school NSL in all the measures, except for English reading in 3rd grade and 5th grade. The CIP students scored higher in English reading, but not significantly higher in the 3rd and 5th grade in school SNL. School NSL was a fluent neighborhood school with EDS of 17.6%, which was much lower than that of the CIP, which is 33%. The CIP was comprised of diverse student population, of which 42.7% were white and more than one third of the students come from poverty (See Table 3), while 73.3% of the student population in school NSL was white and one sixth of the students came from poverty (See Table 3).

The interviews with the three program planners have supported the above statistical findings. The findings from the three program planners indicated that high vigor and active language immersion learning environment, high expectations for all, and hard work have contributed students' academic success to a certain extent. The findings from the Chinese team suggested that the Chinese teachers were struggling with the students who were academically challenged and that their philosophies, that every student could count and do math and every student could get a good grade if they worked hard enough, was challenged with a reality of U.S. public schools: Students who were academically challenged were usually the ones that did not have support at home.

The perception from the director of the magnet office suggested that language immersion in general created academic success. He commented that:

> Academic performance of the language immersion students in a way has always been a surprise to me, because they achieve on such a higher level, although their instructions, [or] so much of their instructions is not in English. It was always fascinated me. This is not just related to Chinese. This is just how the language immersion students in general. In 3rd grade, when you compare the test scores, they are about the same as their peers. When about [the] time they get to their 5th grade, you see outstanding increase in the achievement on part of the immersion students (Director of the Magnet Office, personal communication, June 14, 2013).

He further elaborated, "my assumption is that the immersion process makes the learning a much more active experience for the students. They have to internally understand the concept, not only in the language they are learning, but also translate it to themselves in an English version to be able to retain it and have the connection" (Director of the Magnet Office, personal communication, June 14, 2013).

The interview with the panel Chinese teacher echoed the assumption of the director of magnet office. She indicated that the language immersion by its nature was a challenging environment for the students and that learning language in an immersion environment itself was a constant problem solving process, which led to higher rigor and more active learning in the Chinese language immersion classrooms. It is assumed that these approaches, to a certain extent, explained the high academic achievement of the CIP.

The interview with the panel Chinese teacher also suggested that the Chinese teachers carried the following underlining philosophical assumptions: that everyone could count and do math, that everyone could get a good grade if he or she worked hard enough, that Chinese teachers set high expectations for all of their students, and that the teachers instilled their perspectives of learning philosophy into their students and modeled their students' attitudes and behaviors towards academic successes. The school principal revealed the same observation:

> It is one of the huge blessings that the teachers come from a culture where there are high expectations for the achievement of all kids, not because they are gifted, but because anyone is capable of working hard. The whole culture does not say that you are smart or you are bright, but it is about anyone is capable of working harder. (Principal, personal communication, June 27, 2013)

Based on the scale analysis, four out of 14 (28%) of the teachers agreed that all their students reached the grade level benchmarks in English and math. The perception from this group of the teachers was consistent with the findings of the EOG test results in reading, math, and science. Five out of 14 (36%) of the teachers were in neutral position. Five out of 14 (36%) of the teachers disagreed this survey statement. The perception of this group of teachers was inconsistent with the findings of the various *t*-tests across all subjects. The discrepancy resulted primarily from the observation and perception of the students. For instance, one teacher commented that not all students could reach the grade level benchmark in English and those who could not reach the English grade level benchmark were the ones who struggled in Chinese and Math. Another teacher commented, "I feel that there is a strong connection between learning Chinese and English in general. Based on my experience, students who can successfully master the Chinese language are usually very strong in English literacy as well. Vice versa, students who struggle with learning Chinese were most likely struggled in English fluency and comprehension."

Ten out of 14 teachers (71%) agreed that they observed that studying Chinese improves students' mathematic skills and problems solving skills, which agreed with the findings of EOG test results and findings from the semi-structured interviews. Five out 14 teachers (36%) were in neutral position, and one out of 14 teachers (7%) disagreed with this survey statement. This teacher further stated that, "I do not agree that studying Chinese can improve mathematic skills and problem solving skills for the low academic achievement students."

Ten out of 14 teachers (71%) agreed that they observed that their students were responsive to Chinese cultural nuances, which agreed with the findings from the semi-structured interview. Eleven out of 14 teachers (79%) agreed that they observed that their students appreciated Chinese culture, which also agreed with the findings from the semi-structured interview. Nine out of 14 teachers (64.29%) commented that their students were appreciative of Chinese culture and interested in participating in Chinese cultural events. The interview with school principal illustrated similar finding.

Overall, eight out of 14 teachers (57%) agreed that the Chinese immersion students' academic performance was satisfactory, four out 14 teachers (30.20%) were in neutral position, and two out of 14 teachers (12.80%) disagreed with the survey statements. The disagreement among the perceptions from the teachers about the students' academic success, the perceptions from the program planners, and findings from the EOG and YCT test results indicated the Chinese teachers were struggling with the students who were academically challenged. This incongruity also manifested itself in the Chinese teachers' underlining philosophical assumption that every student could count and do math and every students could get a good grade if they worked hard enough; this was challenged by the reality of U.S. public schools. The school principal pointed out in the interview that:

> The challenges going forward are certainly to have a diverse student population that represents our community. With lottery system and the number of applicants we have, the odds are very good that we'll continue to have a very diverse student population, which then becomes challenge because there is a real demand on the teachers to differentiate and meet the needs of a diverse, urban student population. One third of our students are from poverty, using the measure of economically disadvantaged students. When you consider that those kids are achieving to such a high level in Chinese language, it doesn't happen by accident. (Principal, personal communication, June 27, 2013)

Summary. Findings from various *t*-tests across all subjects and grade level groups showed that the CIP students scored significantly higher than the NSS students and MSS students. Based on the socioeconomic and demographic backgrounds, school NSL was expected to score significantly higher than that of the CIP. On the contrary, the findings of the statistical analysis showed that the CIP students scored higher than the NSL students by all measures. Also the CIP students scored significantly higher than the NSL students by all measures in math, reading, and science, except 3rd and 5th grade reading. According to the teachers' survey, eight out of 14 teachers (57%) agreed that the Chinese immersion students' academic performance was satisfactory, which did not seem to support the t-test findings. Three out of three program planners (100%) agreed that learning Chinese improved students' math and problem solving skills.

Analysis for Evaluation Question 5

Evaluation Question 5. To what extent do the students perform differently in English reading and mathematics (Product)? For answering this question, the EOG test scores in reading and math in the 3rd, 4th, and 5th grade of the Chinese program and of the comparable school NSL were analyzed with descriptive and inferential statistics. The qualitative data collected from semi-structured interview and Chinese Immersion Instructional Environment Survey were transcribed and analyzed following Strauss and Corbin's (1988) approach. The internal reliability was tested for the Chinese Immersion Instructional Environment Survey and its subtopics using Cronbach's alpha. The triangulation of the collected data from various tools was used for answering the evaluation question 5.

In addition, it was expected that the students in the school NSL score significantly higher than that of CIP in all measures, based on the student demographic backgrounds (See Table 3).

Distributive analysis of EOG reading scores and math scores. The CIP students' EOG test scores and that of school NSL were analyzed with descriptive statistics (See Table 48). The summary of the mean scores showed that the CIP students' average math score was higher than that of English in the 3rd, 4th, and 5th grade and that the average NSL students' math score was very close to the average English score (See Table 48).

Table 48

Mean Scores for CIP and School NSL for Reading and Math

Me	3rd Grade		4th Grade		5th Grade		All Grade	
	CIP	NSL	CIP	NSL	CIP	NSL	CIP	NSL
Re	345.2	339.2	349.5	339.9	358.0	348.0	348.8	342.7
Ma	356.1	340.6	357.8	337.4	364.4	344.6	358.1	340.2

Note. Me = Measures; Re = Reading; Ma = Math.

The *t*-test results showed that there was a statistically significant difference between CIP students' reading and math scores in the 3rd, 4th, 5th grade, and CIP students scored significantly higher in math. The same finding was found in CIP students' combined grades reading and math scores, and the students scored significantly higher in math. However, there was no significant difference between the NSL students' reading score and math score in the 3rd, 4th, or 5th grade, or in combined grades respectively. The findings from Chinese instructional survey and the semi-structured interview agreed with the *t*-test results (See Table 49 and Tables 50-57).

Table 49

Summary of t-test Results for Reading and Math Scores

	3rd Grade		4th Grade		5th Grade		Combined Grade	
	t-stat	P	t-stat	P	t-stat	P	t-stat	P
CIP	-7.31	1.70E-11	-4.7	7.85E-06	-4.33	6.87E-05	-8.73	1.73E-16
NSL	0.45	0.655	0.31	0.75	0.31	0.758	0.62	0.536

Inferential analysis between EOG reading scores and math scores. An independent samples *t*-test was used to check the difference between the 3rd grade CIP students' reading and math scores, t(144) = -7.31, p = 0.000000000017. Therefore, a statistically significant difference between the 3rd grade CIP students' reading and math scores was found and the students scored significantly higher in math (See Table 50).

Table 50

t-test Results for Grade 3 CIP Reading and Math Scores

	CIP 3rd Grade Reading	CIP 3rd Grade Math
Mean	345.2317073	356.0853659
Variance	122.5012045	58.30126468
Observations	82	82
Hypothesized Mean Difference	0	
Df	144	
t Stat	-7.309386081	
P(T<=t) one-tail	8.50988E-12	
t Critical one-tail	1.655504177	
P(T<=t) two-tail	1.70198E-11	
t Critical two-tail	1.976575066	

An independent samples *t*-test was used to check the difference between the 3rd grade reading score and math score in school NSL, t(134) = -0.44, p = 0.65. Therefore, no statistically significant difference between the 3rd grade NSL reading score and math score was found, and the students scored higher in the 3rd grade reading in school NSL

(See Table 51).

Table 51

t-test Results for Grade 3 NSL Reading and Math Scores

	NSL 3rd Grade Reading	NSL 3rd Grade Math
Mean	342.7333333	340.5555556
Variance	453.2314607	1680.833958
Observations	90	90
Hypothesized Mean Difference	0	
Df	134	
t Stat	0.447230025	
P(T<=t) one-tail	0.327715526	
t Critical one-tail	1.656304542	
P(T<=t) two-tail	0.655431052	
t Critical two-tail	1.977825758	

Note. The test was conducted with one converted NCEXTEND I test score in school NSL (See Table 14).

An independent samples *t*-test was used to check the difference between the 4th grade CIP students' reading and math scores, t(105) = -4.70, p = 0.0000078. Therefore, a statistically significant difference between the 4th grade CIP student reading and math scores was found, and the students scored significantly higher in math (See Table 52).

Table 52

t-test Results for Grade 4 CIP Reading and Math Scores

	CIP 4th Grade Reading	CIP 4th Grade Math
Mean	349.537037	357.7592593
Variance	91.46086653	73.62019567
Observations	54	54
Hypothesized Mean Difference	0	
Df	105	
t Stat	-4.702593756	
P(T<=t) one-tail	3.92404E-06	
t Critical one-tail	1.659495383	
P(T<=t) two-tail	7.84809E-06	
t Critical two-tail	1.982815274	

An independent samples *t*-test was used to check the difference between the 4th grade reading score and math score in school NSL, t(105) = 0.31, p = 0.75. Therefore, no statistically significant difference between the 4th grade reading and math scores was found and the NSL students scored higher in the 4th grade reading in NSL (See Table 53).

Table 53

t-test Results for Grade 4 NSL Reading and Math Scores

	NSL 4th Grade Reading	NSL 4th Grade Math
Mean	339.9137931	337.362069
Variance	885.7292801	2966.620992
Observations	58	58
Hypothesized Mean Difference	0	
Df	88	
t Stat	0.313101274	
P(T<=t) one-tail	0.37747229	
t Critical one-tail	1.662354029	
P(T<=t) two-tail	0.75494458	
t Critical two-tail	1.987289865	

Note. *t*-test was conducted with one converted NCEXTEND I test score (See Table 14).

An independent samples *t*-test was used to check the difference between the 5th grade CIP students' reading and math scores, t(51) = -4.33, p = 0.000069. Therefore, a statistically significant difference between the 5th grade CIP student reading and math scores was found, and the students scored significantly higher in math (See Table 54).

Table 54

t-test Results for Grade 5 CIP Reading and Math Scores

	CIP 5th Grade Reading	CIP 5th Grade Math
Mean	358.037037	364.962963
Variance	30.57549858	38.34472934
Observations	27	27
Hypothesized Mean Difference	0	
Df	51	
t Stat	-4.334972751	
P(T<=t) one-tail	3.43486E-05	
t Critical one-tail	1.67528495	
P(T<=t) two-tail	6.86972E-05	
t Critical two-tail	2.00758377	

An independent samples *t*-test was used to check the difference between the 5th grade reading score and math score in school NSL, $t(41) = 0.31$, $p = 0.76$. Therefore, no statistically significant difference between the 5th grade NSL student reading score and math score was found, and the students scored higher in the 5th grade reading (See Table 55).

Table 55

t-test Results for Grade 5 NSL Reading and Math Scores

	NSL 5th Grade Reading	NSL 5th Grade Math
Mean	348	344.5517241
Variance	722.0714286	2884.541872
Observations	29	29
Hypothesized Mean Difference	0	
Df	41	
t Stat	0.309208348	
P(T<=t) one-tail	0.379364494	
t Critical one-tail	1.682878002	
P(T<=t) two-tail	0.758728989	
t Critical two-tail	2.01954097	

An independent samples *t*-test was used to check the difference between the aggregated 3rd, 4th, and 5th grade CIP students' reading scores and math scores, t(304) = -8.73, p = 0.00000000000000017. Therefore, a statistically significant difference between the CIP student aggregated reading and math scores was found and the students scored significantly higher in math (See Table 56).

Table 56

t-test Results for Grades 3-5 CIP Reading and Math Scores

	CIP Reading	CIP Math
Mean	348.7791411	358.1104294
Variance	116.9262289	69.33340907
Observations	163	163
Hypothesized Mean Difference	0	
Df	304	
t Stat	-8.729231971	
P(T<=t) one-tail	8.6634E-17	
t Critical one-tail	1.649881428	
P(T<=t) two-tail	1.73268E-16	
t Critical two-tail	1.967798141	

An independent samples *t*-test was used to check the difference between the aggregated 3rd, 4th, and 5th grade NSL students' reading scores and math scores, t(268) = 0.62, p = 0.54. Therefore, no statistically significant difference between the NSL student aggregated 3rd, 4th, and 5th grade reading scores and math score was found, and the students scored higher in the aggregated reading (See Table 57).

Table 57

t-test Results for Grade 3-5 NSL Reading and Math Scores

	NSL Reading	NSL Math
Mean	342.6723164	340.1638418
Variance	638.1079224	2275.490049
Observations	177	177
Hypothesized Mean Difference	0	
Df	268	
t Stat	0.618274769	
P(T<=t) one-tail	0.268459657	
t Critical one-tail	1.650559157	
P(T<=t) two-tail	0.536919314	
t Critical two-tail	1.968855173	

Note. *t*-test was conducted with two converted NCEXTEND I reading and math scores (See Table 14).

Based on the North Carolina School Report Card and the data extracted from the school district, the Chinese immersion program has reduced the achievement gap in mathematics between the majority and minority (African American and Hispanic) students (See Table 58).

Table 58

Percentage of Student Achieved at/above Grade Levels

School Year	Sub-Groups	CIP	NSS	MSS	NSL	District	State
2009-2010	White	100	89.0	95	95	94.6	89.4
	Black	100	76.8	76.3	69	71.1	67.9
	Gap (W/B)	0	12.2	18.7	26	23.5	21.5
	Hispanic	100	90.9	77.8	89.5	78.6	76.9
	Gap (W/H)	0	-1.09	17.2	5.5	16	12.5
2010-2011	White	100	89.0	>95	94.6	94.7	89.6
	Black	100	78.6	77.8	51.6	71.5	69
	Gap (W/B)	0	10.4	17.2	43.0	23.2	20.6
	Hispanic	100	75.0	64.3	81.8	78.5	78.5
	Gap(W/H)	0	14	30.7	12.8	16.2	11.1
2011-2012	White	100	88.8	>95	>95	95	89.7
	Black	95	77.4	75.5	75.4	72.7	70.0
	Gap (W/B)	5	11.4	19.5	19.6	22.3	19.7
	Hispanic	100	73.7	85.7	86.2	79.9	79.3
	Gap (W/H)	0	15.1	9.3	8.8	15.1	10.4

Note. W/B = Caucasian and African-American student sub-groups, and W/H = Caucasian and Hispanic student sub-groups.

In summary, the findings of various *t*-tests showed that there was a significant difference between the CIP students' scores in reading and math, and the students scored significantly higher in math, but there was no significant difference between the NSL students' scores in reading and math. In addition, the CIP students' achievement in mathematics evidenced by their EOG scores suggested that CIP closed the achievement gaps in mathematics between the majority and minority students (See Table 58).

By looking into the semi-structured interview and Chinese Immersion Instructional Environment Survey, the rigor of language immersion instruction, mental discipline in learning, and high expectation for academic success in the Chinese immersion environment have played a critical role in students' academic success in general. In particular, the Chinese teachers embrace the importance of mathematical processes and skills and are skillful in teaching math, which may have consequently contributed into the significant performance difference between reading and math. This phenomenon was not evident in a non-immersion school (NSL) in this study.

Based on scale analysis, ten out of 14 teachers (71%) agreed that they observed that studying Chinese improved student's mathematic skills and problem solving skills, which agreed with the findings of the various *t*-tests and results from the semi-structured interview. Five out of 14 teachers (36%) were in neutral position, and one teacher (7%) disagreed with this survey statement, which was inconsistent with the findings of the various *t*-test results, nor the findings from the semi-structured interviews. The teacher who disagreed commented, "I did not agree that studying Chinese could improve mathematic skills and problem solving skills for the low academic achievement students." Therefore, considering this teacher's comment, nobody in the Chinese team disagreed that studying Chinese improved students' mathematic skills and problem solving skills.

Ten out of 14 teachers (71%) agreed that they observed that their students were responsive to Chinese cultural nuances, which agreed with the findings from the semi-structured interview; and 11 out of 14 teachers (79%) agreed that they observed that their students appreciated Chinese culture, which also agreed with the findings from the semi-structured interview. Nine out of 14 teachers (64.2%) commented that their students were appreciative Chinese cultural and interested in participating in Chinese cultural events. One out of 14 teachers (7%) commented, " I find most of them appreciated Chinese culture, but some required more discipline for learning," which indicated that this teacher's underlining assumption–mental discipline was part of the Chinese culture and the Chinese immersion students ought to have this discipline.

The cultural impact on the students was more than just the excitement for celebrating the Chinese New Year and enjoyment of tasting various types of authentic Chinese food. The Chinese teachers assumed that hard work results in academic success. The combination of excitement and hard work has shaped the students' attitudes towards schooling. The "core cultural impact of the Chinese immersion program" was that the teachers set high expectations for all and provided support for the improvement, and the students took their teachers' high expectations as the norm and strived for the success. The school principal confirmed these ideas in one interview,

> I think we've heard a lot recently on a superficial level about tiger moms and high expectations of parents from Asian cultures. And I think it takes on new meaning when you're a child is in a Chinese immersion program. Because we dream of classes, as an educational leader, I dream of a classroom where every child that every teacher has the same high expectations for every child. No matter what

home they come from; no matter how intellectually gifted they are, or not; and no matter what they bring as resources into the classroom with them, the teacher has high expectations of all kids. Isn't that something that we say really easily, but then what does it look like when you actually get it? And it's one of the huge blessings. The teachers come from a culture where there are high expectations for the achievement of all kids, not because they're gifted but because anyone is capable of working hard. And the whole culture does not say "you're bright", or "you're smart", or "you're not smart". That's not what it's about. It's about "oh, you didn't work hard enough; and anyone is capable of working harder." When American parents who are accustomed to having their kids pushed into athletics and they're very comfortable having coaches pushing their kids. But they're not comfortable having teachers push their kids in the same way—they get into Chinese immersion and their kid gets back a paper with a 95 on it and it doesn't have a star or a sticker. And another parent says "well, that's because there's still room for improvement." Well that has now become a joke among parents who survived the kindergarten year and who are so accustomed to this praise—you show up and you get a trophy. The American culture is that you're going to be praised for being there and you know that is not the Chinese culture . . . If there is a room for improvement, there is a room for improvement; and I will coach you to make that improvement. And so [does] the culture of academic achievement because it becomes just the norm . . . I know there's one student who said "I got all A's except one B, because I had a 92. 37 grade point average . . . that's a third grader who understands that concept in the first place . . . That's what she earned, a 92.37, and you need 93 to get an A. And she was kind of like guess I'll work harder next time. So they have this internal idea of "I'm not blaming she gave me a B". It's like I didn't quite make it over the bar, since that's the system of grading we use . . . It is like the core of the Chinese immersion program. (Principal, personal communication, June 27, 2013)

Teachers have elaborated their perceptions in their comments as well. One teacher commented that not all students could reach the grade level benchmark in English, and that those who could reach the English grade level benchmark were the ones who struggled in Chinese and math. Another teacher commented that, "I feel that there is a strong connection between learning Chinese and English in general. Based on my experience, students who can successfully master the Chinese language is usually very strong in English literacy as well. Vice versa, students who struggle with learning Chinese are most likely struggled in English fluency and comprehension." Overall, ten out 14 teachers (71%) agreed that students performed better in math in the program measured by the EOG tests.

Summary. The findings of *t*-tests showed that there was a significant difference between the CIP students' scores in reading and math, and the students scored significantly higher in math; but there was no significant difference between the NSL students' scores in reading and math. The *t*-test results were supported by the findings from three out of three program planners (100%). Ten out of 14 teachers (71%) agreed that students perform better in math in the program measured by the EOG test.

Analysis for Evaluation Question 6

Evaluation question 6. To what extent do the students of the program perform differently in Chinese compared to the students in the similar program in Minnesota (Product)? For answering this question, the 2012-2013 YCT test results from the 2nd and 3rd grade students in the CIP and that of the CIPL were analyzed with frequency distribution, descriptive, and inferential statistics. The findings were presented after the various statistical analyses. The qualitative data collected from semi-structured interview and Chinese Immersion Instructional Environment Survey were transcribed and analyzed following Strauss and Corbin's approach. The internal reliability was tested for the Chinese Immersion Instructional Environment Survey and its subtopics using Cronbach's alpha. The triangulation of the collected data from various tools was used for answering Evaluation Question 6.

For answering Evaluation Question 6, this section performed the YCT student participant analysis, Chinese student demographic analysis, Chinese immersion model analysis, frequency distribution analysis, descriptive statistical analysis, and inferential statistic analysis. Finally, the statistical findings were triangulated with the findings of the semi-structured interviews, the Chinese Immersion Instructional Environment Survey, and the meta-evaluation survey.

In addition, based on the student demographic analysis, it was expected that CIPL students would score significantly higher in the YCT tests than CIP students.

YCT participant analysis. The YCT test was not a mandatory assessment for the 2nd or 3rd grade CIP students. It was the first year that the 2nd and 3rd grade CIP students take this test voluntarily.

As a result, 31 out of 45 2nd grade CIP students (68.9%) participated in 2012-2013 Level III YCT test (See Figure 1), and 14 out of 45 grade CIP students (31.1%) did not participate in the test (See Figure 2). The 2nd grade CIP YCT participants' report card average score is 84.5 and its standard deviation is 13.66. The 2nd grade CIP non-participants' report card average score is 73.0 and its standard deviation is 13.38

(See Table 59).

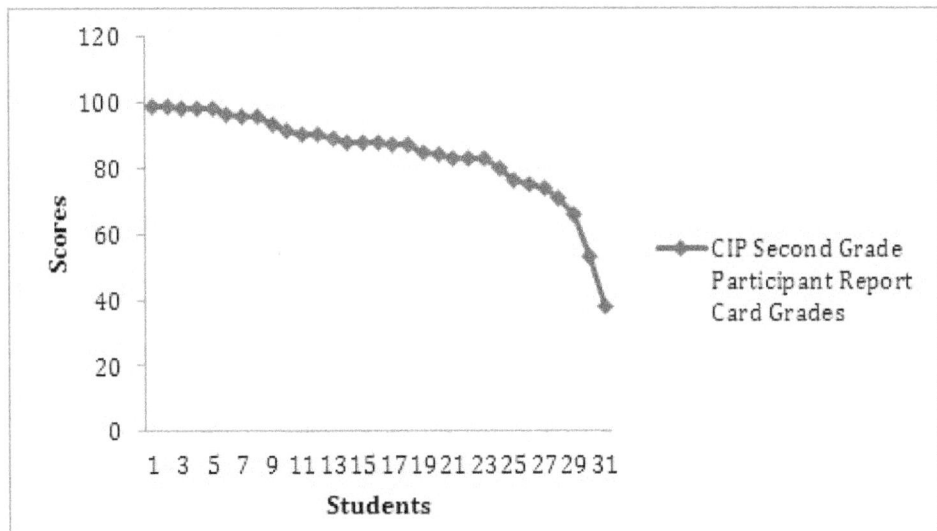

Figure 1. CIP 2nd grade YCT Participant's Chinese Report Card Grade. The scores (%) were extracted from students' report card.

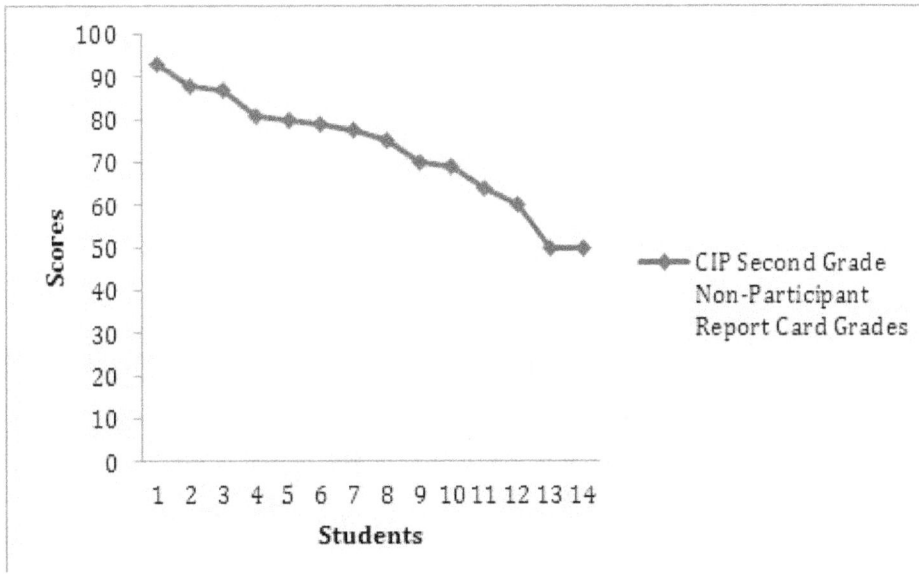

Figure 2. CIP 2nd Grade YCT Non-Participant's Report Card Grades. The scores (%) were extracted from students' report card.

In addition, 26 out of 34 3rd grade CIP students (76.5%) participated in the 2012-2013 YCT Level IV test (See Figure 3). Therefore, 8 out of 34 students (23.5%) did not participate in the test (See Figure 4). The 3rd grade CIP YCT participants' report card average score is 94.3 and its standard deviation is 3.18. The 3rd grade CIP non-participants' report card average score is 91.3 and its standard deviation is 3.46 (See Table 59).

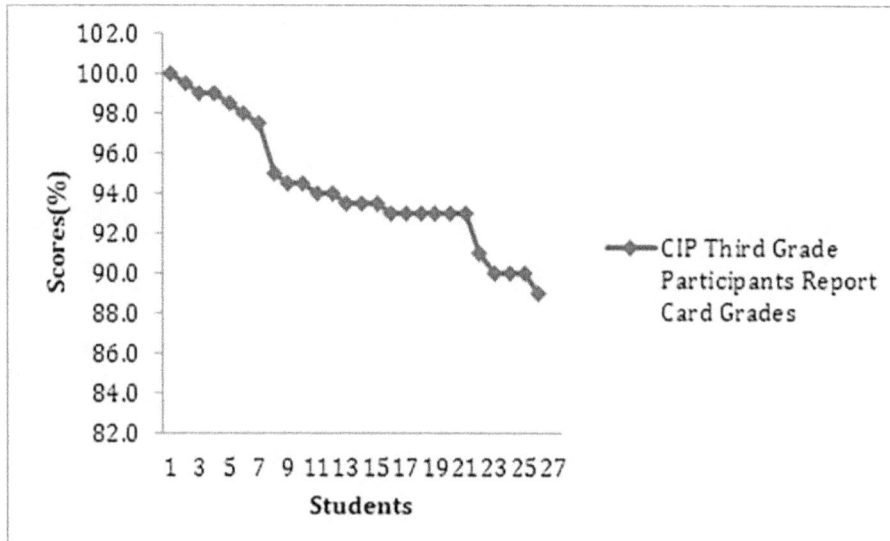

Figure 3. CIP 3rd Grade YCT Participant's Report Card Grades. The scores (%) were extracted from students' report card.

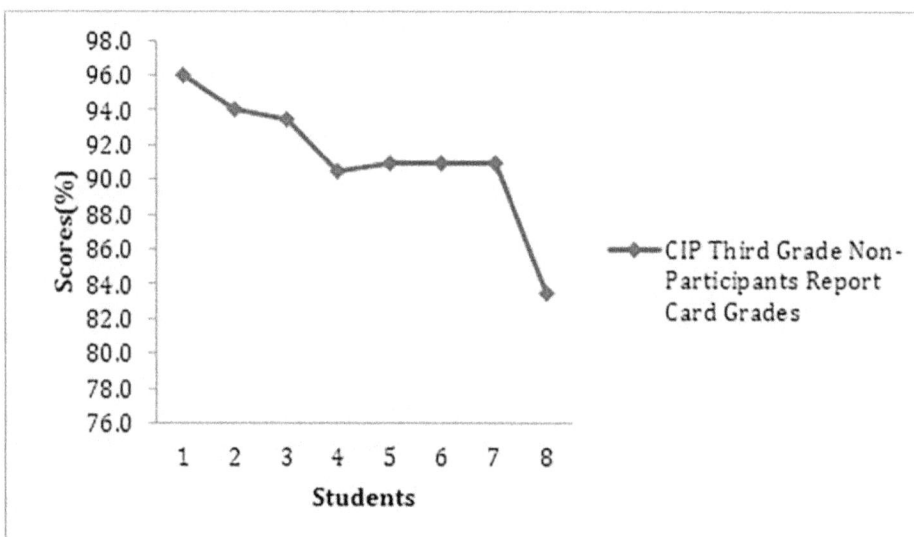

Figure 4. CIP 3rd Grade YCT Non-Participant's Report Card Grades. The scores (%) were extracted from students' report card.

Table 59

Mean Scores and Standard Deviations for CIP Student Chinese Report Cards
Note. n = sample size; M = group mean; SD = Standard deviation.

Measure	n	M	SD	n	M	SD
	Participants			Non-Participants		
2nd Grade	31	85.0	13.66	14	73.00	13.38
3rd Grade	26	94.3	3.18	8	91.30	3.46

The 2nd grade and 3rd grade CIPL students participated in this study. The YCT test was a district mandated summative assessment for all the CIPL Chinese immersion students. This was the 3rd year that CIPL students took the YCT test. However, only the 2012-2013 CIPL students' YCT test scores were used for this study. In 2012-2013 school year, 46 out of 47 2nd grade CIPL students (97.9%) participated in the 2012-2013 Level III YCT test, and 44 out of 44 3rd grade students (100%) participated in the 2012-2013 Level IV YCT test. This study used both the 2nd and 3rd grades listening and reading scores for the analysis. The CIPL students' writing score was excluded from this study due to the fact that the CIPL students' writing score was deemed not comparable to that of CIP. The school district curriculum coordinator stated that it was the first time that the CIPL students took an online YCT writing test this year. The online Chinese writing YCT test format was not compatible with that of the pencil-paper YCT writing test. And hence, the writing test score did not reflect the students' actual writing proficiency level.

Chinese immersion student demographic analysis. The CIP students were more diverse than that of the CIPL students. There were 42% white, 25% African American, 19% Hispanic, 5% Asian, and 9% Multiracial students in CIP; and there were 62.6% white, 6.7% African American, 2.1% Hispanic, 27.6% Asian, and 1.1% Multiracial in CIPL (See Table 3).

Chinese immersion model analysis. The two Chinese programs selected a similar early total Chinese immersion program model. However, CIP slightly modified the early total Chinese immersion model. CIP added 45 minutes of English instruction a day for the Chinese immersion students in Kindergarten, 1st, and 2nd grades. No English instruction was provided in school from Kindergarten to 2nd grade in CIPL. Therefore, the CIP students had 405 hours less Chinese instruction than the CIPL students by the time the students took the YCT test in the 2nd grade and 3rd grade. In addition, the CIPL Chinese student population was less diverse than that of CIP (See Table 3). Therefore, it was expected that the CIPL students would score significantly higher than the CIP students by all measures.

Frequency distribution analysis. For the listening performance, 100 is the highest score. Frequency distribution analysis showed that, 93.5% of the 2nd grade CIP students scored above 90 in listening and 100% of the 2nd grade CIPL students scored above 90; 77.4% of the 2nd grade CIP students have scored above 90 in reading and 80.4% of the 2nd grade CIPL students scored above 90 (See Table 60).

For combined scores, 200 is the highest score. The frequency distribution table showed that 58.1% of the 2nd grade CIP students scored above 190 in combined listening and reading scores and 67.0% of the 2nd grade CIPL students scored above 190 in combined listening and reading scores (See Table 60).

Table 60

The 2nd Grade YCT Frequency Distribution Table for All Measures

Measure	Bins	F	P	A	Bins	F	P	A
		CIP				CIPL		
Lis	100	29	93.5%	93.5%	100	46	100%	100%
	90	2	6.5%	100%	90	0	0	100%
Rea	100	24	77.4%	77.4%	100	37	80.4%	80.4%
	90	7	22.6%	100%	90	5	10.9%	91.3%
	80	0	0	100%	80	4	8.7%	100.0%
Comb	200	18	58.1%	58.1%	200	31	67%	67%
	190	9	29.0%	87.1%	190	10	21.7%	89.1%
	180	4	12.9%	100%	180	2	4.3%	93.5%
	170	0	0	100%	170	3	6.5%	100.0%

Note. Lis = Listening; Rea = Reading; Comb = Combined listening and reading score; Bin = Range of values; F = Frequency; P = Percentage; A = Accumulative percentage.

Frequency distribution analysis showed that 50.0% of the 3rd grade CIP students scored above 90 in listening and 95.5% of the 3rd grade CIPL students scored above 90% in listening. In addition, 92.3% of the 3rd grade CIP students scored above 80 up to 100, while 97.7% of the 3rd grade CIPL students scored above 80 up to 100 (See Table 61).

For the 3rd grade reading, 30.8% of the 3rd grade CIP students scored above 90 and 40.9% of the 3rd grade CIPL students scored above 90. Also, 80.8% of the CIP students scored above 70 up to 100, while 70.5% of the CIPL students scored above 70 up to 100 (See Table 61).

For combined listening and reading scores, the frequency distribution table showed that 23.1% of the 3rd grade CIP students scored above 190 and 40.9% of the 3rd grade CIPL students scored above 190. Moreover, 88.5% of the CIP students scored above 150 up to 200, while 90.9 % of the CIPL students scored above 150 up to 200 (See Table 61).

Table 61

The 3rd Grade YCT Frequency Distribution Table for All Measures

Measure	Bins	F	P	A	F	P	A
			CIP			CIPL	
Lis	100	13	50.0%	50.00%	42	95.5%	95.5%
	90	11	42.3%	92.30%	1	2.3%	97.7%
	80	2	7.7%	100%	1	2.3%	100.0%
Rea	100	8	30.8%	30.80%	18	40.9%	40.9%
	90	8	30.8%	61.6%	8	18.2%	59.1%
	80	5	19.2%	80.8%	5	11.4%	70.5%
	70	2	7.7%	88.5%	7	15.9%	86.4%
	60	2	7.7%	96.2%	2	4.5%	90.9%
	50	1	3.8%	100.0%	0	0	90.9%
	40	0	0	100%	4	9.1%	100.0%
Comb	200	6	23.1%	23.1%	18	40.9%	40.9%
	190	5	19.2%	42.3%	8	18.2%	59.1%
	180	5	19.2%	61.5%	5	11.4%	70.5%
	170	4	15.4%	76.9%	5	11.4%	81.8%
	160	3	11.5%	88.5%	4	9.1%	90.9%
	150	2	7.70%	96.2%	0	0	90.9%
	140	1	3.80%	100%	1	2.3%	93.2%
	130	0	0	100%	1	2.3%	95.5%
	120	0	0	100%	1	2.3%	97.7%
	110	0	0	100%	1	2.3%	100%

Note. Lis = Listening; Rea = Reading; Comb = Combined listening and reading score; Bin = Range of values; F = Frequency; P = Percentage; A = Accumulative percentage.

The YCT Chinese writing test was only available in YCT Level IV. The analysis showed that 88.4% of the 3rd grade CIP students scored above 60 up to 100 and 84.5% of the 3rd grade CIP students scored above 60 up to 90. No comparison was made for writing in this study due to the fact that the CIPL students' writing score was deemed not comparable to that of CIP (See Table 62).

Table 62

The 3rd Grade YCT Frequency Distribution Table for Writing

Bins	F	P	A
100	1	3.8%	3.8%
90	7	26.9%	30.7%
80	6	23.1%	53.8%
70	9	34.6%	88.4%
60	3	11.5%	100.0%

Note. Bin = Range of values; F = Frequency; P = Percentage; A = Accumulative percentage.

Descriptive statistic analysis. The descriptive analysis showed that the CIP students scored highest in listening and lowest in writing.

The descriptive analyses also showed the 2nd grade CIPL students scored higher in listening than the 2nd grade CIP students. The same finding applied for the 3rd grade listening. It also showed that the 2nd grade CIP students scored higher in reading than the CIPL students. The same finding held true for the 3rd grade reading. Finally, it showed that the 2nd grade CIPL students scored higher in the combined listening and reading scores. The same results were found for the 3rd combined listening and reading scores.

The descriptive analysis finally showed that the mean of the YCT writing test scores for 3rd grade CIP student was 74.62 and the standard deviation was 12.71. The writing test results for the 3rd grade CIPL students were deemed not comparable with that of CIP, and hence, were excluded from this study (See Table 63).

Table 63

YCT Mean Scores and Standard Deviations for All Measures

	Measure	n	M	SD	n	M	SD
		CIP			CIPL		
2nd Grade	Listening	31	96.48	4.1	46	98.76	2.15
	Reading	31	94.45	4.92	46	93.04	6.77
	Comb	31	190.94	7.49	46	191.80	8.31
3rd Grade	Listening	26	92.19	5.5	44	96.84	4.71
	Reading	26	82.73	14.9	44	81.25	19.69
	Comb	26	174.92	18.57	44	178.09	22.78
	Writing	26	74.62	12.71			

Note. Comb = Combined listening and reading scores, n = sample size, M = mean, and SD = Standard deviation.

Inferential statistic analysis for 2nd grade YCT test results. The YCT scores for listening between the program CIP and CIPL were compared using an independent *t*-test. The same analysis applied for reading, as well as for the combined listening and reading scores. The *t*-test results were analyzed and reported as follows.

The *t*-test results showed that there was a statistically significant difference between 2nd grade CIP students' listening and that of CIPL, and that CIPL students scored significantly higher in listening. The same finding was found in the 3rd grade students' listening score. It also showed that there was no statistically significant difference in reading score between the 2nd grade CIP students and CIPL students, and the same finding was found in the 3rd grade students' reading score. Finally, it indicated that there was no statistically significant difference in combined listening and reading scores between the 2nd grade CIP students and CIPL students, and that the same finding was found in the 3rd grade students' combined listening and reading scores (See Table 64 and Tables 65-70).

Table 64

Summary of YCT t-test Results

Measure	T-Stat	P	T-Stat	P	T-Stat	P
	Listening		Reading		Combined	
2nd Grade	-2.84	0.00697	1.057	0.294	-0.433	0.667
3rd Grade	-3.60	0.0007	0.356	0.723	-0.633	0.529

An independent samples *t*-test was used to check the difference between the listening test score of the 2nd grade CIP students and that of the 2nd grade CIPL students, $t(41) = -2.84$, $p = 0.0069$. Therefore, a statistically significant difference between the listening test score of the 2nd grade CIP students and that of the CIPL students was found. The 2nd grade CIPL students scored significantly higher in Chinese listening test than the 2nd grade CIP students (See Table 65).

Table 65

t-test Results for the 2nd Grade YCT Listening Scores

	CIP	CIPL
Mean	96.48387097	98.76086957
Variance	16.79139785	4.630434783
Observations	31	46
Hypothesized Mean Difference	0	
Df	41	
t Stat	-2.841104244	
P(T<=t) one-tail	0.003485717	
t Critical one-tail	1.682878002	
P(T<=t) two-tail	0.006971433	
t Critical two-tail	2.01954097	

An independent samples *t*-test was used to check the difference between the reading score of the 2nd grade CIP students and that of the 2nd grade CIPL students, $t(75) = 1.057$, $p = 0.294$. Therefore, the 2nd grade CIP students scored higher than the 2nd grade CIPL students, but no significant difference between the reading score of the two programs was found (See Table 66).

Table 66

t-test Results for the 2nd Grade YCT Reading Scores

	CIP	CIPL
Mean	94.4516129	93.04347826
Variance	24.18924731	45.82028986
Observations	31	46
Hypothesized Mean Difference	0	
Df	75	
t Stat	1.056512969	
P(T<=t) one-tail	0.147062617	
t Critical one-tail	1.665425373	
P(T<=t) two-tail	0.294125234	
t Critical two-tail	1.992102154	

An independent samples *t*-test was used to check the difference between the 2nd grade CIP students' combined listening and reading scores and that of CIPL, $t(62) = -0.43$, $p = 0.667$. Therefore, the 2nd grade CIPL students scored higher than the 2nd grade CIP students, but no statistically significant difference in the 2nd grade combined listening and reading scores between the two programs was found (See Table 67).

Table 67

t-test Results for the 2nd Grade YCT Combined Scores

	Program Under Study	School D
Mean	190.9354839	191.8043478
Variance	78.52903226	69.0942029
Observations	31	46
Hypothesized Mean Difference	0	
Df	62	
t Stat	-0.432530724	
P(T<=t) one-tail	0.333428263	
t Critical one-tail	1.669804163	
P(T<=t) two-tail	0.666856526	
t Critical two-tail	1.998971517	

Inferential statistical analysis for 3rd grade YCT test results. The 3rd grade YCT scores for listening between the program CIP and CIPL were also compared using an independent *t*-test. The same analysis applied for the 3rd grade YCT reading scores, as well as the combined listening and reading scores. The *t*-test results were analyzed and reported as follows.

An independent samples *t*-test was used to check the difference between the YCT listening scores of the 3rd grade CIP students and that of the 3rd grade CIPL students, $t(46) = -3.60$, $p = 0.00078$. Therefore, a statistically significant difference in the 3rd grade YCT listening scores between the two programs was found. The 3rd grade CIPL students scored significantly higher than the 3rd grade CIP students (See Table 68).

Table 68

t-test Results for the 3rd Grade YCT Listening Scores

	CIP	CIPL
Mean	92.19230769	96.84090909
Variance	30.24153846	22.18340381
Observations	26	44
Hypothesized Mean Difference	0	
Df	46	
t Stat	-3.600102494	
P(T<=t) one-tail	0.00038801	
t Critical one-tail	1.678660414	
P(T<=t) two-tail	0.00077602	
t Critical two-tail	2.012895599	

An independent samples *t*-test was used to check the difference between the reading scores of the 3rd grade CIP students and that of the 3rd grade CIPL students, $t(75) = 1.057$, $p = 0.294$. Therefore, the 3rd grade CIP students scored higher in reading than the 3rd grade CIPL students, but no statistically significant difference between the 3rd grade reading scores of the two programs was found (See Table 69).

Table 69

t-test Results for the 3rd Grade YCT Reading Scores

	CIP	CIPL
Mean	82.73076923	81.25
Variance	221.5646154	387.8662791
Observations	26	44
Hypothesized Mean Difference	0	
Df	64	
t Stat	0.355633101	
P(T<=t) one-tail	0.361642433	
t Critical one-tail	1.669013025	
P(T<=t) two-tail	0.723284866	
t Critical two-tail	1.997729654	

An independent samples *t*-test was used to check the difference between the 3rd grade CIP students' combined listening and reading scores and that of CIPL, $t(61) = $ -

0.63, p = 0.529. Therefore, the 3rd grade CIPL students scored higher than the 3rd grade CIP students, but no statistically significant difference between the 3rd grade combined listening and reading scores of the two programs was found (See Table 70). The writing score was excluded in this analysis due to the fact that the CIPL students' writing score was deemed not comparable to that of CIP.

Table 70

t-test Results for the 3rd Grade YCT Combined Scores

	CIP	CIPL
Mean	174.9230769	178.0909091
Variance	344.7138462	518.9217759
Observations	26	44
Hypothesized Mean Difference	0	
Df	61	
t Stat	-0.632909794	
P(T<=t) one-tail	0.264579082	
t Critical one-tail	1.670219484	
P(T<=t) two-tail	0.529158164	
t Critical two-tail	1.999623585	

In summary, the findings of the statistical analyses showed that there was no statistical difference in the 2nd grade combined listening and reading YCT III scores between the program CIP and CIPL. The same finding applied for the 3rd grade combined listening and reading Level IV scores between the two programs. The statistical analysis also showed that the CIPL students scored significantly higher in listening performance than the CIP students.

By looking into the semi-structured interview and Chinese Immersion Instructional Environment Survey, all the interviewees agreed that the high expectations and high rigor of the instruction provided by the Chinese immersion teachers have played a significant impact on student Chinese language proficiency. More specifically, the interviews with the director of the magnet office and school principal indicated that they observed that the students obtained high Chinese language proficiency. The interview with the panel Chinese teacher revealed that the students were consistently demonstrating strong Chinese speaking and listening skills but need improvement in their writing skills. The finding from the Chinese instructional environment also concurred with the YCT results and the findings from the semi-structured interviews. In addition, the Chinese Immersion Instructional Environment Survey also revealed that 13 out of 14 the teachers (91.39%) agreed that they have applied research-based balanced Chinese instructional strategies in their classrooms for developing student speaking, listening, reading, writing skills. For an example, using a real object or picture to introduce new characters or new concepts and using Pinyin to help students pronounce the characters with accurate tones (See Appendix H).

Summary. The CIP student's Chinese proficiency was compared with that of CIPL. Both programs selected the total Chinese immersion program model. However, the CIP made a slight modification that it provided 45 minutes English instruction a day from Kindergarten to 2nd grade, while CIPL did not provide any English instruction in school and all the district curricular contents were delivered in Chinese from Kindergarten to 2nd grades. Also CIPL had less diverse student population than CIP. Therefore, it was expected the CIPL students would score significantly higher in Chinese by all measures than the CIP students.

The CIP's YCT participation rate was lower than that of CIPL. It was the first time that the 2nd and 3rd grade CIP students were offered the opportunity to participate in the YCT Chinese tests voluntarily. As a result, 31 out of 45 2nd grade CIP students (68.9%) participated in the 2012-2013 Level III YCT test. Also 26 out of 34 3rd grade

CIP students (76.5%) participated in the 2012-2013 Level IV YCT test. At the same time, 46 out of 50 2nd grade CIPL students (97.9%) participated in the 2012-2013 Level III YCT test. Moreover, 44 out of 50 3rd grade CIPL students (100%) participated in the 2012-2013 Level IV YCT test.

Firstly, the 2nd grade CIPL students scored better, but not significantly better than the 2nd grade CIP students measured by the combined Chinese listening and reading skills. The same finding from the *t*-test results held true for the 3rd grade students.

Comparing the listening skills between the two Chinese programs, the 2nd CIPL students scored significantly higher than the 2nd grade CIP students. The same finding from the *t*-test results applied for the 3rd grade students.

Comparing the reading skills between the two Chinese programs, the 2nd grade CIP students scored higher, but not significantly higher than the 2nd grade CIPL students. The same finding from the *t*-test results applied for the 3rd grade students.

For writing, no comparison was made due to the fact that the CIPL students' writing score was deemed not comparable to that of CIP. However, the test result showed that the CIP students scored lowest in reading among listening, reading, and writing scores.

As mentioned initially in this chapter, it was expected that the CIPL students score would significantly higher by all the measures in the YCT tests than the CIP students, which was based on the differences of student demographics between CIP and CIPL as well as the differences of Chinese instructional hours between CIP and CIPL. Therefore, the CIP students exceeded the expectation set by this study.

The finding from semi-structured interview agreed with the YCT test results. All the interviewees indicated that they have observed that the student obtained high Chinese language proficiency, though it would be ideal that students could practice more in Chinese writing, according to the panel Chinese teacher. The finding from the Chinese instructional environment also concurred with the YCT results and the semi-structured interviews. In addition, 13 out of 14 teachers (91.39%) agreed that they applied research-based balanced Chinese instructional strategies in their classrooms for developing student speaking, listening, reading, writing skills.

Meta-Evaluation Survey Analysis

There were three steps involved in the meta-evaluation process. Firstly, the methodologies and the expected results were introduced to the advisory panel members after the informed consent form from each member was collected. Secondly, the data collecting processes, the data analyzing procedures, and the findings were presented and discussed with the advisory panel members after the study was done. Thirdly, the advisory panel members were provided with the meta-evaluation survey and were advised to rate each survey question with the consideration of how the semi-structured interview and how the Chinese Immersion Instructional Environment Survey were conducted and analyzed, how the students EOG data and YCT were collected and analyzed, and how each of the six evaluation questions was actually answered in this study. The advisory panel members were provided opportunities to ask any questions during the time they were completing the meta-evaluation survey.

The data collected were organized under the four evaluative standards below (See Table 71) and were used for evaluating the evaluation process for each of the evaluation questions in this study.

Table 71

Meta-Evaluation Survey Results

Panel Member	Utility Standard (%)	Feasibility Standard (%)	Propriety Standard (%)	Accuracy Standard (%)	Total (%)
Member A	98	100	100	98	99
Member B	78	84	78	80	80
Member C	96	98	100	98	98
Total	91	94	92	92	92

Utility standards. According to utility standards developed by members of the joint committee on Standards for Educational Evaluation (2008), ten statements were provided. The average response was 91% (See Table 11), which was calculated based on the formula provided in the meta-evaluation survey (See Appendix E).

Feasibility standards. According to feasibility standards developed by members of the joint committee on Standards for Educational Evaluation (2008), ten statements were provided. The average response was 94% (See Table 11), which was calculated based on the formula provided in the meta-evaluation survey (See Appendix E).

Propriety standards. According to propriety standards developed by members of the joint committee on Standards for Educational Evaluation (2008), ten statements were provided. The average response was 92% (See Table 11), which was calculated based on the formula provided in the meta-evaluation survey (See Appendix E).

Accuracy standards. According to accuracy standards developed by members of the joint committee on Standards for Educational Evaluation (2008), ten statements were provided. The average response was 92% (See Table 11), which was calculated based on the formula provided in the meta-evaluation survey (See Appendix E).

Chapter 5: Discussions

The purpose of this study is to comprehensively evaluate the effectiveness of the Chinese immersion program (CIP) in an urban southeastern setting. This chapter is divided into five sections. The first section provides a brief overview of the findings derived from Chapter 4, which will be organized by Context, Input, Process, and Product of Stufflebeam's (2003) CIPP evaluation model. The second section offers the in-depth discussion of the results in this study, which will be presented through nine discussion topics. These discussion topics have surfaced from the qualitative and quantitative data collected in this study, and each carries certain weight for developing a deeper understanding of the program and Chinese language immersion in general. Moreover, the CIP students' earlier establishment of their consistent higher academic performance by the end of the 3rd grade, the CIP students' significant success in mathematics, CIP reducing the achievement gaps between the majority and minority groups in mathematics, and using the CIP adapted Chinese immersion model as an educational vehicle to improve students' academic achievement are the four major discussion topics among all. The third section presents the conclusion of this study, which will be organized by the six overarching evaluative questions. The criteria for each evaluative question are illustrated in the Chinese Immersion Program Evaluation Plan (See Table 4) and will be used against the findings of this study. The conclusions of the effectiveness of the CIP evaluation have been made consequently. The fourth section proposes recommendations for improving the Chinese immersion program. Finally, section five puts forward the implications of this study.

The Chinese language immersion program was implemented in a school that offers French, German, Japanese, and Chinese instruction to the students in immersion settings. The school made expected growth in the North Carolina ABC's program and met 33/33 AYP goals under No Child Left Behind guidelines (No Child Left Behind, 2001). It was also a NC School of Distinction 2006-2007, 2007-2008, 2008-2009, 2009-2010 and 2010-2011. The standards were based on the North Carolina Standard Course of Study (NCSCOS); the students were assessed in English in the state's mandatory summative assessment, for example, EOG or EOC. The K-5 full immersion Chinese program was implemented in 2006 when the other three language immersion programs had already been up and running. The Chinese language immersion program provided all students with at least 65% of their instruction in Chinese, with English instruction provided at each grade level beginning in Kindergarten. This study evaluated the effectiveness of the CIP program. Various findings from Chapter 4 are briefly reviewed as follows.

Overview of the Findings

This section starts with the overall review of the findings organized by the Context, Input, Process, and Product of the Stufflebeam's (2003) CIPP program evaluation model. Results indicated that the Context included concerns for (a) recruiting licensed native Chinese teachers for the Chinese immersion program and retaining them due to visa issues to sustain CIP, and (b) creating Chinese immersion teaching materials and retaining them to sustain and improve CIP. The Input component of the study revealed that (a) modifying the Chinese immersion program model in order to seek the balance the instruction time between Chinese and English, (b) providing professional development for the Chinese teachers to further develop their expertise in this field, and (c) developing and increasing Chinese immersion teachers' awareness of ethnic and socioeconomic impact on student achievement. The Process component of the evaluation demonstrated that the implementation of the Chinese immersion program was executed with a commitment to continuous improvement of the program model and curriculum with a final goal of achieving high-level success in academic performance, Chinese language acquisition, and Chinese culture competencies. Finally, the Product component revealed through students' EOG test scores that the Chinese immersion program not only has significantly and positively impacted student EOG test results in the 3rd, 4th, and 5th grade years in reading, math, and science administered in English, but also has reduced the achievement gaps in mathematics between the majority and minority (African-American and Hispanic) students (See Tables 3, 19, 26, and 58). In addition, student Chinese proficiency test scores (YCT scores) discovered that the program has significantly and positively impacted each student's Chinese language skills in speaking, listening, reading, and writing.

Discussion of Results

Analysis of student EOG and YCT test data, information from the interviews with the three program planners, and survey results from the Chinese immersion team exposed nine important results: (a) assessing the environment and leading the change in the school system was critical for creating the Chinese immersion program; (b) the program model selection was a challenge; (c) program implementation with fidelity was crucial; (d) the CIP students scored significantly higher by all measures than the two comparable schools with similar socioeconomic backgrounds, and performed significantly better than the neighborhood school with a much higher socioeconomic student backgrounds by all measures, except for the 3rd grade and 5th grade reading; (e) the CIP students scored significantly higher in math than English reading, which was not indicated by the statistical test results in the high-performing neighborhood school NSL; (f) there was no statistical significance between the 2nd grade CIP students' YCT Level III test scores and that of CIPL, and the CIPL students scored significantly higher in the listening test than the CIP students; (g) students demonstrated a deeper level of understanding of Chinese culture; (h) there was a need for identifying and providing appropriate Chinese language immersion professional development opportunities for Chinese language immersion teachers; and (i) retaining Chinese native teachers for CIP was a huge challenge due to various visa issues and required a long-term plan. Each of the discussion topics will be discussed as follows.

Assessing the environment and leading the change. The first critical step for CIP's implementation was to gain the buy-in for the Chinese language immersion program from the leaders at the top of the organizational levels of the school system. Findings of this study clearly delineated that leadership in the public school system played a critical role in making the Chinese program a legitimate entity and getting it on the organizational agenda. As indicated by the director of the magnet office, school principal, and the panel Chinese teacher, global economy and competition has impacted everybody's life, including people of the United States of America. How well the American students would be prepared for this environmental change and how American students could benefit from this trend were the concerns that the district educational leaders had at the beginning of the 21st century. According to Pugh and Hickson (2007), "[t]his [developing concern] involves problem sensing, leading to legitimating the notion of change and getting it on the corporate agenda. It is a time consuming and politically sensitive process and one in which the top management plays a critical role" (p.170). The findings of this study concurred with Pugh and Hickson's view that the environmental concerns, the buy-in, and the support provided by the superintendent, director of the magnet office, and the school principal for creating the Chinese immersion program in the school district were critical elements for moving the program forward. To conclude, in order to implement a Chinese immersion program successfully, the support from the organizational leaders is crucial. The unwavering support at the organizational level ensured the smooth and uninterrupted execution of the Chinese program.

Program model selection. The customized total Chinese language immersion program model along with the Unity-Type Chinese curricula effectively addressed the needs of the diverse CIP student population. Program model selection is situation dependent and a time-consuming process, but it is critical for building a successful Chinese language immersion program. Research showed that language immersion education has been generally accepted as the most effective way to teach students a second language at no apparent cost to their English academic skills (Curtain & Dahlberg, 2004; Fortune, 2012; Genesee, 1987, 1994; Met, 2012). Research also showed that partial or delayed French immersion does not yield greater proficiency in English but does result in reduced French language proficiency (Genesee, 1987). But the research findings were mostly based on study results of alphabet-based languages, not Chinese (Chao, 1993; De Courcy, 1997). Planning a Chinese language immersion program and selecting a program model was a challenging task, as very few Chinese language immersion programs were available in 2005. Fortune (2008) summarized that the most critical step in language immersion program design was to select the immersion model. Fortune (2008) further stated that immersion programs in Canada and the United States have followed a number of different models, which could be defined with reference to two factors: first, the grade level in which the second language was used for instruction (early, delayed, late); and second, the amount of content instruction time in the second language (total or partial). Finally, she defined that an early total immersion program was characterized by 100% of the instruction being given in French in kindergarten and the first grade, about 80% of the instruction day was in French; and for the remaining time English was taught starting with the 2nd grade; and from 60% to 80% of the instruction time was conducted in French and remaining time in English in the 5th and 6th grade. The language immersion model for the comparable school in Minnesota is an early total Chinese immersion model. CIP adopted this early total immersion model with a slight modification in that English instruction was provided 45 minutes a day from Kindergarten to 2nd grade and one hour a day for 3rd to 5th grade students.

The various statistical analyses on student academic performance data and Chinese language proficiency data have indicated the adapted total Chinese immersion model has effectively addressed the needs of the Chinese immersion students and the same conclusion has been made through the CIP teachers and the three program planners. There was no statistically significant difference in the 2nd grade combined listening and reading YCT test scores between the program CIP and CIPL, and the same findings applied for the 3rd grade. Based on the t-test results, the CIP modified total Chinese immersion program model suggested that the reduced 405 hours of Chinese instruction reduced significantly the 2nd and 3rd grade students' listening proficiency, which concurred with the research findings from French language immersion (Genesee, 1987). At the same time it did not significantly impact the students' reading proficiency nor the students' overall Chinese proficiency measured by combined listening and reading YCT tests, which obviously contradicted the researching findings from the French immersion programs (Genesee, 1987). According to He and Jiao (2010), there were three types of Chinese curricula: (a) Unity Type, focusing on developing the unity of listening, speaking, reading, and writing skills; (b) Delay Type, teaching listening, speaking, and reading skills for a prolonged period of time or even during the entire first year using phonetic symbols, Pinyin, to deliver the contents; and (c) Lag Type, focusing the oral-aural skills with a temporary delay in character-learning and speaking more and writing less.

In conclusion, the adapted total Chinese language immersion program model along with the balanced Chinese teaching approach (Unity-Type) is an effective program model for addressing the needs of the diverse CIP student population and strengthening the Chinese language acquisition with regards to the development of the four fundamental Chinese language skills and culture competencies. Further study in this topic can provide more insight on Chinese program design for the field.

Program implementation with fidelity. The continuing support from the organizational leadership and the expertise and dedication at the Chinese team level are the keys to the successful execution of CIP with fidelity, which consequently contributes to students' academic success in Chinese language and cultural competencies. The findings of this study showed that the organizational leaders played a critical role in legitimizing the new CIP and putting it in the organization's agenda. The findings from the interviews with the director of the magnet office, school principal, and the panel Chinese teacher showed that the Chinese immersion program has always been funded as planned–even when the district was enduring dramatic budget cuts–and that the resources for adding the new Chinese immersion classes were available. It also showed that implementing strategic changes at the program level was critical for program success. Implementing the Chinese program was a complex, situation-dependent, and continuous process. Pugh and Hickson (2007) pointed out, "Andrew Pettigrew underlines the particular complexity of the interacting factors of context, content, and process with which managers have to grapple to execute an effective strategic change. Strategic change is a complex, situation-dependent, continuous process" (p. 173). Furthermore, the expertise of educational leaders at the school level and the expertise and the dedication of the teachers have played critical roles in implementing the plans of the Chinese program. Chinese teachers are the change agents and catalysts in the process of transforming the resources and materials into the intellectual assets (See Appendix H).

In conclusion, successful execution of a complex Chinese language immersion program calls for different levels of expertise and dedication. The support from organizational level leadership ensures the funding and resources that feed to CIP; the expertise and support from school leadership clears the obstacles for teaching and instruction; and the expertise and dedication of the Chinese teachers turn all the investment into the intellectual assets, the students' academic success and Chinese language and culture competencies.

Impact on English academic achievement. The Chinese immersion program has evidently improved each student's academic performance in math, reading, and science. In particular, the CIP students have established an unambiguously strong academic performance in their 3rd grade math and reading through their 5th grades (See Tables 19 and 26). In addition, the CIP students have demonstrated clear advancement in mathematic skills evidenced by their EOG test scores, which is even true for students of diverse ethnic backgrounds (See Tables 3, 19, and 26). It suggests that the Chinese immersion program reduced students' achievement gap in mathematics between the majority and minority students (See Tables 3 and 58). The CIP's impact on students' mathematical performance and reducing achievement gaps in mathematic skills will be specifically discussed in the next section.

The study of the academic impact of the Chinese immersion program contributes one addition to the literature of Chinese language immersion education: The CIP students accumulate their academic and linguistic foundation by the end of the 3rd grade year, which enables them to perform significantly higher in mathematics than the students of different socioeconomic and demographic backgrounds, and perform significantly higher in reading than the students of similar socioeconomic and demographic backgrounds. The above claim was evidenced by the fact that CIP students have consistently established significantly higher academic performance than comparison schools with different socioeconomic and demographic student populations, and this strong higher academic performance starts at the 3rd grade and continues through the 5th grade.

The following sections will discuss the findings of the CIP students' academic achievements in reading and math, relevant findings from the literature of alphabet-based language immersion programs, and the findings from perceptions of the program planners.

First, the CIP students significantly outperformed their peers with different socioeconomic and demographic backgrounds in mathematics and significantly outperformed their peers with similar socioeconomic and demographic backgrounds in English reading from the 3rd grade to 5th grade. The statistical results showed that the CIP students scored significantly higher in English reading based on all the EOG tests they have taken in the recent three years, which included 2009-2010, 2010-2011, and 2011-2012, than the NSS students and MSS students. The same finding was applied for math. Additionally, the CIP students scored significantly higher in math than school NSL (See Tables 3 and 26). In short, CIP has significantly impacted students' English academic performance, especially in mathematics.

Second, the research on Chinese language immersion is inadequate. There were limited studies on Chinese language immersion, especially on the impact of the Chinese language immersion program (De Courcy, 2002; Liu, 1992; Tang, 1989). This study has referenced the studies on alphabet-based language immersion programs to gain a deeper understanding of the Chinese immersion program phenomenon. Genesee (1987) concluded that decades of research on English-speaking students of various academic abilities immersed in other languages showed that these learners were capable of achieving high levels of functional proficiency in the immersion language while, at the same time, achieving academically at or above their non-immersion peers on standardized tests administered in English. This concurred with the findings of this study that the Chinese immersion program students scored significantly higher than their peers in non-immersion programs on standardized tests administered in English since the 3rd grade. More specifically, it takes the CIP Chinese students 4 years to establish significantly higher academic performance across subjects, particularly in mathematics. This phenomenon calls for more attention and studies in the field of Chinese language immersion.

Third, the interviews with the program planners established the similar finding with that of French or German language immersion programs that the language immersion student, including Chinese immersion students, gradually demonstrated their significantly higher academic achievement. According to the director of the magnet office, "[in] 3rd grade, when you compare the test scores, they are about the same as their peers. When about the time [they] get to their 5th grade, you will see outstanding increase in the achievement on the part of the immersion students" (Director of the

Magnet Office, personal communication, June 14, 2013). The school principal asked, "Are they [language immersion students] going to be reading at the same level in both languages, by first grade, 2nd grade, or 3rd grade as a child with a monolingual education? [They] may not. By 5th grade they're going to surpass them. By 8th grade [they] are going to blow them out of the water" (Principal, personal communication, June 27, 2013). But there is more to the impact of the Chinese immersion program: as was discussed in the previous section, the CIP students persistently established their significant higher academic performance by the end of the 3rd grade year.

In addition, the CIP students may have gone beyond the threshold of the Chinese language proficiency necessary for their cognitive benefit to develop when they reached the end of the 3rd grade. Research showed that the full immersion students' English development might lag temporarily in reading and spelling while instruction was occurring exclusively in the target language. However, this discrepancy disappeared after a year or two of English literacy instruction (Genesee, 1987). The director of the magnet office and school principal indicated similar perceptions based on their observations from the current French, German, and Japanese immersion programs at the school. However, the findings of studies and observations from the alphabet-based languages were different from the statistical findings in this study. This study clearly found that CIP students have consistently demonstrated stronger and higher academic performance measured by the EOG tests starting from 3rd through 5th grade. Cummins (1981) and Fortune (2008) cautioned that there may be a certain threshold of second language proficiency necessary before cognitive benefits would develop. And hence, the findings in this study may indicate that the Chinese immersion students build the necessary Chinese language proficiency for their cognitive benefit to develop by the time they reached the end of the 3rd grade. This suggestion needs more empirical research in the field of Chinese language immersion.

To conclude, the CIP students consistently demonstrated much stronger academic performance in the 3rd grade and through the 5th grade. More specifically, it takes 4 years for the CIP students to build a foundation that enables them to perform significantly higher than their peers with different demographic and socioeconomic backgrounds. Longitudinal study on the CIP students' academic achievement is recommended.

Impact on student mathematic performance. The findings of the statistical analyses revealed that the CIP students scored significantly higher in math than English reading, but this was not evident in the highly performing neighborhood school NSL (See Table 49 and Tables 50-57). In addition, considering the discussion in the previous section, the CIP has significantly improved students' mathematical skills. This is even true for the students of diverse multicultural backgrounds. The CIP's impact on student academic achievement in mathematics has, to a certain degree, overwritten the socioeconomic impact or reduced the achievement gaps in mathematics between the majority and minority students as evidenced by the fact that the students in the Chinese program have performed significantly better in mathematics than their peers with very different socioeconomic backgrounds in both neighborhood school and magnet school settings. The above claim was clearly supported by the findings from the short-term, medium-term, and long-term English academic impact (See Tables 19, 26, and 58). In addition, the analysis on North Carolina school report cards and the EOG data extracted from the accountability department of the school district settled the argument above (See Tables 3 and 58).

The following sub-sections will discuss the qualitative findings that may justify the CIP students' higher academic success. On the whole, dual-mathematical-process in the Chinese language immersion environment, high expectation, Chinese culture, and cognitive benefits of the language immersion program contribute to the CIP students' higher mathematic achievement.

The dual-mathematic-process in the Chinese language immersion environment leads to a deeper understanding of the mathematical concepts. The students are processing the mathematical concepts in Chinese and referencing with English constantly while the Chinese immersion teachers deliver the mathematic content in Chinese and when they are solving the mathematical problems. This dual-mathematic-process directs deeper understanding of mathematical concepts and processes. The three program planners offered similar explanations. Those, to a certain extent, may have explained why CIP Chinese immersion students scored significantly higher in math.

The cultural perspective of learning philosophy carried by the Chinese teachers has impacted students' attitudes and behaviors towards learning in general and learning in math and science in particular. The panel Chinese teacher indicated the above assumption, and she also revealed that Chinese teachers were passionate for math, skillful for teaching math, and set high expectations for all the students, all of which has set up their students for success in academics, particularly in mathematics. Moreover, the panel Chinese teacher also suggested that the Chinese teachers might carry underlying philosophical assumptions that everybody could count and could do math, and that everyone could obtain math mastery if he or she worked hard enough. This belief was instilled into their students and consequently affected their students' attitudes and behaviors towards academics. According to the school principal,

It is one of the huge blessings that the teachers come from a culture where there are high expectations for the achievement of all kids, not because they are gifted, but because anyone is capable of working hard. The whole culture does not say that you are smart or you are bright, but it is about anyone is capable of working harder. (Principal, personal communication, June 27, 2013)

Chinese teachers, to a certain extent, agreed that studying Chinese has improved students' mathematic skills and problem solving skills (See Tables 10 and 11).

In addition, the data from the Chinese teachers on the Chinese Immersion Instructional Environment Survey described the instructional environment that the Chinese teachers provided for the students (See Appendix H). First of all, the Chinese teachers applied research-based Chinese instructional strategies (See Tables 10 and 11). At the same time, the school principal stressed during the interview that it was a norm that the CIP instructional environment carried high rigor and relevant learning activities in their classrooms.

Finally, studies showed various cognitive benefits for the students in language immersion programs, for instance, verbal and nonverbal abilities, symbolic reasoning abilities, cognitive flexibility, more attentive to structure and details of the tasks, etc. (Hakuta & Diaz, 1985; Ben-Zeev, 1977a; Baker, 1988; and Soderman, 2010), which, to a certain degree, explains the findings of the academic results in math in this study. Soderman (2010) pointed out, "Bilingual children are driven to higher levels of cognitive flexibility than are unilingual children in education settings. Learning a new language is greater than simply acquiring a vocabulary and workable syntax. It's a problem-solving" (p. 57). At the same time, Cummins (1981) and Fortune (2010) cautioned that there might be a certain threshold of second-language proficiency necessary before the cognitive benefit would develop, and cognitive benefit would accrue in relation to the level of the second-language proficiency attained. The findings from this study may indicate that the CIP students might have reached beyond the threshold of Chinese proficiency necessary, which needs more research in the Chinese immersion field. In summary, the CIP students' significantly higher mathematic achievement is substantiated by various statistical tests and qualitative findings. The dual-mathematic-process in the Chinese language and culture, the Chinese language immersion environment, and cognitive benefits of the language immersion program contribute to the CIP students' mathematical success.

Impact on Chinese language performance. The CIP students have achieved higher Chinese language proficiency in speaking, listening, reading, and writing substantiated by the findings of this study. Cummins (1983) concluded that "because most program evaluations focus primarily on academic outcomes, little or no data are available on the impact of bilingual, or heritage language programs on the education system as a whole" (p. 6). Part of this study was intended to collect data and analyze the program impact on student Chinese language proficiency.

This study indicates that the CIP has effectively improved students' Chinese language skills. Statistical analyses on the 2nd grade CIP students' YCT test scores showed that there was no statistically significant difference between the CIP students' YCT combined listening and reading test scores and that of CIPL (See Table 67). The same findings applied for the 3rd grade (See Table 70).

This result not only indicates that the program has effectively improved student Chinese language skills but also reveals that the CIP modified total Chinese language immersion model has effectively addressed the needs of diverse students. Moreover, the CIP model has improved students' English academic performance without significant sacrifices of their Chinese language proficiency.

Identifying a modified total Chinese immersion program model that can possibly produce maximum academic success and result in high Chinese language proficiency in a diverse student population is critical. The study findings may have shed some light on this topic, and more empirical research is strongly recommended for the field.

Impact on developing student cultural awareness. Study results from the three program planners showed that students have demonstrated a deep level of understanding and acceptance of Chinese cultures. The survey from the Chinese immersion team also indicated similar findings. For example, many Chinese language students enjoy practicing Chinese calligraphy. Many Chinese language students also practice Chinese folk dance and have won rewards from local competitions. Moreover, one of the 4th grade students won the grand prize in the 2012 North Carolina Chinese Speech Contest. Her topic was Confucius. In her speech, she said, "Confucius is my Chinese idol" (Smith, 2012). In summary, the Chinese language students have developed cultural competencies in a deep level through learning the languages in the immersion environment.

Diversity and professional development. The Chinese teachers were facing challenges in addressing the needs of a diverse student population. There were gaps between what teachers wanted their students to achieve and what the students were achieving, and the Chinese teachers were frustrated with lower-performing students. Just as the result of the Chinese Immersion Instructional Environment Survey indicated, only eight out of 14 teachers (57%) agreed that the Chinese immersion students' academic performance was satisfactory while their students significantly outperformed their peers of similar and different socioeconomic and demographic backgrounds. In addition, the findings from the three program planners were all in agreement with statistical findings of this study. The discrepancy among the perceptions from the teachers, the perceptions from the program planners, and findings from the EOG and YCT test results indicated that the Chinese teachers were struggling with academically challenged students, which also challenged their underlying philosophical assumptions that every student could count and do math and every student could attain math mastery if they were working hard enough. At the same time, their high expectations for all the students and their consistent support for their students to reach their expectations have produced the results being discussed. Just as the school principal pointed out in an interview,

> The challenges going forward are certainly to have a diverse student population that represents our community. With lottery system and the number of applicants we have, the odds are very good that we'll continue to have a very diverse student population, which then becomes challenge because there is a real demand on the teachers to differentiate and meet the needs of diverse, urban student population. One third of our students are from poverty, using the measure of economically disadvantaged students. When you consider that those kids are achieving to such a high level in Chinese language, it doesn't happen by accident. (Principal, personal communication, June 27, 2013)

Consequently, professional development was needed to improve the Chinese teachers' understanding of the diverse student populations in American public schools and further develop the skills needed to work with students who were academically challenged and were living in poverty households.

Chinese language immersion professional development. Based on the Chinese Immersion Instructional Environment Survey, the Chinese teachers indicated that they needed professional development opportunities for continuing to develop their effectiveness in Chinese instruction, to deepen their understanding of the Chinese immersion pedagogy, and to better prepare them for serving the needs of the diverse student population. For example, the Chinese immersion workshop provided by the University of Minnesota or the breakout sessions provided by the National Chinese Conferences have played an important role in nurturing Chinese language immersion teachers, but these are apparently not sufficient. Currently, professional development for Chinese language immersion teachers is unavailable locally. It is critical for the school district to seek a feasible path of facilitating effective professional development for the Chinese language immersion teachers.

Retaining Chinese language immersion teachers. Retaining highly proficient Chinese teachers is a challenge for the Chinese immersion program due to visa issues. In order to implement the program model with fidelity, Chinese language immersion teachers are required to be native Chinese language speakers with North Carolina licenses. Therefore, some teachers are hired through VIF with a temporary working visa. Both the director of the magnet office and school principal noted that a system of retaining the Chinese language immersion teachers by overcoming visa issues was an immediate need and needed to be addressed. Currently there are VIF Chinese teachers in the CIP program, and these teachers are required to return to China before their visa expires. It takes about 3 years for a new teacher to become proficient in the school system. It is necessary for the school district to seek a long-term plan of retaining the highly proficient Chinese language immersion teachers in order to sustain the quality of the Chinese language immersion program.

In summary, it is apparent that the Chinese immersion students significantly outperformed the students with similar and different socioeconomic and demographic backgrounds. It is evident that CIP has reduced the achievement gaps in mathematics between the majority and minority student groups. It is unmistakable that the CIP students have established consistent higher academic achievement by the end of the 3rd grade year. It is unique that the CIP has created a feasible adapted Chinese immersion model that produced higher student academic success without sacrificing Chinese language proficiency. In addition, the Chinese language immersion program is a complex system. Environmental support from the leaders of the school district level and school level are critical. The Chinese teachers are the change agents and catalysts for transforming the resources and materials provided for the program into intellectual assets—the students' academic achievement. The key is apparently the Chinese language immersion teachers. Therefore, any effort made to retain the Chinese language immersion teachers by overcoming the visa issues and any support to further improve the effectiveness of Chinese language immersion teachers will magnify the outcomes of the CIP program.

Conclusions

Based on the discussion of the results and criteria illustrated in the Chinese Immersion Program Evaluation Plan (See Table 4), the conclusions were made, justified, and presented with the evaluation questions as follows.

Evaluation Question 1: To what extent did the program goals reflect the assessed needs (Context)? The findings of the study showed that three out of three program planners (100%) and 11 out of 14 Chinese teachers (75.91%) agreed that the goals met the addressed needs.

Evaluation Question 2: To what extent were the selected approaches and plans feasible, compatible, potentially successful, and cost effective for meeting the assessed needs (Input)? The findings of the study showed that three out of three program planners (100%) and 12 out of 14 Chinese teachers (83.50%) agreed that the selected approach and plans were feasible, compatible, successful, and cost effective.

Evaluation Question 3: To what extent was the program implemented as designed (Process)? The findings of the study showed that three out of three program planners (100%) and 11 out of 14 Chinese teachers (78.61%) agreed that the program was implemented as designed, that the concerns and ideas for improvement were handled efficiently, that negative side effects were analyzed and minimized; thirteen out of fourteen Chinese teachers (91.39%) agreed that they utilized research-based Chinese language instructional strategies and implemented the selected program model and Chinese curriculum with fidelity.

Evaluation Question 4: To what extent is there a difference in the academic performance of the immersion students when compared to similar students (Product)? It was expected that the students in the Chinese program perform at least at the same level as their peers in the school NSS and school MSS. It was also expected that the NSL students perform significantly better than the CIP students due to the differences of socioeconomic and demographic backgrounds between the two programs (See Table 3).

The findings of the study showed that there was a significant difference in the academic performance of the immersion students when compared to similar students in non-immersion programs and the CIP students scored significantly higher than the similar students in non-immersion programs. The findings also showed that the CIP students scored significantly higher than the NSL students of high socioeconomic background by all the measures except the 3rd and 5th grade reading. The findings of this study also showed clearly that CIP students demonstrated consistently strong higher academic performance measured by the EOG tests starting from the 3rd and continuing through the 5th grade.

In this study, the findings not only indicated that the Chinese immersion students exceeded the threshold of Chinese language proficiency necessary for their cognitive benefit to develop when they reached the end of their 3rd grade, but also suggested that the program reduced the achievement gap in mathematics between the majority and minority student groups (See Tables 3 and 58).

To answer the evaluative Question 4, the findings of the study showed that three out of three program planners (100%) agreed with the statistical results mentioned above. However, only eight out of 14 Chinese teachers (57.0%) agreed that the Chinese immersion students' academic performance was satisfactory, which was not in agreement with the findings of the program planners, nor the findings from the t-tests.

Evaluation Question 5: To what extent do the students perform differently in English reading and mathematics (Product)? The findings of this study showed that the CIP students scored significantly higher in mathematics than English reading, while this phenomenon was not observed nor indicated by the statistical results for the school NSL in this study. This finding is a newly identified feature in the Chinese immersion program, which has not been reported in the studies of French or German language immersion programs. More empirical analysis and study in this topic is needed in the field of Chinese language immersion.

In addition, the CIP students scored significantly higher in mathematics than that of all comparable schools across all the measures. This is even true for students of diverse racial backgrounds. Based on the North Carolina School Report Card and the

EOG data extracted from the district accountability department, CIP has reduced the achievement gap in mathematics between the majority and minority (African American and Hispanic) students (See Tables 3 and 58). This claim was substantiated by 3 years of CIP test results. It needs more empirical study for this assumption to be grounded in the field of Chinese language immersion.

To answer the evaluative Question 5, the findings of the study showed that three out of three program planners (100%) and 10 out of 14 Chinese teachers (71.0%) agreed that the CIP students scored better in math. Both findings agreed with the statistical results.

Evaluation Question 6: To what extent do the students of the program perform differently in Chinese compared to the students in the similar program in Minnesota (Product)? It was expected that the CIPL students would score significantly higher than the CIP students, due to the differences of the Chinese instruction time and student demographic and socioeconomic backgrounds between the two Chinese programs (See Table 3). The findings of this study, however, showed that there was no significant statistical difference between the 2nd grade combined CIP students' YCT listening and reading scores and that of CIPL. The same findings applied for the 3rd grade students. Not only did this finding differ with the research results from French language immersion programs that asserted reduced language immersion time resulted in reduced French language proficiency (Cummins, 1987), but it also suggested that the program has, to a some extent, effectively addressed the needs of diverse students in developing the Chinese language and culture competencies and that the program provided a feasible adapted Chinese total immersion model for improving academic performance for the students of similar and different socioeconomic and demographic backgrounds. More empirical research on this topic is needed for the field.

To conclude the evaluative Question 6, the findings of the study showed that three out of three program planners (100%) agreed that the program had improved the students' Chinese language proficiency, and 13 out of 14 Chinese teachers (91.39%) agreed that they have applied research-based balanced Chinese instructional strategies in their classrooms for developing students' speaking, listening, reading, writing skills. Both findings agreed with the statistical results mentioned above.

Meta-Evaluation Results

Findings suggested average agreement regarding utility standards was 91%, feasibility standards was 94%, propriety standards was 92%, and accuracy standards was 92% (See Table 71). The conclusion derived from the meta-evaluation was that the three members of the advisory panel all agreed that the expectations of all four categories of standards were achieved.

The meta-evaluation results indicated that evaluation results were useful to the stakeholders. The evaluation was conducted with minimal disruption and data burden. The schedule was realistic. The evaluation identified program strengths to build on and weaknesses to correct. The rights of human subjects were respected. The evaluation honored the confidentiality and anonymity agreement. Finally, the evaluation described the context's social, political, organizational, and economic features. It employed a variety of data collection sources and methods. The information was validated and reliable. The analyses of quantitative and qualitative information were validated and reliable, and justified conclusions were made.

Recommendations

Recommendations for the CIP. Based on the discussion of the results and discussions with the advisory panel members, this study enables and substantiates the following recommendations for the CIP:

1. The school district should form a systematic plan for retaining the licensed native Chinese teachers for CIP to overcome visa issues.

2. The school should proactively provide time to create, review, and revise the Chinese teaching materials among the Chinese team members on a yearly basis.

3. The school district and school should formalize a Chinese immersion curriculum review committee to evaluate the program model modifications in order to balance the instruction time between Chinese language and English language. The focus of the Chinese immersion curriculum review committee is to maximize the Chinese language instruction and produce optimal English academic outcomes in the Chinese language immersion environment.

4. The school district and school should be proactive in working with local universities to create professional development opportunities. The professional development workshops should improve Chinese immersion teachers' knowledge in Chinese language immersion pedagogy and develop deeper levels of awareness of ethnic and socioeconomic impacts on students' academic achievement. Just as Genesee (1994) stated, the knowledge available to educators was what made a Chinese program effective.

Recommendations for future research. The discussion of the findings has revealed four distinguished features of the CIP program and its outcomes, which may have shed some light on the Chinese language immersion field. Related empirical studies are strongly recommended for the field as follows.

First, the statistical findings along with qualitative results revealed that the CIP students scored significantly higher than the NSS and MSS students across all measures starting with 3rd grade. This early persistent higher academic establishment was not noted in the existing language immersion literature, which needs further studies.

Second, the findings suggested that CIP reduced the achievement gap between the majority and minority students in the 3rd, 4th, and 5th grade years in mathematics administered in English. The CIP students also scored significantly higher in math than English reading. Finally, the CIP student has achieved the Chinese proficiency level so that there was no statistically significant difference between the program CIP and CIPL measured by combined 2nd grade YCT listening and reading test scores. The same finding applied for the 3rd grade students. This particular finding may have suggested that the CIP modified total Chinese immersion program model might be an effective program model for the Chinese immersion programs designed to address the needs of the diverse student populations in the public school system. Further investigation on this topic is recommended.

Third, the findings of this study indicated that the CIP students attained the Chinese language proficiency necessary for their cognitive benefit to develop by the end of their 3rd grade, which needs more empirical support for this assumption to be grounded in the field of Chinese language immersion. This is another appropriate research topic for the field.

Finally, the Chinese Immersion Instructional Environment Survey has collected abundant information about the CIP Chinese immersion instructional environment. It is critical to conduct a correlated study with different types of Chinese language immersion programs using this survey and to examine to what extent the Chinese instructional environment correlates with the student English academic outcomes, as well as the

Chinese language proficiency in different Chinese program settings.

To conclude, this study recommends four major research topics for the field: early establishment of persistent higher academic achievement, reducing achievement gaps in mathematics between majority and minority groups, exceeding the threshold of Chinese language proficiency necessary for cognitive benefit to develop by the end of the 3rd grade, and correlated study on the effectiveness of Chinese language immersion instructional environment with different program settings.

Implications of Study

Prior to the implementation of this evaluative study, the program had not been evaluated. This study was designed for the purpose of comprehensively evaluating the impact of the Chinese language immersion program. As designed, this evaluative study specifically focused on its prioritized components, which are (a) Chinese immersion program model selection and teacher preparation; (b) Chinese curriculum design; (c) administrative and collegial support; (d) Chinese language specific teaching strategy inputs; and (e) the CIP's outcomes (See Appendix B).

Continuous research studies in the field of Chinese language immersion programs in North America, specifically in five areas illustrated by the findings of this study, which would also benefit CIP, are as follows: (a) identifying the needs of Chinese teacher professional development; (b) examining and isolating the potential influencing factors that have impacted the Chinese immersion student's academic achievement, which will help continuously sustain and improve CIP's effectiveness; (c) examining and isolating the potential influencing factors that have impacted the Chinese student academic achievement in mathematics, which will also help continuously sustain and improve CIP's effectiveness; (d) reviewing and modifying the Chinese language immersion program model to maximize the Chinese language instruction time, which is critical for sustaining and improving CIP; and (e) researching and finding the balance between English and Chinese instruction in this high stakes testing environment for the field. Also, the impact on CIP students' English achievement and Chinese language proficiency without the 45 minutes of English instruction from Kindergarten to 2nd grade is an important topic that is worth further study.

The findings of the study additionally identify three ways that the Chinese language immersion program may be continuously sustained and improved through systemic effort.

First, continuously sustaining the Chinese instructional environment that the Chinese language teachers have created for their Chinese language students is critical for continuously sustaining and improving CIP. The creation of the effective Chinese instructional environment involves (a) acquiring sufficient funding for CIP from the magnet office in the school district, (b) implementing the program model with fidelity, (c) implementing Chinese curriculum with fidelity, (d) ensuring effective administrative and collegial support, (e) employing effective classroom management, and (f) using research-based Chinese instructional strategies.

Second, retaining highly qualified and highly motivated Chinese language immersion teachers in the team is the most important factor for further sustaining and improving the effectiveness of the Chinese language immersion program and must be addressed in a systematic manner.

Third, it is likely that the findings of this study could result in more students and families who want to participate in this program. There are currently over 40 prospective kindergarten students who want to get into the CIP. In addition, it is possible that the findings of this study may get more attention from district and NCDPI, and hence, to expand the Chinese immersion program. The findings may also be used for the acquisition of grant funding for the purpose of systematic improvement at the school site or in the local universities. Through this effort, more study can be supported for sustaining and improving CIP and the Chinese language immersion programs in North America in general. In addition, this study may result in more involvement of local universities in language immersion study and support, for example, providing Chinese language immersion professional development opportunities for the local language immersion schools.

In summary, the implications of this study suggest that Chinese language immersion is not only comparably new in the field of foreign language immersion but also lacks theoretical support in general. The Chinese immersion educational practitioners have borrowed the theories and findings from French and German language immersion programs. However, Chinese language is linguistically different from the alphabet-based languages, and the culture that the Chinese language resides in is farther away from the United States of America than that of the other Western countries. Hence, establishing a research system to support the development of Chinese language immersion education in North America is a need. This study may help to get this voice heard and get funding from different organizations to support further research on Chinese language immersion. This study may also help local universities understand the needs and provide professional development opportunities for improving the effectiveness of Chinese immersion teachers in working with the diverse student populations, for sustaining the academic success the CIP has created in the past 7 years, for supporting the mathematic achievement created by the CIP, and for further analyzing the CIP program model and exploring the balance between Chinese instruction and English instruction in order to create optimal Chinese immersion environment and outcomes.

To conclude, the findings of the study showed the following:

1. Three out of three program planners (100%) and 11 out of 14 Chinese teachers (75.91%) agreed that the goals met the addressed needs.

2. Three out of three program planners (100%) and 12 out of 14 Chinese teachers (83.50%) agreed that the selected approach and plans were feasible, compatible, successful, and cost effective.

3. Three out of three program planners (100%) and 11 out of 14 Chinese teachers (78.61%) agreed that CIP was implemented as designed, that the concerns and ideas for improvement were handled efficiently, that negative side effects were analyzed and minimized, that they utilized research-based Chinese language instructional strategies, and that they implemented the selected program model and Chinese curriculum with fidelity.

4. CIP students scored significantly higher than the similar students in non-immersion programs in English reading, math, and science. Furthermore, CIP students clearly demonstrated consistently strong higher academic performance measured by the EOG tests starting from the 3rd and continuing through the 5th grade.

5. CIP students scored significantly higher in mathematics than in English. In addition, CIP students scored significantly higher in mathematics than that of all comparable schools across all the measures. This is even true for students of diverse racial backgrounds: CIP has reduced the achievement gap in mathematics between the majority and minority students, which was substantiated by three

years CIP EOG test results and school report cards from the state.

6. There was no statistically significant difference between combined CIP students' YCT listening and reading scores and that of a comparable Chinese language immersion program in Minnesota, which had a less diverse student population and higher socioeconomic status. This suggested that the modified CIP Chinese language immersion model served the needs of the diverse students effectively. Finally, 3 out of 3 advisory panel members (100%) scored the evaluation process at least 80% for the utility, feasibility, propriety, and accuracy of the process.

Based on the criteria illustrated in the Chinese Immersion Program Evaluation Plan (See Table 4), the criteria for each of the evaluation questions were met or exceeded by the substantiated results; therefore, although the recommendations for CIP's improvement were made, CIP was successful as designed.

References

Anderson, M., Lindholm-Leary, K., Wilhelm, P., Zeigler, M., & Bourdreaux, N. (2005). Meeting the challenges of No Child Left Behind in immersion education in the U.S. *ACIE Newsletter 8*(3), Bridge Insert, 1-8.

Baker, C. (1988). *Key issues in bilingualism and bilingual education.* Philadelphia: Multilingual Matters Ltd.

Bamford, K., & Mizokawa, D. (1991). Additive-bilingual (immersion) education: Cognitive and language development. *Language Learning 41*(3), 413-429.

Ben-Zeev, S. (1977a). Mechanisms by which childhood bilingualism affects understanding of language and cognitive structures. In P. A. Hornby (Ed.), *Bilingualism: Psychological, social, and educational implications* (pp. 10-19). NY, NY: Academic Press.

Ben-Zeev, S. (1977b). The influence of bilingualism on Cognitive Strategy and cognitive development. *Child Development, 48*(3), 1009-1018. Hoboken, NJ: John Wiley & Sons, Inc.

Bickman, L. (1996). The application of program theory to the evaluation of a managed mental health care system. *Evaluation and program planning, 19*(2), 111-119.

Bruck, M., Lambert, W. E., & Tucker, G. R. (1976). *Cognitive consequences of bilingual schooling: The St. Lambert project through grade 6.* (Unpublished manuscript). Psychology Department, McGill University, Montreal.

Campbell, R. N., Gray, T. C., Rhodes, N. C., & Snow, M. A. (1985). Foreign language learning in the elementary schools: A comparison of three language programs. *Modern Language Journal, 69*(44-54).

Cartwright, K. B. (2008). *Literacy processes.* New York: Guilford Press.

Center for Applied Linguistics. (2012). *CAL activities and resources related to Chinese.* Retrieved from http://www.cal.org/resources/discoverlanguages/chinese/resources.html

Chao, D. (1993). *A case study of learning Chinese in an immersion program through the eye of a teacher-researcher.* (Doctoral dissertation). New York University, New York.

Chan, L., & Nunes, T. (1998). Children's understanding of the formal and functional characteristics of writing Chinese. *Applied Psycholinguistics, 19*(1), 115-131.

Cheung, H. (2003). Pinyin and Phonotactics affect the development of phonemic awareness in English-Cantonese bilinguals. In C. McBride-Chang, & H. C. Chen (Eds.), *Reading development in Chinese children.* Westport, CT: Greenwood Press.

Cheung, H., & Ng, L. K. H. (2003). Chinese reading development in some major Chinese societies: An introduction. In C. McBride-Chang, & H. C. Chen (Eds.), *Reading Development in Chinese Children.* Westport, CT: Greenwood Press.

Charles, C. M., & Mertler, C. A. (2006). *Introduction to educational research* (6th ed.). San Francisco, CA: Allyn & Bacon.

Clarke, J. (1995). Evaluation of the Road Whys program: A road safety education program targeting secondary school students. *Proceedings of the Australasian Evaluation Society Conference,* Sydney.

Collins, K., Onwuegbuzie, A., & Sutton, I. (2006). A model incorporating the rationale and purpose for conducting mixed methods research in special education and beyond. *Learning Disabilities: A Contemporary Journal, 4*(1), 67-100.

Cook, V. (2001). *Second language learning and language teaching.* London: Arnold.

Creswell, J. W. (2003). *Research design: Qualitative, quantitative, and mixed methods approaches* (2nd ed.). Thousand Oaks, CA: Sage.

Creswell, J. W. (2005). *Educational research: Planning, conducting, and evaluating quantitative research.* Upper Saddle River, NJ: Prentice Hall.

Creswell, J. W. (2009). *Research design: Qualitative, quantitative, and mixed methods approaches* (3rd ed.). Thousand Oaks, CA: Sage.

Creswell, J. W. (2012). *Educational Research: Planning, conducting, and evaluating quantitative and qualitative research* (4th ed.). Boston, MA: Pearson.

Creswell, J. W. & Clark, V. L. P. (2007). *Designing and conducting mixed methods research.* Thousand Oaks, CA: Sage.

Collins, K., Onwuegbuzie, A., & Sutton, I. (2006). A model incorporating the rationale and purpose for conducting mixed methods research in special education and beyond. Learning Disabilities: *A Contemporary Journal, 4*(1), 67-100.

Cummins, J. (1981). The role of primary language development in promoting educational success for language minority students: In California State Department of Education (Ed.), *Schooling and language minority students: A theoretical framework.* Los Angeles: California State University, Evaluation, Dissemination, and Assessment Center.

Cummins, J. (1983). *Heritage language education: A literature review* (Information Analyses: 70). Toronto, Ontario M5S1V6 Canada: Ontario Institute for Studies in Education.

Cummins, J. (1998). Immersion education for the millennium: What we have learned from 30 years of research on second language immersion. Retrieved on from http://carla.acad.umn.edu/cobaltt/modules/strategies/immersion2000.pdf.

Curtain, H., & Dahlberg, C. A. (2004). *Languages and children: Making the match* (3rd ed). Boston, MA: Pearson Education, Inc.

De Courcy, M. (1997). Benowa high: A decade of French immersion in Australia. In R. K. Johnson, & M. Swain (Eds.), *Immersion education: International perspectives* (pp. 44-62). Cambridge, UK: Cambridge University Press.

De Courcy, M. C. (2002). Learners' experiences of immersion education: Case studies in French and Chinese. Clevedon, UK: Multilingual Matters.

Duncan, S. E., & DeAvila, E. A. (1979). Bilingualism and cognition: Some recent findings. *The Journal for the National Association for Bilingual Education. 4*(1), 15-50.

Duvall, A. L. (2011). *An examination of facilitated mentoring on school performance within an urban middle school* (Unpublished doctoral dissertation). Capella University.

Felderman, C., & Shen, M. (1971). Some language-related cognitive advantages of bilingual five-year-olds. *Journal of Genetic Psychology, 118*(2), 235-244.

Finnamore, S. M. (2006). *Immersion in a language of power: A case study of the English immersion pedagogy of an elementary school in China.* (Unpublished doctoral dissertation). University of Minnesota, Minneapolis.

Fitzpatrick, J. L., Sanders, J. R., & Worthen, B. R. (2004). *Program evaluation alternative approach and practical guidelines*. 3rd ed. Boston, MA: Pearson.

Fitzpatrick, J. L., Sanders, J. R., & Worthen, B. R. (2011). *Program evaluation alternative approach and practical guidelines*. (4th ed.). Boston, MA: Pearson.

Fortune, T. (2008). Immersion benefits and challenges: A research review. *Immersion 101 for Chinese and Japanese*. Minneapolis: University of Minnesota, Center of Advanced Research on Language Acquisition.

Fortune, T. W. (2012). What the research says about immersion. In Asia Society (Ed.), *Chinese language learning in the early grades: A handbook of resources and best practices for Mandarin immersion* (pp. 9-13). Retrieved from http://asiasociety.org/education/chinese-language-initiatives/chinese-language-learning-early-grades

Fortune, T., & Tedick, D. (2003). What parents want to know about foreign language immersion programs. (CAL Digests, EDO-FL-03-04). Retrieved from http://www.cal.org/resources/digest/0304fortune.html

Friedman, T. L. (2005). *The world is flat: A brief history of the twenty-first century.* New York, NY: Farr, Straus, & Firoux.

Fung King Lee, J. (2001). International field experience-What do student teachers learn? *Australian Journal of Teacher Education. 36*(10). Retrieved from http://ro.ecu.edu.au/ajte/vol36/iss10/1

Funnel, S. (1997). Program logic: An adaptable tool. *Evaluation News & Comment, 6*(1), 5-17.

Genesee, F. (1984). Historical and theoretical foundations of immersion education. In California Department of Education (Ed.), *Studies on immersion education: A collection for United States educators* (pp. 32-57). California: California State Department of Education.

Genesee, F. (1985). Second language learning through immersion: A review of U.S. programs. *Review of Education Research, 55*(4), 541-561.

Genesee, F. (1987). *Learning through two languages: Studies of immersion and bilingual education.* Cambridge, MA: Newbury House.

Genesee, F. (1994). *Integrating language and content: Lessons from immersion.* (Educational Practice Report No. 11). Montreal: McGill University. Retrieved from http://escholarship.org/uc/item/61c8k7kh#page-2

Genesee, F., & Jared, D. (2008). Literacy development in early French immersion programs. *Canadian Psychology, 49*(2), 140-147. Retrieved from http://www.psych.mcgill.ca/perpg/fac/genesee/19.pdf.

Gibbs, G. R. (2007). Analyzing qualitative data. In U. Flick (Ed.). *The sage qualitative research kit.* London: Sage.

Gottardo, A., Yan, B., Siegel, L. S., & Wade-Woolley, L. (2001). Factors related to English reading performance in children with Chinese as a first language: More evidence of cross-language transfer of phonological processing. *Educational Psychology, 93*(3), 530-542.

Greene, J. C. (2006). Toward a methodology of mixed methods social inquiry. *Research in the Schools. 13*(1), 93-99.

Gudykunst, W. B. (1998). *Bridging Differences: Effective Intergroup Communication.* Thousand Oaks, CA: SAGE Publications.

Hagel, C. (2012). State of the field: Proficiency, sustainability, and beyond. 2012 National Chinese Language Conference [Conference]. Washington D.C.

Hakuta, K. (1985). Cognitive development in bilingual instruction. In *Issues in English Language Development* (pp. 63-67). Rosslyn, VA: National Clearinghouse for Bilingual Education.

Hakuta, K., & Diaz, R. M. (1985). The relationship between degree of bilingualism and cognitive ability: A critical discussion and some new longitudinal data. In E. Nelson (Eds.), *Children's language* (pp. 320-344). Hillsdale, NJ: L. Erlbaum Associates.

He, W. W., & Jiao, D. (2010). Curriculum design and special features of computer Chinese and Chinese for tomorrow. In J. Chen, C. Wang, & J. Cai (Eds.), *Teaching and learning Chinese: Issues and perspectives* (pp. 217-235). NC: Information Age Publishing, Inc.

Hu, G. (2002). Potential cultural resistance to pedagogical imports: The case of communicative language teaching in China. *Language, Culture and Curriculum, 15*(2), 93-105.

Huang, H. S., & Hanley, J. R. (1997). A longitudinal study of phonological awareness, visual skills, and Chinese reading acquisition among first-graders in Taiwan. *International Journal of Behavioral Development, 20*(2), 249-268.

Institute of Linguistics, Chinese Academy of Social Sciences. (2004). *Xinhua Dictionary* (10th ed.). Beijing: The Commercial Press.

Jin, L., & Cortazzi, M. (1998). Dimensions of dialogue: Large classes in China. International Journal of Educational Research, 29, 739-761.

Johnson R. K, & Swain, M. (1997). Immersion education: A category within bilingual education. In R.K. Johnson, & M. Swain (Eds.), *Immersion education: International perspectives* (pp. 1-17). Cambridge, UK: Cambridge University Press.

Jordan, D. (1971). *Guide to the Romanization of Chinese.* Taipei: Mei Ya Publications Inc.

Kanagy, R., & Hai, G. D. (2001). Doing fine in a Japanese immersion classroom. In D. Christian, & F. Genesee (Eds.), *Bilingual education* (pp. 139-150). Alexandria, VA: Teachers of English to Speakers of Other Languages.

Kissau, S., Yon, M., & Algozzine, B. (2011). The beliefs and behaviors of international and domestic foreign language teachers. *Journal of National Council of Lesson Commonly Taught Languages, 10*, 21-56

Ku, Y., & Anderson, R. C. (2001). Chinese children's incidental learning of word meanings. *Contemporary Educational Psychology, 26*(2), 249-266.

Kubler, C., Biq, Y., Henrichson, G. C., Walton, A. R., Wong, M. M., Wu, W., et al. (1997). *NFLC guide for basic Chinese language programs.* Published cooperatively by the Ohio State University National Foreign Language Resource Center and the OSU Foreign Language Publications Office, Columbus, Ohio, and the National Foreign Language Center, Washington, DC.

Lei, H., & Moreira, A. (2001). *Teaching English modal verbs with cognitive flexibility hypertext.* Aveiro, Portugal: Department of Didactics and Educational Technology, University of Aveiro.

Li, W., Anderson, R. C., Nagy, W., & Zhang, H. (2002). Facets of metalingisitic awareness that contribute to Chinese literacy. In W. Li, J. S. Gaffney, & J. L. Packard (Eds.), *Chinese children's reading acquisition: Theoretical and pedagogical issues,* (pp. 87-106). Boston, MS: Kluwer Academic Publishers.

Lin, D., McBride-Chang, C., Shu, H., Zhang, Y., Li, H., Zhang, J., Aram, D. & Levin, I. (in press). Small wins big: Analytic Pinyin skills promote character reading. Psychological Science.

Liedtke, W. W., & Nelson, L. D. (1968). Concept formation and bilingualism. *Alberta Journal of Educational Research. 14*, 225-232.

Lichtman, M. (2006). *Qualitative research in education: A user's guide.* Thousand Oak, CA: Sage Publications.

Liu, J. L. (1992). *When the students stopped speaking English: A case study of teaching and learning Chinese in an intensive summer immersion program.* (Unpublished doctoral dissertation). University of Oregon, Oregon.

Loke, K. (2002). Approaches to teaching and learning of Chinese: A critical literature review and proposal for semantic, cognitive, and metacognitive approach. *Journal of Chinese Language Teachers Association, 37*(1), 65-112.

McBride-Chang, C., Cho, J.R., Liu, H. Y. Wagner, R. K., Shu, H., Zhao, A. B., et al. (2005). Changing models across cultures: associations of phonological awareness and morphological structure awareness with vocabulary and word recognition in second graders from Beijing, Hong Kong, Korea, and the United States. *Journal of Experimental Child Psychology, 92*(2), 140-160.

Met, M. (2000). School immersion in less commonly taught languages. In R. D. Lambert, & E. Shohamy (Eds.), *Language policy and pedagogy in honor of A. Ronald Walton* (pp. 139-146). Philadelphia: John Benjamin Publishing Co.

Met, M. (2012). Basics of program design. In M. Abbott & M. Bacon (Eds.), *Chinese language learning in the early grades: A handbook of resources and best practices for Mandarin immersion* (pp. 16-21). Asian Society: AsianSociety.org/Chinese.

Met, M., & Lorenz, B. E. (1997). Lessons from U.S. immersion programs. In R. K. Johnson & M. Swain (Eds.), *Immersion education international* perspectives (pp. 243-264). NY: Cambridge University Press.

McMillan, J. H., & Schumacher, S. (2006). *Research in education: Evidence-based inquiry* (6th ed.). Boston, MA: Pearson.

McNeil, K., Newman, I., & Steinhauser, J. (2005). *How to be involved in program evaluation: What every administrator needs to know.* Lantham, MD: Scarecrow Education.

Morgan, G. (2006). *Images of organization.* New Delhi India: Sage Publication India.

Nagy, W. E., & Anderson, R. C. (1995). *Metalinguistic awareness and literacy acquisition in different languages* (Technical Report No. 618). Illinois: University of Illinois at Urbana-Champaign. Center for the Study of Reading.

NCDPI, (2010). North Carolina world language essential standards: Classical, dual & heritage, and modern languages. Retrieved from http://www.ncpublicschools.org/acre/standards/new-standards/#worldlang.

NCDPI, (2011). The North Carolina State Testing Results. Retrieved on from http://www.ncpublicschools.org/docs/accountability/reports/green/1112/achlevelranges.pdf.

NCDPI, (2012). The ABCs of Public Education 2012 accountability report backgrounds packet. Retrieved from http://www.ncpublicschools.org/docs/accountability/reporting/abc/2011- 12/backgroundpacket.pdf.

NCDPI, (2013). Education acronyms: READY. Retrieved from http://www.ncpublicschools.org/acronyms/.

National Chinese Language Conference. (2012). *State of the field: Proficiency, sustainability and beyond.* Retrieved from http://sites.asiasociety.org/nclc2012/presentations/

National Council of Less Commonly Taught Languages. (2012). *Shared solutions for common problems.* Retrieved from http://www.ncolctl.org/

Negroponte, J. (2012). State of the field: Proficiency, sustainability, and beyond. *2012 National Chinese Language Conference.* Washington: Asian Society and College Board.

Nelson, M. & Eddy, R.M. (2008). Evaluative thinking and action in the classroom. In T. Berry & R.M. Eddy (Eds). *Consequences of No Child Left Behind for education. New Directions for Evaluation. 117,* 37-46.

No Child Left Behind Act (2001). Washington, DC: U.S. Department of Education. Pub. L. No. 107-110(2002).

Paige, R. (2002). Stronger accountability. [Key policy letters signed by the Education Secretary or Deputy Secretary]. Retrieved from http://www2.ed.gov/policy/elsec/guid/secletter/020724.html

Peng D. L., Xu S. Y., Ding G. S., Li E. Z., & Liu Y. (2003). Brain mechanism for the phonological and semantic processing of Chinese character. *Chinese Journal of Neuroscience. 19,* 287–291.

Perfetti, C. A. (2003). The Universal Grammar of Reading. *Scientific Studies of Reading, 7*(1). 3-24. Lawrence Eribaum Associates, Inc.

Pettigrew, A. (1972). Organizational change and learning. In D. S. Pugh, & D. J. Hickson (Eds.), *Writers on organizations* (pp. 169-175). Thousand Oaks: SAGE Publishing.

Piaget, J., (1952). *The child's conception of number.* London: Routledge and Kegan Paul.

Pugh, D. S. & Hickson, D. J. *Writers on Organizations.* London: SAGE Publications, 2007.

Rogers, P. J. (2000). Program theory: Not whether programs work but how they work. In D. L. Stufflebeam, G. F. Madaus, & T. Kellaghan (Eds.), *Evaluation models: Viewpoints on educational and human services evaluation* (pp. 232). Boston: Kluwer Academic Publishers.

Roybal, V. M. (2011). *A summative evaluation of a comprehensive 9th grade transition.* (Doctoral dissertation). Retrieved from http://search.proquest.com.ezproxy.gardner-webb.edu/pqdthss/index?accountid=11041

Sandell, E. J. (2007). Impact of international education experiences on undergraduate students. *Delta Kappa Gamma Bulletin, 73*(4), 12-39.

Senge, P. (1992). Organizational change and learning. In D. S. Pugh, D. J. Hickson (Eds.), *Writers on organizations* (pp. 178-181). Thousand Oaks: SAGE Publishing.

Shu, H. (2003). Reading acquisition in Chinese: Behavior and brain imaging approach. In A. Kelly (Ed.), *A report on the literacy network and numeracy network deliberations* (pp. 46-48). Brockton, MA: OCED.

Shu, H., & Anderson, R. C. (1997). Role of radical awareness in the character and work acquisition of Chinese children. *Reading Research Quarterly, 32*(1), 78-89.

Shu, H., Chen, X., Anderson, R. C., Wu, N., & Xuan, Y. (2003). Properties of school Chinese: Implications for learning to read. *Child Development, 74*(1), 27-47.

Shu, H., Peng, H., McBride-Chang, C. (2008). Phonological awareness in young Chinese children. *Developmental Science. 11*(1), 171-181.

Siok, W.T., & Fletcher, P. (2001). The role of phonological awareness and visual-orthographic skills in Chinese reading acquisition. *Developmental Psychology, 37*(6), 886-899.

Smith, A. H. (2007). *Chinese Immersion: A study of effective elementary school programs.* (Unpublished doctoral dissertation), Fielding Graduate University, Santa Barbara, CA.

Smith, E. (2012). Waddell Language Academy students win at NC State's Chinese Speech Contest. Retrieved from http://www.cipfeiffer.org/english/news/waddell-language-academy-students-win-nc-states-chinese-speec/.

Snow, M. A. (1990). Instructional methodology in immersion foreign language education. In A. M. Padilla, H. H. Fairchild, & C. M. Valdez (Eds.), *Foreign language education: Issues and strategies* (pp. 156-171). Newbury Park, CA: Sage Publications.

Soderman, A. K. (2010). Language immersion program for young children? Yes . . . but proceed with caution. *Phi Delta Kappan, 90*(8), 54-61.

Spiro, R. J., Feltovich, P. J., Jacobson, M. J., & Coulson, R. L. (1995). Cognitive flexibility, constructivism and hypertext: Random access instruction for advanced knowledge acquisition in ill-structured domains. In L.P. Steffe & J.E. Gale (Eds.), *Constructivism in education* (pp. 85-107). Hillsdale, NJ: Erlbaum.

Strauss, A., & Corbin, J. (1988). *Basics of qualitative research: Techniques and procedures for developing grounded theory.* Thousand Oaks, CA: Sage Publications.

Stufflebeam, D. L. (1999). Program Evaluation Metaevaluation Checklist. Retrieved from http://www.wmich.edu/evalctr/checklists/metaevaluation/

Stufflebeam, D. L. (2000a). Foundation models for 21st century program evaluation. In D. L. Stufflebeam, G. F. Madaus, & T. Kellaghan (Eds.), *Evaluation models: Viewpoints on educational and human services evaluation* (pp. 35). Boston: Kluwer Academic Publishers.

Stufflebeam, D. L. (2000b). Professional standards and principles for evaluations. In D.L. Stufflebeam, G. F. Madaus, & T. Kellaghan (Eds.), *Evaluation models: Viewpoints on educational and human services evaluation* (pp. 440-448). Boston: Kluwer Academic Publishers.

Stufflebeam, D. L. (2000c). The CIPP Model for evaluation. In D. L. Stufflebeam, G. F. Madaus, & T. Kellaghan (Eds.), *Evaluation models: Viewpoints on educational and human services evaluation* (pp. 279-317). Boston: Kluwer Academic Publishers.

Stufflebeam, D. L. (2000d). The methodology of metaevaluation. In D. L. Stufflebeam, G. F. Madaus, & T. Kellaghan (Eds.), *Evaluation models: Viewpoints on educational and human services evaluation* (pp. 458). Boston: Kluwer Academic Publishers.

Stufflebeam, D. L. (2002). *CIPP Evaluation model checklist: A tool for applying the Fifth Installment of the CIPP Model to assess long-term enterprises.* Retrieved from http://www.wmich.edu/evalctr/archive_checklists/cippchecklist_mar07.pdf.

Stufflebeam, D. L. (2003). The CIPP Model for evaluation. In T. Kellaghan, D. L. Stufflebeam, & L.A. Wingate (Eds.), *International handbook of educational evaluation* (pp. 31-62). Boston: Kluwer Academic Publishers.

Stufflebeam, D. L. (2004). The 21st century CIPP model: Origins, development, and use. In M. Alkin (Ed.), *Evaluation roots: Tracing theorists' views and influences* (pp. 245-262). Thousand Oaks, CA: Sage.

Stufflebeam, D. L., & Madaus, G. F. (1983). The standards for evaluation of educational programs, projects, and materials: A description and summary. In G. F. Madaus, M. Scriven, & D.L. Stufflebeam (Eds.), *Evaluation models: Viewpoints on educational and human services evaluation (p. 395).* Norwell: Kluwer–Nijhoff Publishing.

Swain, M., & Lapkin, S. (1981). *Bilingual education in Ontario: A decade of research.* Queen's Park, Ontario: Ministry of Education.

Tang, W. S. L. (1988). *A study of the Chinese language immersion program in San Francisco: The first two years.* (Unpublished doctoral dissertation). University of the Pacific, Stockton, CA.

Thomas, W. P., & Colliers, V. P. (2002). *A national study of school effectiveness for language minority students' long-term academic achievement.* (ERIC document Reproduction Service No. ED 475048)

Vengraf, T. (2001). *Qualitative research interviewing.* Thousand Oak, CA: SAGE Publications Ltd.

Vygotsky, L. S. (1962). *Thinking and Speaking.* Cambridge, MA: The M.I.T. Press.

Walker, R. G. (1996). Designing an intensive Chinese curriculum. In. S. McGinnis (Ed.), *Chinese pedagogy: An emerging field* (pp. 181-223). OH: Foreign Language Publishing.

Wang, S. C. (2007). Building societal capital: Chinese in the United States. *Language Policy*, 6(1), 27-52.

Wang, S. C. (2010). Chinese language education in the United States: A historical overview and future directions. In J. Chen, C. Wang, & J. Cai (Eds.), *Teaching and learning Chinese: Issues and perspectives* (pp. 3-32). NC: Information Age Publishing, Inc.

Wang, T. T. (2008). *Instructional strategies and teacher-student interaction in the classroom of a Chinese immersion school.* (Doctoral dissertation). Retrieved from http://search.proquest.com.ezproxy.gardner-webb.edu/pqdthss/index?accountid=11041.

Wen, X. (2009). Teaching listening and speaking: An interactive approach. In M. E. Everson, & Y. Xiao (Eds.) *Teaching Chinese as a foreign language: Theories and applications* (pp. 131-149). MA: Cheng & Tsui Company.

Xiao, Y. (2009). Teaching Chinese Orthography and Discourse: Knowledge and pedagogy. In M. E. Everson, & Y. Xiao (Eds.), *Teaching Chinese as a foreign language: Theories and applications* (pp. 131-149). MA: Cheng & Tsui Company.

Yiu, E. M., Van Hasselt, C. A., Williams, S. R., & Woo, J. K. S. (1994). Speech intelligibility in tone language (Chinese) laryngectomy speakers. *European Journal of Disorders of Communication, 29*(4), 339-347.

Zhu, Z. (2010). A historical perspective of teaching Chinese as a second language. In J. Chen, C. Wang, & J. Cai (Eds.), *Teaching and learning Chinese: Issues and perspectives* (pp. 33-69). NC: Information Age Publishing, Inc.

Appendix A

The 5th National Chinese Language Conference 2012

The 5th National Chinese Language Conference 2012

This video was made by the researcher (The 5th National Chinese Language Conference 2012.asf) based on the videos captured during the 5th National Chinese Language Conference held in April 2012 in Washington and was used as a reference tool. There are four speakers in this video: John D. Negroponte, Chuck Hagel, Wishakha N. Desai, and Whuhan Wang. The highlights of the speeches and the backgrounds of the speakers are listed below.

John Negroponte points out that United States and China relationship is critical for the global prosperity and stability. The Asia Society is committed to prepare the young American leaders to be able to engage their Chinese counterparts on their own terms and in their own languages. These young leaders and their Chinese counterparts will be stewards of cooperative relationship going forward. John Negroponte is a United States career diplomat and national security official. He held government positions abroad and in Washington between 1960 and 1997 and again from 2001 to 2008.

Chuck Hagel states that the bilateral relationship between China and United States becomes more critical than ever in the history, at least in the modern history. He emphasizes that United States and China don't have to agree on everything, but need to build up a common ground to benefit the future of the world. Chuch Hagel is a distinguished professor at Georgetown University. He serves on the boards of directors of Chevron Corporation and Zurich's Holding Company of America; he is also a co-chairman of the President's Intelligence Advisory Board, co-chair of the Defense's Policy Board.

Wishakha N. Desai stresses that it is time to think about how to sustain the Chinese immersion programs in the United States and how to ensure the accountability of the Chinese programs. Wishakha Desai is president and CEO of Asia Society, a global organization committed to strengthening partnerships among the people, leaders, and institutions of Asia and the United States.

Shuhan C. Wang calls for a standardized online Chinese assessment tool in United States for assessing students' Chinese language proficiency. Shuhan Wang is deputy director of the National Foreign Language Center at the University of Maryland. She is co-principal investigator of the STARTALK project, a multiyear, federal funded initiative that promotes the studying and teaching of critical languages as Arabic, Chinese, Dari, Hindi, Persian, Portuguese, Russian, etc.

Appendix B

Comprehensive Chinese Language Immersion Program Sequence Model

241

Comprehensive Chinese Language Immersion Program Sequence Model

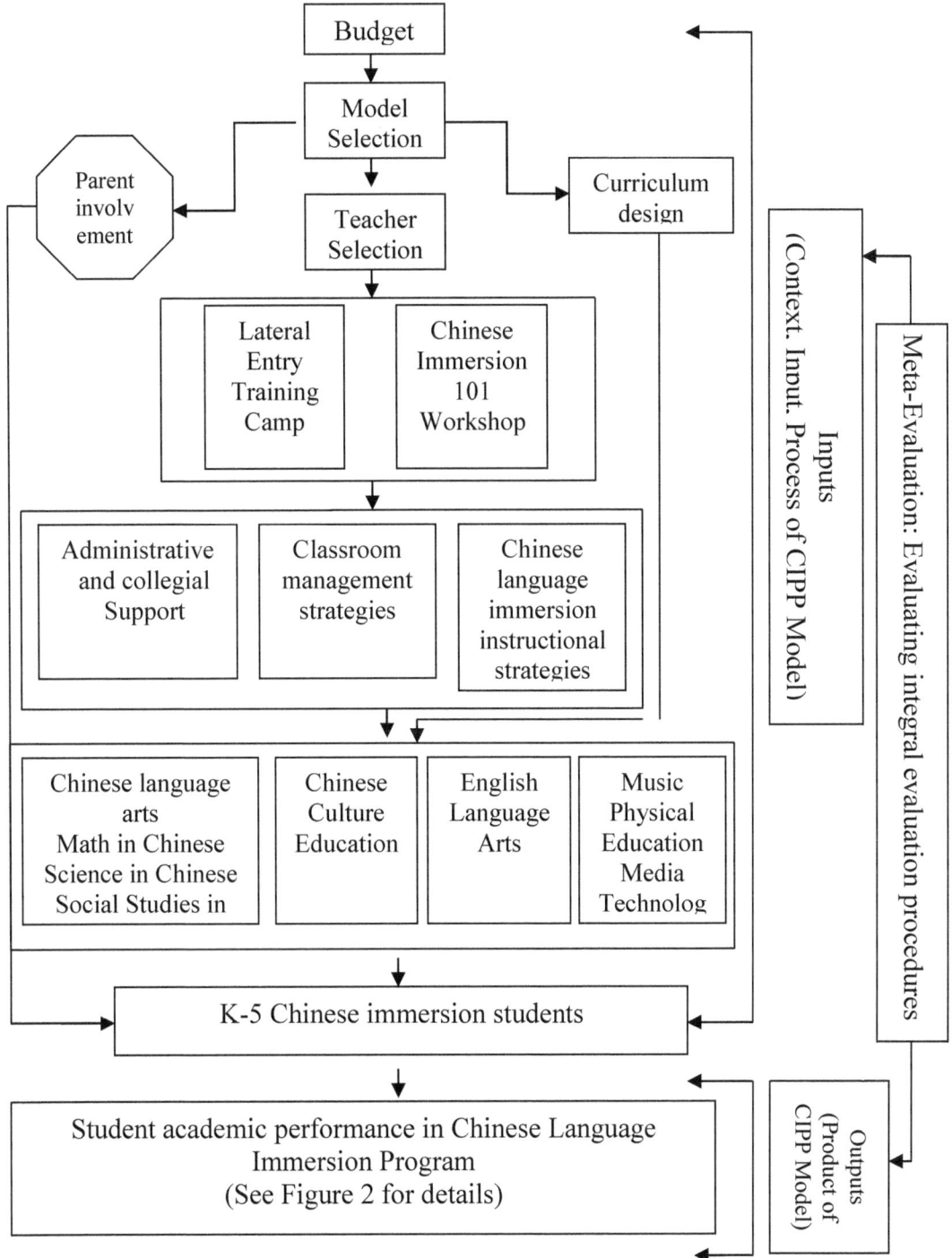

Appendix C

Chinese Curriculum Articulation

Chinese Curriculum Articulation

	Chinese Literacy Focus	**Word Production Benchmarks**	**Word Production Accumulation**	**Hanban Chinese Proficiency Tests Standards**
K	<ul><li>Focusing on oral language development</li><li>Focusing on character recognition</li><li>Introducing Chinese character in the 4th quarter</li></ul>	50	50	
1st Grade	<ul><li>Focusing on critical Chinese words and radicals</li><li>Starting to introduce Pinyin from 3rd quarter</li><li>New Change in 2013-2014—Systematically introducing Pinyin in the 3rd and 4th quarter</li><li>Starting free writing and creative writing to cultivate students' writing skills</li></ul>	150 2013-2014: 100	200	YCT Level 1: 150+
2nd Grade	<ul><li>Teaching Pinyin systematically—move to 1st grade</li><li>New Change in 2013-2014 – Teaching application of Pinyin and typing skills</li><li>Teaching dictionary skills</li><li>Focusing reading and listening comprehension</li><li>Introducing time and location modifiers in the sentence</li><li>Introducing the order of the time units and locative units</li><li>Applying whole language strategies in teaching Chinese literacy</li><li>Using LEA approaching in introducing writing</li></ul>	150 2013-2014: 300	500	YCT Level 2: 300+

	• Chinese story • Continuing free writing and creative writing to cultivate students' writing skills. • Developing oral language fluency			
3rd Grade	• Reinforcing time and location modifiers in the sentence • Reinforcing the order of the time units and locative units • Introducing measuring words and parts of a sentence • Introducing simple sentence structures • Paying explicit attention to oral/vocabulary development, and direct teaching writing skills • Addressing the conventions and genres of writing • Continuing developing fluency with Pinyin-input method	450	950	**YCT Level 3:** **600+**
4th Grade	• Reinforcing measuring words and parts of a sentence • Reinforcing simple sentence structures • Systematically teaching measuring words • Addressing simple and compound sentence structures • Focusing on the convention and genres of writings • Continuing fluency with Pinyin-input method	450	1400	**Level 4: 1200+**
5 Grade	• Systematically teaching compound sentence structures • Developing students' oral, reading and writing language fluency as a whole	450	1850	

| | - Applying students' Chinese language skills into a real-world situation—Trip to China!
- Continuing developing fluency with Pinyin-input method | | | |

Appendix D

Chinese Tri-Input Model

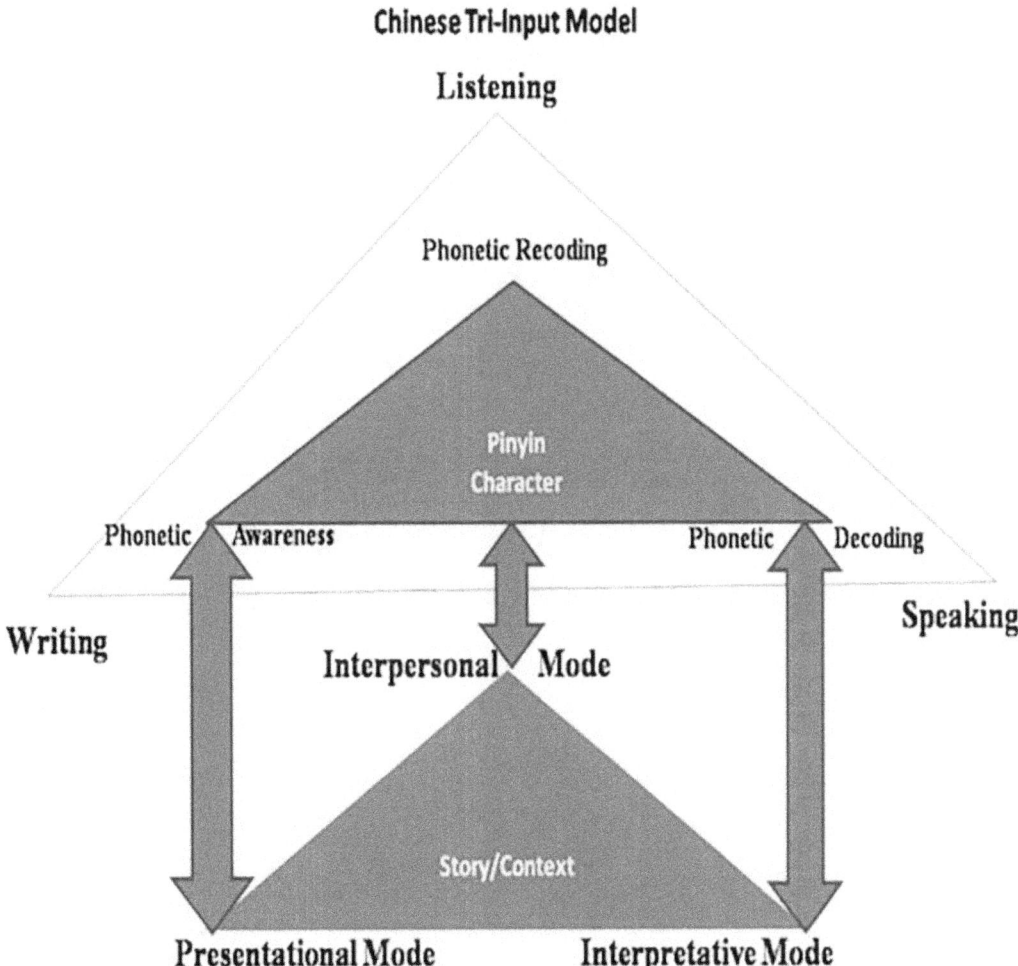

Note. The Chinese Tri-Input Model depicts the process of Chinese curriculum and instruction design and the flow of instructional input in the Chinese immersion program.

Appendix E

Meta-Evaluation Survey

Meta-Evaluation Survey

Part I: To Meet the Requirement for Utility, Program evaluations should

1 2 3 4 5 6   1. Clearly identify the evaluation client

1 2 3 4 5 6   2. Assign priority to the most important questions

1 2 3 4 5 6   3. Allow flexibility for adding questions during the evaluation

1 2 3 4 5 6   4. Obtain sufficient information to assess the program's merit

1 2 3 4 5 6   5. Obtain sufficient information to assess the program's worth

1 2 3 4 5 6   6. Consider all relevant sources of values for interpreting evaluation findings, including societal needs, pertinent laws, institutional mission, and program goals

1 2 3 4 5 6   7. Determine the appropriate party for value judgments

1 2 3 4 5 6   8. Take into account the stakeholders' values

1 2 3 4 5 6   9. Write and present the findings simply and directly

1 2 3 4 5 6   10. To the extent appropriate, conduct feedback sessions to go over and applying findings.

Scoring the Evaluation for Utility
Using scale of 6 - Excellent, 5 - Very Good, 4 - Good, 2-3 - Fair, and 0-1 - Poor
Adding to the followings:
Number of Excellent: _____ X 1.0 = _____
Number of Very Good: _____ X 0.8 = _____
Number of Good: _____ X 0.6 = _____
Number of Fair: _____ X 0.25 = _____
Total score: _____
(6 Excellent, 5 Very Good, 4 Good, 2-3 Fair, 0-1 Poor)
Strength of the evaluation 's provisions for UTILITY:
9 (90%) to 10: Excellent
7 (70%) to 8: Very good
5 (50%) to 6: Good
4 (25%): Fair
0 (0%) to 3: Poor

_____**(Total score) / 10 X 100 =** _____

Comments:

Part II: To Meet the Requirement for Feasibility, Program evaluations should

1 2 3 4 5 6   1. Minimize disruption and data burden

1 2 3 4 5 6   2. Make a realistic schedule

1 2 3 4 5 6   3. As feasible and appropriate, engage locals to help conduct the evaluation

1 2 3 4 5 6   4. As appropriate, make evaluation procedures a part of routine events

1 2 3 4 5 6   5. Anticipate different positions of different interest groups

1 2 3 4 5 6   6. Be efficient

1 2 3 4 5 6   7. Inform decisions

1 2 3 4 5 6   8. Foster program improvement

1 2 3 4 5 6   9. Provide accountability information

1 2 3 4 5 6   10. Generate new insights

Scoring the Evaluation for FEASIBILITY
Using scale of 6 - Excellent, 5 - Very Good, 4 - Good, 2-3 - Fair, and 0-1 - Poor
Adding to the followings:
Number of Excellent: _____ X 1.0 = _____
Number of Very Good: _____ X 0.8 = _____
Number of Good: _____ X 0.6 = _____
Number of Fair: _____ X 0.25 = _____
Total score: _____
(6 Excellent, 5 Very Good, 4 Good, 2-3 Fair, 0-1 Poor)
Strength of the evaluation's provisions for FEASIBILITY:
9 (90%) to 10: Excellent
7 (70%) to 8: Very good
5 (50%) to 6: Good
4 (25%): Fair
0 (0%) to 3: Poor
_____**(Total score) / 10 X 100 =** _____

Comments:

Part III: To Meet the Requirement for Propriety, Program evaluations should

1 2 3 4 5 6   1. Assess program outcomes against targeted and non-targeted customer's assessed needs

1 2 3 4 5 6   2. Identify program strengths to build on

1 2 3 4 5 6   3. Identify program weaknesses to correct

1 2 3 4 5 6   4. Rights of human objects are respected

1 2 3 4 5 6   5. Follow due process and uphold civil rights

1 2 3 4 5 6   6. Respect human object

1 2 3 4 5 6   7. Honor confidentiality/anonymity agreements

1 2 3 4 5 6   8. Minimize harmful consequences of the evaluation

1 2 3 4 5 6   9. Honor participants' privacy rights/time commitments

1 2 3 4 5 6   10. Report intended and unintended outcomes

Scoring the Evaluation for PROPRIETY
Using scale of 6 - Excellent, 5 - Very Good, 4 - Good, 2-3 - Fair, and 0-1 - Poor
Adding to the followings:
Number of Excellent: _____ X 1.0 = _____
Number of Very Good: _____ X 0.8= _____
Number of Good: _____ X 0.6 = _____
Number of Fair: _____ X 0.25 = _____
Total score: _____
(6 Excellent, 5 Very Good, 4 Good, 2-3 Fair, 0-1 Poor)
Strength of the evaluation 's provisions for PROPRIETY:
9 (90%) to 10: Excellent
7 (70%) to 8: Very good
5 (50%) to 6: Good
4 (25%): Fair
0 (0%) to 3: Poor
_____ **(Total score) / 10 X 100 =** _____

Comments: _____

Part IV: To Meet the Requirement for Accuracy, Program evaluations should

1 2 3 4 5 6   1. Describe the context's social, political, organizational, and economic features

1 2 3 4 5 6   2. When interpreting findings, take into account the extent to which the intended procedures were effectively executed

1 2 3 4 5 6   3. As appropriate, employ a variety of data collection sources and methods

1 2 3 4 5 6   4. Document, justify, and report the means used to obtain information from each source

1 2 3 4 5 6   5. Information are validated and reliable

1 2 3 4 5 6   6. Analysis of quantitative information are validated and reliable

1 2 3 4 5 6   7. Analysis of qualitative information are validated and reliable

1 2 3 4 5 6   8. Justified conclusions are made

1 2 3 4 5 6   9. Limit conclusions to the applicable time periods, contexts, purposes, questions, and activities

1 2 3 4 5 6   10. Evaluate all important aspects of the evaluation, including the instrumentation, data collection, data handling, coding, analysis, synthesis, and reporting.

Scoring the Evaluation for ACCURACY
Using scale of 6 - Excellent, 5 - Very Good, 4 - Good, 2-3 - Fair, and 0-1 - Poor
Adding to the followings:
Number of Excellent: _____ X 1.0 = _____
Number of Very Good: _____ X 0.8 = _____
Number of Good: _____ X 0.6 = _____
Number of Fair: _____ X 0.25 = _____
Total score: _____
Strength of the evaluation's provisions for ACCURACY:
9 (90%) to 10: Excellent
7 (70%) to 8: Very good
5 (50%) to 6: Good
4 (25%): Fair
0 (0%) to 3:   Poor
_____(Total score) / 10 X 100 = _____

Comments:

Note. This Meta-Evaluation Survey is adapted from Program Evaluation Metaevaluation checklist (Stufflebeam, 1999). The researcher has modified this checklist based on the needs of Chinese language immersion program evaluation under study.

Appendix F

Interview Questions

Interview Questions

I want to thank you for taking the time to participate in my study. This should take approximately 45 minutes. I will be recording the interview so that I can focus on your responses rather than taking notes. The first thing I will ask you to do is that you give me a pseudonym for use on this recording, which I will also use in my evaluation to keep your identity confidential. What would you like me to call you? Get response.
Thank you. The focus of this study is to evaluate the effectiveness of Chinese immersion program. The evaluation will specifically focus on eight subtopics: (a) program funding and resources, (b) program model implementation, (c) curriculum implementation, (d) professional development, (f) administrative and collegial support, (f) classroom management, (g) Chinese instructional environment, and (h) Chinese immersion program output. I will begin by taking you back to the time before the Chinese immersion program began to be implemented. I will ask follow-up questions at the end to fill in any blanks as needed. The idea is to get a good description of your perceptions related to the creation, implementation, and academic impact of the program.

1. First of all, please tell me a little bit about your professional background. How did you get here?

(The following questions will be repeated, as needed, if not brought up by the participant: (a) program funding and resources, (b) program model implementation, (c) curriculum implementation, (d) professional development, (f) administrative and collegial support, (f) classroom management, (g) Chinese instructional environment, and (h) Chinese immersion program output). I would like you to think back to the time when the Chinese immersion program was first being discussed.

2. When was that?
3. What was going on?
4. Who thought of it?
5. What made that person think about Chinese language immersion program?
6. Why did you choose this particular model?
7. What resources were identified for this program?
8. How did it actually happen?
9. Who all was involved?
10. Which students participate in this program?
11. What were the challenges?
12. What surprised you?
13. If you could redo the process, what would you change?
14. Tell me about the first year. Did you set any goals?
15. In your opinion, have resources been used effectively?
16. In your opinion, how well has this program been implemented?
17. What are the limits and negative side effects of the program, from your point of view?
18. How are concerns and ideas for improvement handled?
19. Is there anything else you would like to add? Anything that I didn't ask but you would like to discuss?

This is adapted from Roybal's (2011) Dissertation, APPENDIX B Interview Questions.

Appendix G

Proposal Timetable

Proposal Timetable

Events	Data Collections	Analyses
Defending proposal		May 17 2013
Semi-structured interviews	July 2013	August 2013
Chinese Immersion Instructional Environment Survey	July 2013	August 2013
EOG results collecting	July 2013	July 2013
EOG results collecting from Comparable school	July 2013	July 2013
YCT result collecting	July 2013	July 2013
YCT result collecting from MN	July 2013	July 2013
Meta-evaluation collection from Advisory Panel	August 2013	August 2013
Chapter 4 & 5	August 2013	August 2013
Editing Dissertation	September 2013	October 2013
Defending Dissertation		November 2013

Appendix H

Chinese Immersion Instructional Environment Survey

The Chinese Immersion Instructional Environment Survey

Using the following 1-5 scale, please indicate, by circling the most correct response, the degree to which you agree with the statement listed below:

1	2	3	4	5
Strongly Agree	Agree	Neutral	Disagree	Strongly Disagree

Funding and Resources

1 2 3 4 5   1. I have teaching materials needed for my students to learn Chinese.
1 2 3 4 5   2. My class has the technologies needed to promote effective teaching and learning in Chinese.
1 2 3 4 5   3. My students were provided resources for cultural activities, such as, Chinese calligraphy instructions, Chinese New Year celebrations, etc.

Comments:
_____

Program Model Implementation

1 2 3 4 5   4. I use Chinese most of the time and English only when needed. I am a _____ teacher (please indicate your grade level).
1 2 3 4 5   5. I use Chinese only.
1 2 3 4 5   6. I allow mixture of language use by the students.
1 2 3 4 5   7. It is helpful for me to observe my language immersion colleagues in Japanese, French, or German teaching students in the same building.
1 2 3 4 5   8. I can get immediate support from the experienced Japanese, French or German language immersion colleagues in the same building.

Comments:
_____

Curriculum Implementation

1 2 3 4 5   9. I teach my students subject contents based on NCSCOS and world language standards
1 2 3 4 5   10. I participated the discussion of what I should teach at my grade Level.
1 2 3 4 5   11. I teach my students based on what I should teach at my grade level.
1 2 3 4 5   12. I know the articulation of the Chinese curriculum across K-5 levels.
1 2 3 4 5   13. Chinese team has discussed and revised the Chinese curriculum annually.
1 2 3 4 5   14. The concerns and ideas for improvement have been handled satisfactorily.
1 2 3 4 5   15. The Chinese teachers share teaching materials at the same grade level.

Comments:
_____

Professional Development

1 2 3 4 5   16. I am satisfied with the professional development opportunities available to me.

1 2 3 4 5   17. CMS lateral entry training camp was useful for me to start my teaching practice in CMS.

1 2 3 4 5   18. Chinese immersion 101 or National Chinese Conference is informative for me to teach Chinese in language immersion settings.

Comments: _____

Administrative and collegial support

1 2 3 4 5   19. I know what my principal expect of me.

1 2 3 4 5   20. I feel respected and supported by school administration regarding promoting Chinese language and cultural in the program.

1 2 3 4 5   21. I feel supported by administration regarding behavioral challenges.

1 2 3 4 5   22. The people I work with care about each other on a personal level.

1 2 3 4 5   23. I feel that people around me are collaborative.

Comments: _____

Classroom Management

1 2 3 4 5   24. My students learn the classroom rules and expectations from the first day of the school.

1 2 3 4 5   25. My classroom management plan was implemented with fidelity.

1 2 3 4 5   26. My students follow their daily routines.

1 2 3 4 5   27. My students observe the rewarding and consequence system in my class.

Comments: _____

Chinese Instructional Strategies

1 2 3 4 5   28. I use teacher-fronted and student-centered instructional strategy.

1 2 3 4 5   29. Mastery of Pinyin and tone at the 1st and 2nd grades is critical for students to develop their phonological awareness.

1 2 3 4 5   30. I use real objects or pictures to introduce new characters or new concepts, use Pinyin to help them pronounce the new characters with accurate tone.

1 2 3 4 5   31. I read aloud corresponding character prints to facilitate character recognition.

1 2 3 4 5   32. I use body language to assist students understand my input in Chinese.

1 2 3 4 5   33. I use context clues to help students understand the story.

1 2 3 4 5   34. I make connection to students' lives

1 2 3 4 5	35. I make repetitive comprehension check.
1 2 3 4 5	36. I ask students to read aloud for enhancing their pronunciation.
1 2 3 4 5	37. I ask students to read aloud for enhancing reading fluency.
1 2 3 4 5	38. I ask students to read aloud for developing reading comprehension.
1 2 3 4 5	39. I teach students the basic writing rule for composing the Chinese characters: from top to bottom, from left to right.
1 2 3 4 5	40. I ask students to practice the characters with its pinyin, tones, radicals, stroke orders, and stroke numbers.
1 2 3 4 5	41. I instruct students to identify the radical.
1 2 3 4 5	42. I ask students to practice the formation and pronunciation of the new characters, phrases, sentences and summary of the passages.
1 2 3 4 5	43. I ask students to demonstrate their comprehension of the characters by making phrases related to the characters and using them in sentences for meaningful communication.
1 2 3 4 5	44. I allocated time for students to act out what they read from the textbook.
1 2 3 4 5	45. I allocated time for students to share their group Chinese projects findings with the class.

Comments:
_____

Chinese Immersion Output

1 2 3 4 5	46. All my students reached the grade level bench mark in Chinese.
1 2 3 4 5	47. All my students reached the grade level benchmark in English and math.
1 2 3 4 5	48. I observed that studying Chinese improves students' mathematic skills and problem solving skills.
1 2 3 4 5	49. I observed that my students are responsive to Chinese cultural nuances.
1 2 3 4 5	50. I observed that my students appreciate Chinese culture.

Comments:
_____

Thank you for your participation and candid responses.
Please return your survey in the enclosed envelop before _____.

Appendix I

Quantitative Data Collection & Analysis Organization Chart

Quantitative Data Collection & Analysis Organization Chart
(Evaluating the Product component of the CIPP Model: the impact of Chinese language immersion program on student academics)

	Short-term (3rd grade)	Medium-term (4th grade)	Long-term (5-grade)	Questions Answered	Total Tests
	Student academic performance in Math and English Language Arts				
2009-10	Class06 CCP06				
2010-11	Class07 CCP07	Class06 CCP06			
2011-12	Class08 CCP08	Class07 CCP07	Class06 CCP06		
SPSS test	t-test/math t-test/English	t-test/math t-test/English	t-test/math t-test/English	Q4 Q4	6 t-tests
	Student academic performance in Chinese language arts				
2012-13	Class10YCT3 MN10YCT3	Class09YCT4 MN09YCT4			
SPSS test	t-test for Chinese	t-test/Chinese		Q5	2 t-tests
	Student academic performance trends in different instructional settings				
2012-13 SPSS test	Class09, Class 08, Class07, CCP09, CCP08, CCP07 t-tests for English and math for each school			Q6 Q6	2 t-tests
Total Tests					10

Note. Class06 = Students who were Kindergarten in 2006-2007 school year and took their EOG test in 3rd grade in 2009-2010 school year; CCP = Comparable class participants; Q1 = Evaluation question 1; t-test = independent t-test; Class09YCT4 = Students who were Kindergarten in 2009-2010 school year and took Youth Chinese Test Level 4 in their 3rd grade; MN09YCT4 = Minnesota students who were Kindergarten in 2009-2010 school year and take Youth Chinese Test Level 4 in their 3rd grade.

Appendix J

Informed Consent Forms

Request for Permission for On Site Research

Dear Sir/Madame,

I am a student in a doctorate of education program with Gardner-Webb University. As a student, I am doing program evaluation research in Chinese language immersion program at CMS. The title of my dissertation is a comprehensive program evaluation of a Chinese language immersion program.

At national level, there are 75,000 K-12 students and 50,000 college students are studying Chinese, yet only one comprehensive Chinese language immersion program evaluation was done and was report by Center of Applied Linguists (CAL, 2012). It is time to think about how to sustain the Chinese immersion programs in the United States and how to ensure the accountability of the Chinese programs (National Chinese Language Conference, 2012).

My study is to comprehensively evaluate the effectiveness of a Chinese language immersion program in CMS using the CIPP evaluation model (Stufflebeam, 2003). This study will focus on collecting data on Context, Input, Process, and Product of the program and make a summative data-driven report on the four components of the program to the stakeholders, and make suggestions on improvement of the program.

The information provided will be kept strictly confidential. The informed consent forms and other identification information will be kept separate from the data. All materials will be kept at the researcher's home. The researcher will destroy any records that would identify participants in this study approximately 3 years after the study is completed. Participants will be asked to provide a different name for any quotes that might be included in the final research report. If any direct quotes will be used, permission will be sought from participants first.

Participation is voluntary, and participants can withdraw from the project at any time without consequence. There are no risks or discomfort involved in this study to the participants.

No compensation will be provided for participants.

If you have any questions about this study, please ask the researchers before or after signing the form.

I am asking your permission to complete this Chinese immersion program evaluation at _____. I will be happy to answer any questions.

By signing below, you are giving me permission to carry out my research with students, teachers, and principals at _____.
Please keep one copy for your file and return the signed copy.

Thank you very much for your time.

_____
Signature

_____   _____
Principal/School District Official Signature   Date

Shoufen A. Jacobson
Doctorate Program of Education Department
Gardner-Webb University

Contact information for XXXXXX:

Work: XXXXXX
Cell: XXXXXX
Fax: XXXXXX
Address: XXXXXX

Center for Applied Linguistics. (2012). *CAL activities and resources related to Chinese.*
 Retrieved April 5, 2012, from
 http://www.cal.org/resources/discoverlanguages/chinese/resources.html

Stufflebeam, D. L. (2003). The CIPP Model for evaluation. In T. Kellaghan, D. L.
 Stufflebeam, & L. A. Wingate (Eds.), Wingate (Eds.), *International handbook of
 educational evaluation* (31-62). Boston: Kluwer Academic Publishers.

Informed Consent Form
For Program Planners

To Whom It May Concern,

You are being asked to participate in an evaluation study.

The purpose of this study is to comprehensively evaluate the district Chinese language immersion program using CIPP model (Stufflebeam, 2003). This will provide summative data driven information about the levels of effectiveness of the program under study to the stakeholders.

The information about the needs, resources, process, and academic impacts of the Chinese language immersion program will be collected from you through an interview. It takes approximately 45 minutes of your time. I will begin by taking you back to the time before the program began to be implemented. I will ask follow-up questions at the end to fill in any blanks as needed. The idea is to get a good description of your perceptions and experiences related to the creation, implementation, and academic impact of the program.

Please do not hesitate to ask questions about the study before participation or during study. I would be happy to share the findings with you after the evaluation is completed. Your name will not be associated with the evaluation findings in any way, and only the evaluator knows your identity.

There are no known risks and/or discomforts associated with this study. The expected benefits associated with your participation are the information about the experience, perceptions in the planning, creating, and implementing the program. Your participation is voluntary. If you do not want to continue to be in the study, you may stop at any time without penalty or loss of benefits to which you are otherwise entitled.

Please sign this consent form if you decided to participate in this study. You are signing it with full knowledge of the nature and purpose of the procedures. A copy of this form will be given to you to keep.

_____   _____
Signature   Date

Evaluator's Name: XXXXXX

Work: XXXXXX   Cell: XXXXXX   Fax: XXXXXX
Address: XXXXXX

Stufflebeam, D. L. (2003). The CIPP Model for evaluation. In T. Kellaghan, D. L. Stufflebeam, & L. A. Wingate (Eds.), Wingate (Eds.), *International handbook of educational evaluation* (31-62). Boston: Kluwer Academic Publishers.

Informed Consent
For Chinese Language Immersion Team Members

To Whom It May Concern,

You are being asked to participate in an evaluation study.

The purpose of this study is to comprehensively evaluate the district Chinese language immersion program using CIPP model (Stufflebeam, 2003). This will provide summative data driven information about the levels of effectiveness of the program under study to the stakeholders.

The information about the Chinese language instructional environment of the program will be collected from you through a survey. It takes approximately 30 minutes of your time. The idea is to get a good description of your perceptions and experiences related to the Chinese language instructional environment of the program.

Please do not hesitate to ask questions about the study before participation or during study. I would be happy to share the findings with you after the evaluation is completed. Your name will not be associated with the evaluation findings in any way, and only the evaluator knows your identity.

There are no known risks and/or discomforts associated with this study. The expected benefits associated with your participation are the information about the experiences, perceptions about your Chinese language instructional environment in your classroom. Your participation is voluntary. If you do not want to continue to be in the study, you may stop at any time without penalty or loss of benefits to which you are otherwise entitled.

Please sign this consent form if you decided to participate in this study. You are signing it with full knowledge of the nature and purpose of the procedures. A copy of this form will be given to you to keep.

_____   _____
Signature   Date

Evaluator's Name: XXXXXX

Work: XXXXXX   Cell: XXXXXX   Fax: XXXXXX
Address: XXXXXX

Stufflebeam, D. L. (2003). The CIPP Model for evaluation. In T. Kellaghan, D. L. Stufflebeam, & L. A. Wingate (Eds.), Wingate (Eds.), *International handbook of educational evaluation* (31-62). Boston: Kluwer Academic Publishers.

Informed Consent
For Members of Advisory Panel

To Whom It May Concern,

You are being asked to participate as a member of Advisory Panel in this evaluation study.

The purpose of this study is to comprehensively evaluate the district Chinese language immersion program using CIPP model (Stufflebeam, 2003). This will provide summative data driven information about the levels of effectiveness of the program under study to the stakeholders.

Your role as an Advisory Panel member is to (a) meet twice in this program evaluation process either through email or in person; (b) provide ongoing oversight and guidance throughout the evaluation period; and (c) complete a 6-points Likert Scale survey to assess collective program evaluation processes, which takes approximately 30 minutes of your time. The idea is to get a good description of your professional judgment related the merit, feasibility, propriety, and utility (Joint Committee on Standards for Educational Evaluation) of program evaluation process underwent.

Please do not hesitate to ask questions about the study before participation or during study. I would be happy to share the findings with you after the evaluation is completed. Your name will not be associated with the evaluation findings in any way, and only the evaluator knows your identity.

There are no known risks and/or discomforts associated with this study. The expected benefits associated with your participation are the information about the experiences, perceptions about this program evaluation process. Your participation is voluntary. If you do not want to continue to be in the study, you may stop at any time without penalty or loss of benefits to which you are otherwise entitled.

Please sign this consent form if you decided to participate in this study. You are signing it with full knowledge of the nature and purpose of the procedures. A copy of this form will be given to you to keep.

_____   _____
Signature   Date

Evaluator's Name: XXXXXX

Work: XXXXXX   Cell: XXXXXX   Fax: XXXXXX
Address: XXXXXX

Stufflebeam, D. L. (2003). The CIPP Model for evaluation. In T. Kellaghan, D. L. Stufflebeam, & L. A. Wingate (Eds.), Wingate (Eds.), *International handbook of educational evaluation* (31-62). Boston: Kluwer Academic Publishers.

www.ingramcontent.com/pod-product-compliance
Lightning Source LLC
Chambersburg PA
CBHW081211230426
43666CB00015B/2711